THE

LOST PRINCIPLE;

OR THE

SECTIONAL EQUILIBRIUM:

HOW IT WAS CREATED—HOW DESTROYED—HOW IT MAY BE RESTORED.

By "BARBAROSSA."

"And therefore it is ever good to relie upon the books at large, for many times *compendia sunt despendia* and *melius est petere fontes, quam sectari rivulos.*"

[COKE—LITTLETON.

RICHMOND, VA.
JAMES WOODHOUSE & CO.
1860.

C. H. WYNNE, PRINTER.

DEDICATION.

I wish to dedicate this little volume to the memory of the Hon. JOHN MACPHERSON BERRIEN, late Senator in Congress from the State of Georgia; not for his eminent abilities, his private worth, nor yet for his great public character, but as an humble tribute of gratitude for an important service which he rendered to me.

It chanced some years ago that I was introduced to that distinguished statesman at one of the public tables in Washington city. The conversation turned on the question of slavery, then vexing Congress, and in terms stronger than good manners would warrant, I expressed my aversion to that form of labor. The sentiment which I uttered elicited no response, and the conversation glided on to other topics. When I was about to depart, Judge Berrien, in the most polite and obliging manner, invited me to remain and take wine with him, an invitation which I gladly accepted, for already I felt strongly attracted to him.

With some abruptness, he turned to me and expressed his surprise that I, a young man from Virginia, should entertain sentiments of so remarkable a character about slavery. I attempted to defend them, and he listened to me with respectful attention. In the ablest manner, the Senator then explained the whole subject to me, in its social, political and economical connexions, and after illustrating its conservative and ameliorating influences on the Federal Government, demonstrated its absolute necessity, in a democratic society, to preserve the empire of law, of virtue and of religion, and predicted that for the want of that restraining power the Northern Republics, so soon as they should be disconnected with the Slave States, even if not sooner, would fall into anarchy, and, treading the old circle, would, to escape the despotism of the mob, seek refuge in the despotism of a single will.

His discourse produced on me the most profound impression; and when I arose to withdraw, I grasped his hand cordially and thanked him for redeeming me from so weak and dangerous an error. I had never seen Judge Berrien before; I never saw him again. A few years later I heard that the Hunter Death had struck him down, and sure he never struck a nobler quarry.

BARBAROSSA.

TO THE

YOUNG MEN OF THE SLAVE-HOLDING SECTION.

I presume to address this publication to you, though it is not without trepidation that I appeal to so intelligent a tribunal. It broaches a new theory of the Constitution. If it shall be considered well founded, upon your courage and intelligence must the Southern people rely for its vindication; but if it shall be deemed fanciful and pleasing from its novelty, rather than valuable for its truth, my apology is a conviction of its importance to the South, and that here in Virginia, we all have a proclivity towards politics, and, in the words of Sir Francis Bacon, where "every one plays the philosopher out of the small treasury of his own fancy."

But let it be remembered that *youth* is not always determined by the period of life. There are old young men, whilst there are those who like Hecla wear crowns of snow, and yet like Hecla have souls of flame.

Respectfully,

BARBAROSSA.

PREFACE.

Soon after its establishment, by Mr. Pryor, in Richmond city, I communicated to *The South* newspaper the theory of an equilibrium in the Federal Constitution, which is the principal subject of this volume. As far as I am informed, the intention on the part of its framers to introduce that principle, had not been suggested by any one since the government went into operation. Subsequent examination confirmed me in the belief of the sectional nature of the compact, and the intention of the Federal Convention to balance power between the North and the South. The means by which that end was to be achieved, together with the means adopted by Congress to prevent it, I thought worthy of a more extended investigation, and therefore have written this book. In the chapter which relates to the ratification of the Constitution by Virginia, several threads of history have been woven in, together with an enquiry into the cause of the decline of that Commonwealth; and in this connection I beg leave to acknowledge the advantage that I have derived from consulting the pages of Mr. Grigsby—I mean with reference to the source from which the bulk of the population of Virginia was derived.

The different parts have been written at different times, as inclination might prompt or business allow, and are now hastily thrown together because of a supposed application of this subject to the present state of public affairs.

I will not apologize for my subject, as though by any comparison it were unimportant; but I will confess a diffidence of the value added by my own handling. In the remarks on our own history, the order of time is neither strictly observed, nor greatly neglected.

"Yet it is designed, slight and imperfect as it is, for the service of *Truth*, by one who would be glad to attend and grace *her* triumphs; as her soldier, if he has had the honor to serve successfully under her banner; or as a captive tied to her chariot wheels, if he has, though undesignedly, committed any offence against her."

FEBRUARY 25, 1860.

THE SECTIONAL EQUILIBRIUM.

PART I.

How it was Created.

CHAPTER I.

When a broad table is to be made and the edges of the planks do not fit, the artist takes a little from both and makes a good joint. In like manner, here, both sides must part with some of their demands.—Dr. FRANKLIN.

In the Constitutional Convention of 1829, WATKINS LEIGH said: "*The Federal Convention of* 1787 *had, for the first time, to arrange a representation of the people in Congress. What was the origin of the Federal number I do not certainly know. I have had recourse, in vain, to every source of information accessible to ascertain how that precise proportion of slaves*—THREE-FIFTHS—*came to be adopted, what mode or principle of estimate led to it. Some reason there must have been.*"

It is my purpose, in the following pages, to solve this question of constitutional history—to ascertain the reason that operated on the Convention which constructed the government under which we live, to adopt in the popular basis the fractional representation which was awarded to the servile population of the South. The Report of "The Debates of the Convention of 1787," by Mr. Madison, enables me to do this. It is the only source from which that information can be derived, for the fragment of those proceedings preserved by Judge Yates, affords no clue whatever to the solution of this interesting problem. "The Debates," in 1829, were not published, but slept in manuscript, at Montpelier, until the death of Mr. Madison broke the seal.

This part of the organic law has excited but little curiosity, and yet it is the ground-work of the political edifice, with reference to which every other part was made. A just understanding of this part of the Constitution will furnish, if I mistake not, an explanation of many of those questions that have convulsed the North and South, and will supply us with the means of ascertaining how far we have departed from the true meaning of that instrument—how far the ship of State has drifted from the intended course.

Mr. Madison was himself a member of the Convention of 1829, and heard the enquiry of Mr. Leigh, but said nothing. Why he stood mute on that occasion, when a true account of the fractional basis would have added strength to the side which he himself advocated, I know not. Let those who reverence the character and eulogize the memory of Madison divine his motives. His explanation of that fundamental part of the federal charter, might not have accorded well with his declared opinions in federal politics, and it is possible that he shrunk from the keen and searching analysis of the powerful minds that illustrated that assemblage.

The Constitution of the United States is generally understood to be a compact to which the several States are parties; and hence, that all the rights which it provides are State rights, and the remedies for the violation of those rights, State remedies. In consequence of this view of the Constitution, State secession and State interposition have been suggested as the modes of redress in the several cases to which they apply. But I shall attempt to prove, by authentic evidence, that this is not true in the exclusive sense in which it has been stated.

The Constitution is, indeed, a compact between States, but it is also a compact between the slaveholding and non-slaveholding sections; and those sections are susceptible of obligations and injuries. This is not the least interesting light in which the Constitution presents itself, and thus viewed is a Great Treaty between two nations of opposite civilizations, and, in many respects, opposite interests, making the federal system even more complex than it has been generally supposed to be.

The true character of the Constitution, and the government which has grown out of it, is illustrated by the political parties which have arisen under it. At first, a consolidating tendency threatened to absorb the States. This produced the State Rights party—a school founded by Jefferson and Madison, and afterwards sustained by a succession of great men, of whom Calhoun was the most illustrious. Calhoun devoted the energies of his wonderful intellect to developing this theory of the Constitution. Perceiving that the congressional or departmental checks were of a subordinate character, and did not operate to restrain the ruling power of the Constitution, he attempted to eliminate from the government a veto power in the hands of the States, which he denominated an Equilibrium, but so denominated for no better reason, as I conceive, than that its originator would have employed it as an imperfect substitute for that wise and healing principle.

An Equilibrium, properly so called, enters into the government and is its living principle. It is ever present; it assists in the deliberations of the Legislature and partakes of the enactment of laws; it moderates the Judicial power, and in the execution of the laws tempers the Executive. But the States, acting as Tribunes, as they have been called from their fancied resemblance to that Roman officer, are not present in the legislative chambers to arrest the passage of bills, but are to be invoked to unravel that which has been woven, to repeal that which has been enacted, to undo that which has been done, and that only within the narrow limits of a State jurisdiction, and *in case of a deliberate, palpable and dangerous exercise of powers, not granted by the Constitution.* But the Equilibrium is confined by no bounds to its discretion, nor even to cases where the Constitution is supposed to be infracted, but decides upon the equity and policy as well as the constitutionality of political action, and is omnipotent to repress corruptions and prevent extravagant expenditures of public money.

But, since the death of Mr. Calhoun, and even a little before, parties have undergone a remarkable change. They are now drawn up on the sectional line. They are no longer characterized by old names. Those distinctions have been blotted out, and parties now are purely geographical. So true is it that every government, in its development, will proclaim the principles upon which it is founded! A war of sections has begun, because the constitutional rights of the Southern section have been invaded. The natural expansion of the South has been limited by Federal law, and it is in vain that we have recourse to State Rights' principles for the means of redress; that school of politics having been formed exclusively with reference to the Constitution regarded as a compact between States. The third of the Virginia Resolutions declares: "In case of a deliberate, dangerous, and palpable exercise of other powers not granted by the said compact, *the States, who are the parties thereto*, have the right, and are in duty bound, to interfere for arresting the progress of the evil, and for *maintaining, within their respective limits*, the authorities, rights and liberties appertaining to them." This is nullification. It is the exercise of State sovereignty within State jurisdiction, but it cannot move an inch beyond those consecrated limits. State secession is evidently derived from the same source, and is circumscribed by the same bounds. If the government attempts to collect protective duties in the port of Charleston, South Carolina has an unquestionable right to annul the law in virtue of which those duties are collected. If South Carolina should deem that Congress had committed a dangerous inroad on the Constitution, for which secession would furnish the only adequate redress, she would have, in virtue of her State sovereignty, the unquestionable right to withdraw from the political association. But if the Federal Goverment attempts to expunge slavery from the District of Columbia, or to exclude it from Kansas, would that be an invasion of the sovereignty of South Carolina? Her State remedies would not be co-extensive with the right. The rule of the common law, which ascertains the existence of a right by the existence of an appropriate remedy for its violation, would apply to cases like this. The common law has been called the perfection of reason, and in nothing does it appear more than in this. Any blow dealt at slavery by the central government, outside of that State, is certainly a wrong done to South Carolina, but to South Carolina considered as a portion of the slave section. The remedy, in such a case, if redress could not be obtained by constitutional methods, would be by the overthrow of the Government, the aggressive power. By the destruction of the wrong-doer the prevention of all future wrong would be accomplished.

This doctrine is not only true, but wholesome. It tends to obliterate, wherever their common civilization is threatened, State lines, and to resolve the Southern States into one community. In case of a dissolution of the Union, they would be held together by a common bond, and would be led to frame, under better auspices, a common government.

Mr. Calhoun discovered, before the close of his life, which was snuffed out before the great drama had fully opened, that he should have to take broader ground and invoke other agencies than those which he had hitherto used in his contests with Congress. He did not resort then to the nullifying powers of a State, but he called upon the South to defend herself from the systematic aggressions of the North, acting through the government at Washington. But his constitutional creed underwent no corresponding change.

The nature of the Constitution is imprinted on its face, and bears unmistakable traces of its two-fold origin. The States, in their sovereign capacity, are represented in the Senate; for, wherever sovereignty exists, equality necessarily prevails. But the sections are represented, and their existence acknowledged in the Electoral College, and in the constitution of the first branch of Congress. It will be seen, hereafter, that the Senate was constituted on its present basis by a conflict between the great and small States, and that the basis upon which the other branch of Congress was founded was the result of a collision between the North and South, and that the differences, in both cases, were adjusted upon the principle of equality.

The difference between a simple compact among the States, and one to which sections and States are equally parties, in respect to the range of powers with which it was thought expedient to invest government, is illustrated by the Articles of Confederation and that Constitution under which we live.

In remarking upon that part of the Constitution which contains the provision for a slave representation, a recent intelligent writer says: "This was the first step, and the next was the formation of the present Constitution, when a contest arose as to the ratio of representation. Should the South have as many representatives, in proportion to her population, as the North? It was just and right that she should. The Federal Government had no concern with the relations between blacks and whites, the different classes of her population. It had not the right to inquire whether the negro was a slave or free. The slaves were a better population than the free negroes, and if the latter were to be counted at their full number in the apportionment of representation, so ought the former. The right could not be refused, because the slaves were naturally or legally unequal to the whites; for so are the free negroes. It could not be refused, because they have no political rights; for neither have the free negroes, paupers, women and children. They are an essential part of the population; if absent, their places must be filled by other laborers, and if they are property as well as population, it is an additional reason for giving their owners the security of full representation for them. But the South, as usual, yielded to Northern exorbitance, and agreed that five slaves should count only as three free negroes. Therefore, instead of 105 representatives in Congress, we have only 91." *

If, indeed, the Constitution is to be regarded in the light of a compact between two nations, it is impossible to say that it was just and right that the South should have a full representation of her slaves, without first ascertaining what effect that would have upon the distribution of the powers of government between the parties. If the effect of a full representation of slaves would place the government under the dominion of the South, the slave power, who can say that there is any principle of natural justice that would have required the North to agree to any such stipulation? If their total or partial exclusion would have produced the contrary effect, and placed the South under the control of the free-soil power, as little could be said in defence of such an arrangement. Each party was entitled to a safe representation in the government, which could result alone from introducing the principle of equality in the division of power; for in nature, as it is in the court of chancery, equality is equity. The idea that the partial exclusion of slaves from the representative basis was due to their moral and legal inferiority is wholly unfounded, as will hereafter be proved, although that doctrine is inculcated by the respectable authority of the Federalist. The Southern delegates in the Federal Convention will likewise, in the progress of this narrative, be vindicated from the insinuated charge of having submitted to *Northern exorbitance;* but the integrity of their motives will be vindicated at the expense of their political sagacity.

The sectional line between the North and South was almost as deeply drawn in 1787, as it is at the present time. This will be clearly exhibited by an inspection of that part of the debates of the Convention now about to pass under review. It contradicts the notion entertained by some, that this sectional

---

* The Union, Past and Future, p. 1, 2.

antagonism is of recent growth and consequently that the Constitution of the United States was not made with reference to it. The States to the northward of Virginia and Maryland were either already free States or were preparing to become so, and it was apparent to every one that they would soon consummate their intention. The Northern delegates in the Convention of 1787, all acted in the free-soil interest, and the delegates from the South were unanimous in the defence of the interests of slavery. To reconcile that difference constituted the chief labor of the Convention. The year following, in the South Carolina Convention of ratification, Gen. Pinckney said:

"But striking as this difference is, it is not to be compared to the the difference that there is between the inhabitants of the *Northern and Southern* States; when I say Southern, I mean Maryland, and the States southward of her. There we may truly observe that nature has drawn as strong marks of distinction in the habits and manners of the people, as she has in her climates and productions. The Southern citizen beholds with a kind of surprise the simple manners of the East, and is too often induced to entertain undeserved opinions of the purity of the Quaker, while they, in their turn, seem concerned at what they term the extravagance and dissipation of their Southern friends, *and reprobate, as an unpardonable moral and political evil, the dominion they hold over a part of the human race.*" Elliot's Debates, vol. iv, p. 310.

This feeling, which existed to so great a degree among the people in the two sections, was ever showing itself in Congress whenever the interests or power of either was involved. The Northern members objected to the admission of Kentucky into the Union, the Southern States objected to the admission of Vermont. That fraternal love which many have supposed to have existed at that period between the North and South, is purely imaginary; instead, a strong and deep-rooted antagonism characterized them both. Already had any affiliation between a Northern member of Congress and the Southern members been put under the ban of the North. General Sullivan thus writes to Washington: "The choice of minister of war was postponed to the first of October. *This was a manœuvre of Samuel Adams and others from the North, fearing that, as I was in nomination, the choice would fall on me, who having apostatized from the true New England faith, by sometimes voting with the Southern States, am not eligible.*"

CHAPTER II.

FEDERAL CONVENTION.

Man, as the minister and interpreter of Nature, does and understands as much as his observations on the order of nature, either with regard to things or the mind, permit him, and neither knows nor is capable of more.

The subtlety of nature is far beyond that of sense or of the understanding: so that the specious meditations, speculations and theories of mankind, are but a kind of insanity, only there is no one to stand by and observe it.—NOVUM ORGANON.

The wit and mind of man, if it work upon matter, which is the contemplation of the creatures of God, worketh according to the stuff, and is limited thereby; but if it work upon itself, as the spider worketh his web, then it is endless and brings forth indeed cobwebs of learning, admirable for the fineness of thread and work, but of no substance or profit.—ADVANCEMENT OF LEARNING.

When you assemble a number of men to have the advantage of their joint wisdom, you invariably assemble with those men all their prejudices, their passions, their errors of opinion, their local interests and their selfish views.—DR. FRANKLIN.

On Friday, the 25th May, 1787, the Convention, professedly to reform, but as it proved to reconstruct, the Constitution, began its sessions at Philadelphia, and adjourned to the 17th September following, having been engaged in their arduous task something over three months. It was composed, for the most part, of the men under whose courageous counsels the country had passed through the travail of the Revolution; they had all taken part in public affairs, either on the theatre of State or Federal politics, and had brought with them much

2

of that knowledge which is acquired only in the school of experience.

The question of Representation chiefly engaged the attention, excited the animosities, and consumed the time of that great synod. Other parts of the Constitution were more readily agreed upon. Nor is this surprising; for the experience of the country had been instructive. It had satisfied every mind that the government of the confederacy was in some particulars defective; and had indicated those in which it needed reform. The consultation in consequence began with a number of conclusions which needed not the aid of argument. Had the Convention confined itself to reforms of this nature, the work would have been rapidly dispatched; but they undertook to re-cast the Constitution and to alter its frame, and this attempt produced new questions of the first moment to the country, and violent agitations which threatened on more than one occasion to dissolve the body.*

So soon as it was determined by the Convention to create a government of great powers, it is not wonderful that the adjustment of the question of representation should have been found to be attended with such difficulty and delay. Upon it depended the question of empire—what should be the relation which the two great sections, the North and South, were to occupy to the central power.

There are those who look back upon the Convention with a romantic eye, and regard the able men of whom it was composed as beings of a superior order, devising, under the enlightened influence of reason and justice, political institutions for themselves and their posterity. But this is only the idolatry of admiration. If we draw near, and through the medium by

---

* Luther Martin, in his address to the Maryland Legislature, says, with respect to the animosities engendered by the slavery discussion in the Convention: "I believe near a fortnight, perhaps more, was spent in the discussion of this business, during which we were on the verge of dissolution, *scarce held together by a hair*, though the public papers were announcing our extreme unanimity."

which it has reached us, attend to the grave debate, it will be discovered that they were men struggling, sometimes fiercely and sometimes unfairly, for particular objects and particular opinions which they wished the government to subserve and embody. The marvel is, not that jealousies and irritations should have arisen, but that they could have been composed.

The business of the Convention was opened by Edmund Randolph, one of the delegates from Virginia, "a child of the Revolution," as on a subsequent occasion he styled himself. After giving an outline of the system which he wished to be adopted, he submitted a plan of government, which was taken as a basis on which to begin work. Mr. Charles Pinckney, a delegate from South Carolina, also submitted a plan of government, which is remarkable for the near resemblance which it bears to the Constitution, not only in phraseology, but in substance. These plans no otherwise concern us here except on account of the different bases of representation which they contained. That of Mr. Randolph provided: "That the right of suffrage in the National Legislature ought to be proportioned to the quotas of contribution, or the number of free inhabitants, as the one or the other rule may seem best in different cases." But Mr. Pinckney proposed to proportion representation in Congress according to the number of inhabitants taken in the gross. These two propositions respectively contain the extreme pretensions of the two sections. It will be discovered, in the course of this narration, what alterations each was in the end subjected to, and what expedient was resorted to, to bring these rival and jealous parties together. Of the first proposition it may be remarked, that it was at best but an ill-digested and double-headed project, and contained conclusive proof that its projector had not very maturely, certainly not very profoundly, considered the weighty question. It rested on alternatives which were based on opposite principles. If the first were adopted, and wealth or contribution made the measure of power, the government, in all its departments, would pass under the dominion of the South; but if the other, the North would have the preponderance. But the crude suggestion so far abandoned just principles as to leave it to Congress to decide between the two—thus throwing upon Congress the responsible duty of the Convention, and conferring upon it, in that particular, an almost unlimited range of power. Alexander Hamilton, a deputy from New York, proposed to simplify Mr. Randolph's proposition, and proportion representatives to the number of free inhabitants alone; but sectional opposition being about to burst forth, the subject was laid over, it being evident that the most delicate and irritable part of the Constitution had been rudely touched.

It is naturally a subject of surprise, that the darling project of the North should have originated with a gentleman representing the largest and most influential member of the Southern community. It was calculated to excite surprise and spread consternation in the ranks of his friends. So important a defection, in the outset, was fraught with ill-omen to the success of the Convention; it can only be explained in the way above indicated, and that the distinguished gentleman was one of that small band who had been entangled in the mazes of the anti-slavery philosophy, then first lifting up its head. But at a later stage in the business, after the question had been discussed in its political applications, and had come to be viewed solely as a question of sectional power, Mr. Randolph promptly abandoned his own offspring, and assumed his proper place in the Southern ranks. That sudden revulsion in the position of a leading character upon a subject of such engrossing importance, is extremely significant, and affords conclusive evidence of the attitude and complexion of parties. Such was the importance attached to negro slavery, as a political element, and so strong the bias of parties in respect to it, that Southern men, who were most averse from it, buried their prejudices, and rallied to its support. This prompt and thorough recantation places Mr. Randolph in the most favorable light. Notwithstanding that he had all the severity of character which belonged to a leader in those bustling times, yet he was not of that bigoted and inflexible turn which would induce him to cling to a dangerous error, after that error had been exposed. Indeed, he appears to have been of a more flexible temper;—and when the alarm of sections was rung, he retraced his steps, and with Madison, Pinckney, and the clear-headed and ever-faithful George Mason, was among the most unflinching advocates of the South, and inflexible opponents of Northern ambition.

But the truce was of short duration. The business was at a stand. No progress could be made until a distribution of power had first been effected. Neither the South nor the North, neither the large States nor the small States, could say with what authorities they were willing to entrust the government, until it was first determined what measure of influence each was to wield. This, of itself, shows the supreme importance attached to that question. But the time had not been thrown away. In private an adjustment had been agreed upon. This is evident from the direction from which the adjustment came. On the 11th of June, when the Constitution of the first branch of the Legislature was again taken up, Mr. Wilson, from Pennsylvania, a leader of great talents, seconded by Mr. Chas. Pinckney, from South Carolina, justly entitled from his abilities and activity to be esteemed a leader from the South, submitted a proposition that slaves should be admitted into the representative basis in the proportion of five slaves to three freemen. From this, it is clear that a compromise had been effected, and that each party had receded from its extreme pretensions. The vote on that compromise reveals most strikingly the healing influences that had been at work. The States of New Jersey and Delaware alone voted against it. Their motive evidently was to keep the whole question open, so as to prevent any combination being made between the large States and the slave States; a combination which was, nevertheless, afterwards effected, and to defeat which, in part, the small States were finally compelled to assume the most decided attitude. From this single instance, it may be collected how great a part of the business was really transacted in private, no memorandum of which has been preserved. It will explain, too, how it happened that many questions of the deepest import were settled by the Convention with but little debate, and in some instances, without debate at all.

I wish here to state, that when Mr. Wilson introduced his proposition, that he added, by way of explanation and recommendation, that it embraced the same ratio which, on a former occasion, had been proposed in an act of Congress as a measure of taxation, and which had commanded the concurrence of eleven out of thirteen States. The reason of this, and the connexion between the two propositions, will hereafter be examined, or rather the same proposition examined in its two-fold application. It will be found to throw a strong light on the purpose and meaning of that ratio as applied to representation.

In the committee of the whole house, the principle of representation agreed upon for the first branch of Congress, was applied likewise to the second branch; and that conclusion was reported to the Convention.

On Wednesday, the 27th June, "Mr. Rutledge moved to postpone the sixth resolution defining the powers of Congress, in order to take up the seventh and eighth, which involved the most fundamental points, the rules of suffrage in the two branches. Agreed to *nem. con.*" The seventh and eighth resolutions of the report, were in the words following:

"7. *Resolved*, That the right of suffrage in the first branch of the National Legislature, ought not to be according to the rule established in the Articles of Confederation, but according to some *equitable* ratio of representation, namely, in proportion to the whole number of white and other free citizens and inhabitants, of every sex, age and condition, including those bound to servitude for a term of years, and *three-fifths of all other persons* not comprehended in the foregoing description, except Indians not paying taxes in each State.

"8. *Resolved*, That the right of suffrage in the second branch of the National Legislature, ought to be according to the rule established for the first."

It will be remarked, that the whole question, which was ultimately divided into two branches, was, by these resolutions, presented in one point of view. The debate which ensued was extremely interesting, and shows, even in the condensed and imperfect account of it which has reached us, the difficulties which the Convention encountered. The proposed settlement was first assailed by the small States; and one of the expedients proposed by that interest for the settlement of the dispute exhibits, in striking colors, the deep-seated apprehension, unfounded as it was then pronounced, and has since turned out to be, of an absorption of the lesser by the greater States. It was proposed by the delegates from New Jersey and Deleware to confound all State lines and throw them into one mass, or into *hotchpot*, as the lawyers of the Convention called it, and then re-partition the territory into equal parts among the States. But the old difficulty would still have existed. Some of those equal allotments would have been greatly superior to others in wealth and population, which would have caused, to borrow a passage from Burke respecting a similar plan in the French Constitution of 1789, "such infinite variations between square and square, as to render mensuration a ridiculous standard of power in the Commonwealth, and equality in geometry the most unequal of all measures in the distribution of men." New Jersey and Delaware demanded such a consolidation and re-distribution of territory, or an equality of representation for the States in every department of government. But the more moderate were content with an equal vote in the Senatorial department, which they insisted upon as a negative "to save them from being destroyed." *Self-protection* was their avowed object. It was in this connection, and in reply to Mr. Edgeworth of Connecticut, that Mr. Madison delivered a speech, from which the following extract is made. It bears directly on the object of this publication, and states, in the most explicit language, the purpose and meaning of the fractional representation awarded to the South in both the legislative departments by the 7th and 8th resolutions then under discussion. It is to the ratio which they contained that Mr. Madison alludes:

"He admitted that every peculiar interest, whether in any class of citizens, or any description of States, ought to be secured as far as possible. Wherever there is danger of attack, there ought to be given a constitutional power of defence. But he contended that the States were divided into different interests, not by their difference of size, but by other circumstances; the most material of which resulted partly from climate, but principally from the effects of their having, or not having slaves. These two causes concurred in forming the great division of interests in the United States. It did not lie between the large and small States. It lay between the Northern and Southern; and if any defensive power were necessary, it ought to be mutually given to these two interests. He was so strongly impressed with this important truth, that he had been casting about in his mind for some expedient that would answer the purpose. The one which had occurred, was, that instead of proportioning the votes of the States in both branches, to their respective number of inhabitants, computing the slaves in the ratio of five to three, they should be represented in one branch according to the number of free inhabitants only; and in the other according to the whole number, counting the slaves as free. By this arrangement, the Southern scale would have the advantage in one house, and the Northern in the other. He had been restrained from proposing this expedient by two considerations; one was his unwillingness to urge any diversity of interests on an occasion where it is but too apt to arise of itself; the other was the inequality of powers that must be vested in the two branches, and which would destroy the equilibrium of interests."

This speech, so admirable for its correct appreciation of the true principles of representative government, opens the discussion, so far as the debates show, upon the subject of slavery. It exhibits the principles by which the speaker as a constitution maker was guided, and especially sets forth the principles upon which he had, as a Southern delegate, insisted. There could not be produced more undeniable evidence—evidence amounting to the clearest proof—that the ratio of three-fifths, as it stood in the report of the committee of the whole, then under the consideration of the Convention, was looked upon as designed to produce an equilibrium between the two sections. This is fortified, and if any doubt remained, would be rendered certain, by the narrative of the introduction of that compromise heretofore given. This is but the contemporaneous exposition of the purpose of the proposed basis, by a single member of the Convention, but, let it be borne in mind, a member speaking for the whole South, and speaking to the whole North. I will proceed to collect all the passages from the succeeding debate, which concern this point, in order to prove that it was universally looked upon in the same light in which it was viewed by Mr. Madison. By this means, the purpose which that body had in view, in establishing that fractional basis, that mode of distributing power between jealous and at length irritated sections, will be established—established, it is believed, to the satisfaction of every sound understanding.

The debate on the eighth resolution, which constituted the second branch of the legislature on the three-fifths ratio, was continued between the larger and the smaller States until the 2nd July, when the Convention divided, by an equal vote, on that question. Maryland voted with the North, because she considered herself in the interest of the small States. But, with that exception, the whole South voted for that resolution. Sectional considerations produced that unity on the part of the South, because, as heretofore observed, to have yielded that department to the control of the small States would have been to place it under Northern control, the Southern policy then being to have the legislature divided equally between the sections, a determining motive with them, as will be disclosed towards the end of the debate. Pennsylvania and Massachusetts, on that occasion, voted with the South; because of the proportional representation which the ninth section embraced. The contest then was between the large and small States, an issue upon which the South, Maryland excepted, invariably voted with Massachusetts and Pennsylvania. The smouldering fires of sectional jealousy had not then burst forth. But, after they had burst forth, so fierce was the heat with which they burned, and so strong the sympathy that linked the Northern States together, that Mr. Gouverneur Morris, of Pennsylvania, threatened to desert to the small States, or rather proclaimed that he would be compelled to vote for "the vicious principle of equality in the second branch," in order to give the North a counterpoise against the South, to whom the three-fifths ratio, in his opinion, would deliver the first branch of the legislature. The advantage which an equal vote in the Senate would secure to the North will explain the following speech of Mr. Charles Pinckney in opposition to it, which was delivered immediately on the announcement of the vote just alluded to:

"Mr. Pinckney thought an equality of votes in the second branch inadmissible; at the same time, candor obliged him to admit that the large States would feel a partiality for their own citizens, and give them a preference in appointments; that they might also find some common points in their commercial interests, and promote treaties favorable to them. *There is a real distinction between Northern and Southern interests.* North Carolina, South Carolina and Georgia, in their rice and indigo, had a peculiar interest which might be sacrificed. How, then, shall the larger States be prevented from administering the general government as they please, without being themselves unduly subjected to the will of the smaller? By allowing them some, but not a full proportion. He was extremely anxious that something should be done, considering this as the last appeal to a regular experiment. Congress have failed in almost every effort for an amendment of the Federal system. Nothing has prevented a dissolution of it but the appointment of this Convention; and he could not express his alarms for the consequence of such an event."

General Pinckney then proposed that a committee, consisting of a member from each State, should be appointed. The proposition to refer covered only the eighth resolution; as yet the seventh resolution had not been assailed. But the bile of anti-slavery rising in the heart of Mr. Strong, a Northern delegate, he proposed that the whole question, embracing both resolutions, should go to committee. Thus the entire ground which had been gained was lost, and the Convention was again at sea.

Whilst the proposition of Gen. Pinckney was pending, Mr. Gouverneur Morris, of Pennsylvania, spoke, and, without submitting any distinct plan, advocated a government in which the Senate and the Executive should be appointed for life, with a House of Commons framed on liberal ideas. The scheme, itself, was but the re-production of that which already had been brought forward by Col. Hamilton, and thoroughly exposed by Mr. Charles Pinckney. It was the reflection, and nothing more than the reflection, of the English Constitution. By its adoption it was probably the hope of its projector that corresponding interests would, after a while, grow up in the country. But the mind of Mr. Morris seemed filled with other ideas. He turned away from sectional interests, and even denied their existence; but with what candor, the reader will hereafter discover. Burke has said, that there is a class of public men whose patriotism is altogether historical. This was eminently true of the political wisdom of Mr. Morris; for he walked with Solon. Unable or unwilling to recognise the strongly marked differences of the country for which he presumed to suggest a Constitution, his eyes were riveted on the Republics of Antiquity, patterns which stood ready shaped to his hand. He proposed to construct the government with reference alone to the distinctions of the rich and the poor. Between these two classes the legislature, as we have seen, was to be divided. According to his philosophy, these two elements in society were continually at war, and could not dwell in amity together; that the rich man feared the poor man because he was poor, and the poor man hated the rich man because he was rich; and that there was but one way to avoid oppression on the one hand, or confiscation on the other. If things had been as they were in the antique models which filled the imagination and monopolized the thoughts of Mr. Morris; or even, as according to his opinion, they threatened then to become in Pennsylvania, framed, as society then was, on the substratum of free-soil, his suggestion would have been well founded. As it was, he gave very good reasons for a very bad thing. In respect to the aristocratic house which he proposed to establish, he said: "In the first place, the checking branch must have a personal interest in checking the other branch. *One interest must be opposed to another interest.* Vices, as they exist, must be opposed to each other." In short, he proposed to arm each of those social elements with a defensive power in the government. This shows how prevalent, among all reading and thinking men, was the opinion of the necessity of that principle in popular government—to establish between them an equilibrium. It is a fact worthy of notice, that in all the various schemes broached in the Convention, that principle, under one modification or another, was embraced. They seemed to look upon it, as in truth it was, a back of steel; that, with it, representative government was the greatest blessing of society; but, without it, that it was a bubble that would rise to the surface, glisten for a moment, and be dispersed forever; nor is it surprising that this opinion should have so universally prevailed. It was inculcated by the classical authors, then much read; was taught by Montesquieu, a great authority, and oftener quoted than any other in the Convention; and, above all, was incorporated into the English Constitution, which was thought, at that time, to be the best government which the world had ever seen. With that superb model before their eyes, they ever acted.

The proposition of General Pinckney was concurred in. Of that committee, known in the annals of the Convention as the Grand Committee, Mr. Gerry, of Massachusetts, was chairman. The day following, being the fourth of July, the Convention rested from their labors. But the committee devoted the holiday to settling the conditions of an adjustment. No angry collisions had as yet taken place, but, from the following observations of Mr. Williamson, from North Carolina, it is to be inferred that the temper of the respective parties boded a fierce contest: "If we do not concede on both sides, our business must soon be at an end. He approved of the commitment, supposing that, as the committee would be a smaller body, a compromise would be pursued with more coolness." The next day, Mr. Gerry made his report, from which it is clearly visible how intimately connected was the question of representation in both branches:

"That the subsequent propositions be recommended to the Convention, on condition that both shall be generally adopted:

"1. That in the first branch of the legislature each of the States now in the Union shall be allowed one member for every forty thousand inhabitants, of the description reported in the seventh resolution of the committee of the whole house; that each State, not containing that number, shall be allowed one member; that all bills for raising or appropriating money, and for fixing the salaries of the officers of the government of the United States, shall originate in the first branch of the legislature, and shall not be altered or amended by the second branch; and that no money shall be drawn from the public treasury, but in pursuance of appropriations to be originated in the first branch.

"2. That in the second branch each State shall have an equal vote."

It is to be remarked of the first proposition of this report, that it contains evidence of the mutual concessions between the larger States and the slave States, not only in the proportional representation embraced in the three-fifths ratio, but in the exclusive privilege reserved to that branch of the legislature in which the large States are represented, to originate money bills. This was regarded by the large States as an important provision.

Those who construe the three-fifths ratio, contained in Mr. Gerry's report, into a capitulation of the South, will not only have been astonished at the construction heretofore put on it, but will have their astonishment increased by perusing the debate which took place on that report.

"Mr. GORHAM, of Massachusetts, observed, that as the report consisted of propositions mutually conditional, he wished to hear some explanations touching the grounds on which the conditions were estimated.

"Mr. GERRY.—The committee were of different opinions, as well as the deputations from which the committee were taken; and agreed to the report, merely in order that some ground of accommodation might be proposed. Those opposed to the equality of votes have only assented conditionally; and if the other side do not generally agree, will not be under any obligation to support the report."

After some heated discussion, in which the members from the small States talked of appealing to foreign intervention, in case their pretensions were not admitted, it was determined by the Convention to consider separately the propositions of the report. The first proposition was then taken up. Particular attention is invited to the following remarks of Mr. Morris, of Pennsylvania, and of Mr. Rutledge, of South Carolina. They show one of the lights in which the fractional representation was regarded. It is sometimes contended that the representation of slaves was adopted only as a mode of representing property; but it will be seen that slaves were treated as persons, it being left to the laws of the States in which they were to declare their *status*.

"Mr. GOUVERNEUR MORRIS objected to the scale of apportionment. *He thought property ought to be taken into the estimate, as well as the number of inhabitants.* Life and liberty were generally said to be of more value than property. An accurate view of the matter would, nevertheless, prove that property was the main object of society.

"Mr. RUTLEDGE.—The gentleman last up had spoken his sentiments precisely. Property was certainly the principal object of society."

He concluded by proposing to apportion representation according to the contributions paid into the general treasury. But this proposition was voted down. Thus it was determined to rest the government upon population, not upon property,—blacks, equally as whites, being treated as persons. As far as representation was concerned, they were put on the same ground. This ought to put at rest the idea, that the Constitution treats slaves in any other light than as persons, whose status is fixed by the States which they inhabit. This point will be important in another connection, and, therefore, it is noted here. Mr. Morris subsequently moved to commit so much of the report as related "to one member for every forty thousand inhabitants." His view was, that they might absolutely fix the number for each State in the first instance; *leaving the legislature at liberty to provide for changes in the relative importance of the States and for the case of new States.*

It will be observed of this proposal, that it would have made a free-soil government, with power in that government to perpetuate the domination of the Northern interest. It was a favorite plan with Mr. Morris, to leave the basis of representation subject to the discretion of Congress. It will be seen, however, that when the question came to the vote, it was solemnly determined by the Convention, that the Constitution ought to settle that question, thereby refusing to vest in Congress so extraordinary a power. The proposition to commit, however, was adopted; and Mr. Morris was appointed chairman of the committee. His report, when handed in, pleased nobody, and was chiefly remarkable for embracing the idea before thrown out by him. It secured, at the same time, a Northern preponderance, and drew forth from Mr. Randolph the following observation: "He was apprehensive that, as the number was not to be changed till the National legislature should please, a pretext would never be wanting to postpone alterations, and *keep the power in the hands of those possessed of it.* He was in favor of a commitment." So another committee, consisting of five members, was appointed to take into consideration the constitution of the first house of the legislature; and of this committee, Mr. King, of Massachusetts, was chairman. On the 10th July,* Mr. King reported, "that the States, at the first meeting of the general legislature, should be represented by sixty-five members, in the following proportions, to wit: New Hampshire, by three; Massachusetts, eight; Rhode Island, one; Connecticut, five; New York, six; New Jersey, four; Pennsylvania, eight; Delaware, one; Maryland, six; Virginia, ten; North Carolina, five; South Carolina, five; Georgia, three."

It will be seen, from the subsequent explanation of Mr. King, that this apportionment was based upon the ratio, already agreed upon, of three-fifths. But, as no provision was

---

* On this day, Washington thus wrote to Alexander Hamilton, who was absent from the Convention: "I thank you for your communication of the 3d instant. When I refer you to the state of the counsels which prevailed at the period you left this city, and add that they are now, if possible, in a worse train than ever, you will find but little ground on which the hope of a good establishment can be formed. In a word, I almost despair of seeing a favorable issue to the proceedings of our Convention, and do, therefore, repent having had any agency in the business." * * * * * * * "I am sorry you went away. I wish you were back. The crisis is equally important and alarming." This account of the temper of the Convention agrees well with the debate as transmitted to us by Madison.

made for a census, it was a naked proposition to place the control of the government under the free-soil section. The debate will discover how far the Southern delegates agreed to that humiliating condition. It was the universal belief, that the South was destined to be, as it then was, the most populous region, and this explains why the North objected to a full representation of slaves, and why Mr. Randolph and Mr. Mason insisted so strenuously upon a census.

"Mr. RUTLEDGE moved that New Hampshire be reduced from three to two members. Her numbers did not entitle her to three, and it was a poor State.

"Gen. PINCKNEY seconds the motion.

"Mr. KING.—New Hampshire has probably more than one hundred and twenty thousand inhabitants, and has an extensive country of tolerable fertility. Its inhabitants may, therefore, be expected to increase fast. He remarked, that the four Eastern States, having eight hundred thousand souls, have one-third fewer representatives than the four Southern States, having not more than seven hundred thousand souls, rating the blacks five to three. The Eastern people will advert to these circumstances, and be dissatisfied. He believed them to be very desirous of uniting with their Southern brethren, but did not think it prudent to rely so far on that disposition, as to subject them to any gross inequality. *He was fully convinced that the question concerning a difference of interest did not lie, where it had hitherto been discussed, between the great and small States, but between the Southern and Eastern; for this reason he had been ready to yield something in the proportion of representatives for the security of the Southern. No principle would justify giving them a majority. They were brought as near equality as possible.* He was not adverse to giving them a still greater security, but did not see how it could be done.

"Gen. PINCKNEY.—The report, before it was committed, was more favorable to the Southern States than as it now stands. *If they are to form so considerable a minority, and*

3

the regulation of trade is to be given to the General Government, they will be nothing more than overseers for the Northern States. He did not expect the Southern States to be raised to a majority of representatives; but wished them to have something like an equality. At present, by the alterations of the committee, in favor of the Northern States, they are removed further from it than they were before. One member, indeed, had been added to Virginia, which he was glad of, as he considered her a Southern State. He was glad also that the members of Georgia were increased.

"Mr. WILLIAMSON was not for reducing New Hampshire from three to two, but for reducing some others. The Southern interest must be extremely endangered by the present arrangement. The Northern States are to have a majority in the first instance, and the means of perpetuating it.

"Mr. DAYTON, from New Jersey, observed, that the line between the Northern and Southern interest had been improperly drawn; that Pennsylvania was the dividing State, there being six on each side of her.

"Gen. PINCKNEY urged the reduction; dwelt on the superior wealth of the Southern States, and insisted on its having its due weight in the government.

"Mr. GOUVERNEUR MORRIS regretted the turn of the debate. The States, he found, had many representatives on the floor. Few, he feared, were to be deemed the representatives of America. He thought the Southern States have, by the report, more than their share of representation. Property ought to have its weight, but not all the weight. If the Southern States are to supply money, the Northern States are to spill their blood. Besides, the probable revenue from the Southern States has been greatly overrated. He was against reducing New Hampshire.

"Mr. RANDOLPH was opposed to a reduction of New Hampshire, *not because she had a full title to three members; but because it was in his contemplation, first, to make it the duty, instead of leaving it to the discretion, of the legislature to regulate the representation by a periodical census;* secondly, to recognize more than a bare majority of votes in the legislature, in certain cases, and particularly in commercial cases. On the question for reducing New Hampshire, it passed in the negative."

Then followed motions to increase the representatives from the Southern States, all of which were negatived, Virginia and North Carolina voting against the motions, which discloses the fact, that both Virginia and North Carolina looked to a periodical census to rectify such inequalities in representation as might exist at first. Accordingly, and in pursuance of his declared intent, Mr. Randolph moved, as an amendment to the report of the committee of five, "that, in order to ascertain the alterations in the population and wealth of the several States, the legislature should be required to cause a census and estimate to be taken within one year after its first meeting, and every —— years thereafter; and that the legislature arrange the representation accordingly.

"Mr. GOUVERNEUR MORRIS opposed it, as fettering the legislature too much."

On Wednesday, the 11th of July, Mr. Randolph's motion, requiring the legislature to take a periodical census, for the purpose of redressing inequalities in the representation, was resumed.

"Mr. SHERMAN, of Connecticut, was against shackling the legislature too much. We ought to choose wise and good men,* and then confide in them."

How cunningly he puts it—*wise and good men*—that is, *Northern* men. But Col. Mason and Mr. Randolph did not

* Mr. Gerry, in the Federal Convention, gave a glowing picture of the moral condition of Massachusetts, which was a part of the Northern community from which the wise and virtuous men of whom Mr. Sherman speaks were to be selected: "In Massachusetts, the worst men get into the legislature; several members of that body had lately been convicted of infamous crimes. Men of indigence, ignorance and baseness spare no pains, however dirty, to carry their point against men who are superior to the artifices practised."—*Madison Papers*, p. 801.

appear to have had the same unlimited confidence in a free-soil Congress. They continued to press the census, which clearly proves that it was not their purpose to put the South in the condition of a minority, and so dependent on the forbearance of the North.

"Mr. MASON. The greater the difficulty we find in fixing the proper rule of representation, the more unwilling ought we to be to throw the task, from ourselves, on the general legislature. He did not object to the conjectural ratio which was to prevail in the outset; but considered a revision from time to time, according to some permanent and precise standard, as essential to the fair representation required in the first branch. According to the present population of America, the Northern part of it had a right to preponderate, and he could not deny it; but he wished it not to preponderate hereafter, when the reason for it no longer continued. From the nature of man, we may be sure that those who have power in their hands will not give it up while they can retain it. On the contrary, we know that they will always, when they can, rather increase it. If the Southern States, therefore, should have three-fifths of the people of America within their limits, the Northern will hold fast the majority of representatives. One-fourth will govern the three-fourths. The Southern States will complain; but they may complain, from generation to generation, without redress. Unless some principle, therefore, which will do them justice hereafter, shall be inserted in the Constitution, disagreeable as the declaration was to him, he must declare he would neither vote for the system here, nor support it in his own State.

"Mr. WILLIAMSON was for making it a duty of the legislature to do what was right; and not leaving it at liberty to do or not to do it. He moved that Mr. Randolph's propositions be postponed, in order to consider the following: 'That, in order to ascertain the alterations that may happen in the population and wealth of the several States, a census shall be taken of the free white inhabitants, and three-fifths of those of other descriptions, on the first year after this Government shall have been adopted, and every —— years thereafter; and that the representation be regulated accordingly.'

"Mr. RANDOLPH agreed that Mr. Williamson's proposition should stand in place of his. He observed, that the ratio fixed for the first meeting was a mere conjecture; that it placed the power in the hands of that part of America which could not always be entitled to it; that this power would not be voluntarily renounced; and that it was, consequently, the duty of the Convention to secure its renunciation by some constitutional provisions.

"Mr. BUTLER and Gen. PINCKNEY insisted, that the blacks be included in the rule of representation, equally with the whites; and, for that purpose, moved that the words 'three-fifths' be struck out."

It will be remembered that it was Mr. Chas. Pinckney who, along with Mr. Wilson, had introduced the three-fifths ratio. Gen. Pinckney, however, appears, through the whole course of the debate, to have aimed at a Southern preponderance.

"Mr. GERRY thought that three-fifths of them was, to say the least, the full proportion that could be admitted.

"Mr. GORHAM. This ratio was fixed by Congress, as a rule of taxation. Then it was urged by the delegates representing the States having slaves, that the blacks were still more inferior to freemen. At present, when the ratio of representation is to be established, we are assured that they are equal to free men. The arguments on the former occasion had convinced him that three-fifths was pretty near the just *proportion*, and he should vote according to the same opinion now.

Mr. BUTLER insisted that the labor of a slave in South Carolina was as productive and valuable as that of a free man in Massachusetts; that as wealth was the great means of defence and utility to the nation, they were equally valuable with freemen; and that, consequently, an equal representation ought to be allowed for them in a government which was instituted principally for the protection of property, and was itself to be supported by property.

"Mr. MASON could not agree to the motion, notwithstanding it was favorable to Virginia, because he thought it unjust. It was certain that the slaves were valuable, as they raised the value of land, increased the exports and imports, and, of course, the revenue, would supply the means of feeding and supporting an army, *and might, in cases of emergency, become themselves soldiers.* As, in these important respects, they were useful to the community at large, they ought not to be excluded from the representation. He added, as worthy of remark, *that the Southern States have this peculiar species of property,* over and above the other species of property, common to all the States.

Mr. WILLIAMSON reminded Mr. Gorham that if the Southern States contended for the inferiority of blacks to whites, when taxation was in view, the Eastern States, on the same occasion, contended for their equality.* He did not, however, either then, or now, concur in either extreme ; but approved of the ratio of three-fifths."

Mr. Butler's motion, for considering blacks equal to whites, was rejected—Delaware, South Carolina and Georgia voting

* In the Congress of 1776, "John Adams observed, that the numbers of people were taken by this article, as the index of the wealth of the States, and not as subjects of taxation. That, as to this matter, it was of no consequence by what name you called your people, whether by that of freemen, or of slaves. That, in some countries, the laboring poor were *called* freemen ; in others, they were *called* slaves : but that the difference was imaginary only. What matters it, whether a landlord, employing ten laborers on his farm, gives them annually as much as will buy the necessaries of life, or gives them those necessaries—at short hand ? The ten laborers add as much wealth annually to the State, increase its exports as much in the one case as the other. Certainly five hundred freemen produce no more profits, no greater surplus for the payment of taxes, than five hundred slaves. Therefore the State in which the laborers are called freemen should be taxed no more than that in which are those called slaves. Suppose, by any extraordinary operation of nature or of law, one half the laborers of a State could, in the course of one night, be transformed into slaves, would the State be made the poorer, or more unable to pay taxes ?

in the affirmative. I cannot explain Delaware's vote on this occasion, except by her extreme jealousy of Pennsylvania. Like most small bodies, she was extremely sensitive on the score of her importance; and, as it was clear that a proportional representation would be established in, at least, one branch of the legislature, she preferred that the supremacy should be lodged with the slave States, from whom she entertained no such apprehension. This, however, was only one of the complications which embarrassed that vital point.

The debate on Mr. Williamson's resolution was continued.

"Mr. Gouverneur Morris said, he had several objections to the proposition of Mr. Williamson. In the first place, it fettered the legislature too much; in the second place, it would exclude some States altogether who would not have a sufficient number to entitle them to a single representative; in the third place, it will not consist with the resolution passed on Saturday last, authorizing the legislature to adjust the representation, from time to time, on the principles of population and wealth; nor with the principles of equity. If slaves were to be considered as inhabitants, and not as wealth, then the said resolution would not be pursued; if as wealth, then why no other wealth, but slaves, included? These objections may perhaps be removed by amendments. His great objection was, that the number of inhabitants was not a proper standard of wealth.

"Mr. King thought there was great force in the objections of Mr. Morris. He would, however, accede to the proposition for the sake of doing something.

"Mr. Rutledge contended for the admission of wealth in the estimate, by which representation should be regulated."

In accordance with this view he moved that the legislature, from time to time, should proportion the representation according to the principles of wealth and population. A debate took place on Mr. Rutledge's proposition, in the course of which Mr. Gouverneur Morris advocated the proposition.

In reply to him, Mr. Madison said: "He was not a little

surprised to hear this implicit confidence urged by a member, who, on all occasions, had inculcated so strongly the political depravity of men, and the necessity of checking one vice and interest by opposing them to another vice and interest. If the representatives of the people would be bound by the ties he had mentioned, what need was there of a Senate, what of a revisionary power? But his reasoning was not only inconsistent with his former reasoning, but with itself. At the same time that he recommended *this implicit confidence to the Southern States, in the Northern majority*, he was still more zealous in exhorting all to a jealousy of a Western majority. To reconcile the gentleman with himself, it must be imagined that he determined the human character by the points of the compass. *The truth was, that all men, having power, ought to be distrusted to a certain degree.*" This reveals the principle of Mr. Madison's political philosophy. He appears to have thought that no section could be safely entrusted with the power to dominate over another section. Certainly, it is not to be inferred that he was willing to trust a Northern majority with a dominion over the South. He was opposed to any discrimination against the equality of the New States, as it did not appear that they would be divided by any peculiar interest from the other States.

Mr. Rutledge's motion was lost. On the question on the first clause of Mr. Williamson's motion, as to taking a census of the *free* inhabitants, it passed in the affirmative. The next clause, as to three-fifths of the negroes, being considered—

"Mr. KING, being much opposed to fixing numbers as the rule of representation, was particularly so on account of the blacks. He thought the admission of them along with the whites at all, would excite great discontents among the States having no slaves. He had never said, as to any particular point, that he would, in no event, acquiesce in and support it; but he would say, *that if, in any case, such a declaration was to be made by him, it would be in this.* He remarked that in the temporary allotment of representatives, made by the committee, the Southern States had received more than the number of their white, and three-fifths of their black, inhabitants entitled them to.

"Mr. SHERMAN.—South Carolina had not more beyond her proportion than New York and New Hampshire; nor either of them more than was necessary for them to avoid factions, or reducing them below their proportion. Georgia had more; but the rapid growth of that State seemed to justify it. In general, the allotment might not be just, but, considering all the circumstances, he was satisfied with it.

"Mr. GORHAM supported the propriety of establishing numbers as the rule. He said that, in Massachusetts, estimates had been taken in the different towns, and that persons had been curious enough to compare these estimates with the respective numbers of people; and it had been found, even including Boston, that the most exact proportion prevailed between numbers and property. He was aware that there might be some weight in what had fallen from his colleague, as to the umbrage which might be taken by the people of the Eastern States. But he recollected, that when the proposition of Congress for changing the eighth article of the Confederation was before the legislature of Massachusetts, the only difficulty then was to satisfy them that the negroes ought not to have been counted equally with the whites, instead of being counted in the ratio of three-fifths only.

"Mr. WILSON did not see on what principle the admission of blacks, in the proportion of three-fifths, could be explained. Are they admitted as citizens—then why are they not admitted on an equality with white citizens? Are they admitted as property—then why not other property admitted into the computation? *These were difficulties, however, which he thought must be overruled by the necessity of compromise.* He had some apprehensions, also, from the tendency of the blending of the blacks with the whites, to give disgust to the people of Pennsylvania, as had been intimated by his colleague (Mr. Gouverneur Morris), but he differed from him in thinking the number of inhabitants so incorrect a measure of wealth. He had seen the western settlements of Pennsylvania, and, on a comparison of them with the city of Philadelphia, could discover little other difference, than that property was more unequally divided here than there. Taking the same number in the aggregate of the two situations, he believed there would be little difference in their wealth and ability to contribute to the public wants.

"Mr. GOUVERNEUR MORRIS was compelled to declare himself reduced to the dilemma of *doing injustice to the Southern States* or to human nature; he must, therefore, do it to the former. For he could never agree to give such encouragement to the slave trade as would be given by allowing them a representation for their negroes; and he did not believe these States would ever confederate on terms that would deprive them of that trade."

On the question for agreeing to include three-fifths of the blacks,—Connecticut, Virginia, North Carolina, Georgia, aye—4; Massachusetts, New Jersey, Pennsylvania, Delaware, Maryland, South Carolina, no—6. On the question for taking the census, "the first year after the meeting of the legislature," the proposition passed in the affirmative. It is to be observed, in the foregoing vote, that South Carolina voted against the three-fifths ratio, on account of her preference for a full representation of slaves. And "Mr. Carroll explained the vote of Maryland, on the ground that her delegation objected to its phraseology."

It is to be observed in this debate, that Mr. Wilson avowedly accepted the three-fifths ratio as a compromise; and that Mr. Morris objected to it, on the ground of the encouragement it would give to the slave trade—thereby establishing a direct connection between the basis of representation and the importation of slaves. It will be remarked, likewise, that Mr. Wilson pointed out the impropriety of admitting slaves into the basis as property, without, at the same time, including other species of property.

From the period of the rejection of Mr. Williamson's substitute for Mr. Randolph's proposition, the war of sections burst forth in its greatest violence—a war which was not composed until the restoration of the compromise by a full and conclusive vote of the Convention. The next succeeding debate turned upon the sectional issue; and then the sectional collision was fiercest.

On Thursday, the twelfth of July, the struggle again began.

"*In Convention*, Mr. GOUVERNEUR MORRIS moved to add to the clause empowering the legislature to vary the representation according to the principles of wealth and numbers of inhabitants, a proviso, 'that taxation shall be in proportion to representation.'

"Mr. BUTLER contended again, that representation should be according to the full number of inhabitants, including all the blacks; admitting the justice of Mr. Gouverneur Morris' motion.

"Mr. MASON also admitted the justice of the principle, but was afraid embarrassments might be occasioned to the legislature by it. It might drive the legislature to the plan of requisitions.

"Mr. GOUVERNEUR MORRIS admitted that some objection lay against his motion, but supposed they would be removed by restraining the rule to *direct* taxation. With regard to indirect taxes on *exports* and imports, and on consumption, the rule would be inapplicable.

"Gen. PINCKNEY liked the idea. He thought it so just, that it could not be objected to; but foresaw that if the revision of the census was left to the discretion of the legislature, it would never be carried into execution. The rule must be fixed, and the execution of it enforced, by the Constitution. He was alarmed at what was said yesterday concerning the negroes. He was now again alarmed at what had been thrown out concerning the taxing of exports. South Carolina has, in one year, exported to the amount of six hundred thousand pounds sterling, all of which was the fruit of the labor of her blacks. Will she be represented in proportion to this amount? She will not. Neither ought she then to be subject to a tax on it. He hoped a clause would be inserted in the system, restraining the legislature from taxing exports.

"Mr. WILSON approved the principle, but could not see how it could be carried into execution, unless restrained to direct taxation.

"Mr. GOUVERNEUR MORRIS having so varied his motion, by inserting the word 'direct,' it passed *nem. con.*, as follows: 'provided always that direct taxation ought to be proportioned to representation.'

"Mr. DAVIS said it was high time now to speak out. He saw that it was meant by some gentlemen to deprive the Southern States of any share of representation for their blacks. He was sure that North Carolina would never confederate on any terms that did not rate them, at least, as three-fifths. If the Eastern States meant, therefore, to exclude them altogether, the business was at an end.

"Mr. GOUVERNEUR MORRIS. It had been said that it was high time to speak out. As one member, he would candidly do so. He came here to form a compact for the good of America. He was ready to do so with all the States. He hoped, and believed, that all would enter into such a compact. If they would not, he was ready to join with any States that would. But, as the compact was to be voluntary, it is in vain for the Eastern States to insist on what the Southern States will never agree to. It is equally vain for the latter to require, what the other States can never admit; and he verily believed the people of Pennsylvania will never agree to a representation of negroes. What can be desired of these States more than has been already proposed—that the legislature shall, from time to time, regulate representation according to population and wealth.

"Gen. PINCKNEY desired that the rule of wealth should be ascertained, and not left to the pleasure of the legislature; and that property in slaves should not be exposed to danger, under a government instituted for the protection of property.

"The first clause in the report of the first Grand Committee was postponed.

"Mr. ELLSWORTH, of Connecticut, in order to carry into effect the principle established, moved to add to the last clause adopted by the House, the words following: 'And that the rule of taxation, for the support of the government of the United States, shall be the number of white inhabitants, and three-fifths of every other description in the several States, until some other rule, that shall more accurately ascertain the wealth of the several States, can be devised and adopted by the legislature.'

"Mr. BUTLER seconded the motion, in order that it might be committed.

"Mr. RANDOLPH was not satisfied with the motion. The danger will be revived, that the ingenuity of the legislature may evade or pervert the rule, so as to perpetuate the power where it shall be lodged in the first instance. He proposed, in lieu of Mr. Ellsworth's motion, 'that, in order to ascertain the alterations in representation that may be required, from time to time, by changes in the relative circumstances of the States, a census shall be taken within two years from the first meeting of the general legislature of the United States, and once within the term of every —— years afterwards, of all the inhabitants, and in the manner, and according to the ratio recommended by Congress in their resolution of the 18th day of April, 1783, (rating the blacks at three-fifths of their number); and that the legislature of the United States shall arrange the representation accordingly.' *He urged strenuously, that express security ought to be provided for including slaves in the ratio of representation. He lamented that such a species of property existed. But, as it did exist, the holders of it would require this security.* It was perceived that the design was entertained, by some, of excluding slaves altogether. The legislature, therefore, ought not to be left at liberty.

"Mr. Ellsworth withdraws his motion, and seconds that of Mr. Randolph.

Mr. Wilson observed, that less umbrage would, perhaps, be taken against an admission of the slaves into the rule of representation, if it should be so expressed as to make them indirectly only an ingredient in the rule, by saying that they should enter into the rule of taxation; and, as representation was to be according to taxation, the end would be equally attained. He accordingly proposed an amendment embodying this alteration.

"Mr. King. Although this amendment varies the aspect somewhat, he had still two powerful objections against tying down the legislature to the rule of numbers; first, they were at this time an uncertain index of the relative wealth of the States; secondly, if they were a just index at this time, it cannot be supposed always to continue so. He was far from wishing to retain any unjust advantage whatever in one part of the Republic. If justice was not the basis of the connection, it could not be of long duration. He must be short-sighted, indeed, who does not foresee that, whenever the Southern States shall be more numerous than the Northern, they can, and will, hold a language that will awe them into justice. *If they threaten to* separate now, in case injury shall *be done them, will their threats be less urgent or effectual when force shall back their demands? Even in the intervening period, there will be no point of time at which they will not be able to say, do us justice, or we will separate.* He urged the necessity of placing confidence, to a certain degree, in every government, and did not conceive that the proposed confidence, as to a periodical re-adjustment of the representation, exceeded that degree.

"Mr. Pinckney moved to amend Mr. Randolph's motion, so as to make 'blacks equal to whites in the ratio of representation.' This, he urged, was nothing more than justice. The blacks are the laborers, the peasants, of the Southern States. They are as productive of pecuniary resources as those of the

Northern States. They add equally to the wealth, and, considering money as the sinew of war, to the strength of the nation. It will also be politic with regard to the Northern States, as taxation is to keep pace with representation.

"Gen. PINCKNEY moved to insert six years instead of two, as the period, computing from the first meeting of the legislature, within which the first census should be taken."

General Pinckney's motion was adopted. That of Mr. Chas. Pinckney was rejected. On the question on the whole proposition, as proportioning representation to direct taxation, and both to the white and three-fifths of the black inhabitants, and requiring a periodical census, six States voted in the affirmative, two, only, in the negative.

It is to be remarked of this debate, that the idea of proportioning representation to wealth was in the ascendant. This will account for the change of position on the part of Mr. Charles Pinckney, one of the proposers of the three-fifths ratio. It is manifest, that when you take population as the measure of wealth, that every description of population would have to be included—as well the black as the white. This explains the readiness with which the delegates from South Carolina accepted that proposition—inasmuch as that would have created a Southern preponderance in the government. But a sectional preponderance, created by whatever means, was not the object of search of a majority of the States—particularly of the State of Virginia. It appears to have been the conviction that an inequality, in favor of or against either of the parties, would doom the Union to a short existence. That a sectional domination, although it rested on superior wealth, would not reconcile either the North or the South to the grievous yoke.

"FRIDAY, July 13th.

"On motion of Mr. Randolph, the vote of Monday last, authorizing the Legislature to adjust, from time to time, the representation upon the principles of *wealth* and numbers of inhabitants, was reconsidered by common consent, in order to strike out wealth and adjust the resolution to that requiring periodical revisions, according to the number of whites and three-fifths of the blacks.

"Mr. Gouverneur Morris opposed the alteration, as leaving still an incoherence. If negroes were to be viewed as inhabitants, and the revision was to proceed on the principle of numbers of inhabitants, they ought to be added in their entire number, and not in the proportion of three-fifths. If as property, the word wealth was right; and striking it out would produce the very inconsistency which it was meant to get rid of. The train of business and the late turn which it had taken, had led him, he said, into deep meditation on it, and he would candidly state the result. A distinction had been set up, and urged, between the Northern and Southern States. He had, hitherto, considered this doctrine as heretical. He still thought the distinction groundless. He sees, however, that it is persisted in; and the Southern gentlemen will not be satisfied unless they see the way open to their gaining a majority in the public councils. The consequence of such a transfer of power from the maritime to the interior and landed interest, will, he foresees, be such an oppression to commerce that *he shall be obliged to vote for the vicious principle of equality in the second branch, in order to provide some defence for the Northern States against it.* But to come more to the point, either this distinction is fictitious or real; if fictitious, let it be dismissed, and let us proceed with due confidence. If it be real, instead of attempting to blend incompatible things, let us at once take a friendly leave of each other. There can be no end of demands for security, if every particular interest is entitled to it. The Eastern States may claim it for their fishery, and for other objects, as the Southern States claim it for their peculiar objects. In this struggle between the two ends of the Union, what part ought the Middle States, in point of policy, to take? To join their Eastern brethren, according to his ideas. If the Southern States get the power in their hands, and be joined, as they will be, with the interior country, they will inevitably bring on a war with Spain for the Mississippi. This language is already held. The interior country, having no property or interest exposed on the sea, will be little affected by such a war. He wished to know what security the Northern and Middle States will have against this danger. It has been said that North Carolina, South Carolina, and Georgia, only, will in a little time have a majority of the people of America, they must in that case include the great interior country, and every thing was to be apprehended from their getting the power into their hands.

"Mr. BUTLER. The security the Southern States want is, that their negroes may not be taken from them, which some gentlemen within or without doors have a very great mind to do. It was not supposed that North Carolina, South Carolina and Georgia would have more people than all the other States, but many more relatively to the other States, than they now have. The people and strength of America are evidently bearing southwardly and south-westwardly."

The proposition of Mr. Randolph passed, Delaware only voting against it, and Delaware was divided. Thus, after a sectional collision that equalled in violence any that we have witnessed in our day, the compromise, as originally proposed, with the single addition of a periodical census, was adopted into the Constitution. It is not too much to call that compromise, in virtue of which power was ratably distributed between the North and South, the ground-work of the whole system.

But the quarrel between the sections was not yet ended. It broke out again when representation in the Senate came to be adjusted. The delegates from the smaller States made a firm stand for their cherished principle of equality of representation in that chamber of the Legislature. Luther Martin here rose in the ascendant, but he was vigorously opposed by Mr. Madison, who struggled to apply the sectional compromise throughout the government. His speech was an able one. In it he stated five objections to the principle of State equality, the fifth being—"*The perpetuity it would give to the Northern against the Southern scale, was a serious consideration. It seemed now to be pretty well understood that the real difference of interest lay, not between the large and small, but between the Northern and Southern States. The institution of slavery, and its consequences, formed the line of discrimination. There were five States on the Southern, eight on the Northern side of this line. Should a proportional representation take place, it was true, the Northern would still outnumber the other; but not in the same degree, at this time; and every day would tend towards an equilibrium.*" It is believed, if to the evidences contained in the debates heretofore submitted, this speech of Mr. Madison be added, that no doubt can remain on any reasonable mind as to the object of the fractional representation.

In his endeavor to extend the equilibrium to the Senate, Mr. Madison failed. But it must have been apparent to his mind, that enough had been gained already to provide for the safety of the South. The great sectional struggle was over, the distribution of federal population between the sections had been settled. That struggle had resulted to the satisfaction of the South. They, who were so wise in all things else, must have foreseen that finally power in the Senate would be according to population, and for that reason, doubtless, the Southern leaders were content to allow a temporary Northern preponderance in that branch of the Legislature. Although the smaller States talked about a withdrawal from the Convention if their demands were not complied with, it was still apparent that, disconnected as they were territorially, that no such result would follow in the event upon which they threatened to act. It is an interesting part of the history of the Constitution, to enquire by what influences the Senatorial equality was in the end produced. It was produced by the jealousy of the Northern section. It will be remembered, that in the outset the larger States of the North co-operated with the slave section against the equality claimed throughout the government by the lesser States. But this alliance did not last long. It gave rise to sectional jealousies. After the fractional representation had been agreed upon, it appears to have been apprehended by some that it would result in creating a Southern preponderance in the government. As had been intimated by Mr. Gouverneur Morris, the large States of the North wheeled into line with the small States, and carried the principle of Senatorial equality, "to provide some defence for the Northern States against" the evils which were apprehended from the government being put under Southern control. This is revealed not only by the debates above cited, but also by a note appended by Mr. Madison.

CHAPTER III.

There is nothing more unlike than analogy, and nothing more apt to mislead.—MANSFIELD.

They commit the whole to the mercy of untried speculations; they abandon the dearest interests of the public to those loose theories, to which none of them would choose to trust the slightest of his private concerns.—BURKE.

When the ratio of three-fifths was proposed by Wilson and Pinckney as a mode of dividing political power between the North and South in even proportions, it was stated to have been selected because that ratio had been proposed by Congress as a measure of taxation. It is a necessary inference that it was believed that it would be productive of an equal distribution of the burdens of government between those sections. But we are not left to surmise, for Mr. Gorham explicitly stated that it had been devised by Congress because it would result in giving that "proportion" of taxes.

As soon as the North and South, in the Convention of 1776, undertook to construct a federal government, the question of slavery presented itself at the threshold—but it presented itself as a question of taxation. The committee appointed to draught a constitution proposed, in the eleventh article, that the expenses of the government should be defrayed out of a treasury to be supplied by the States, in proportion to the number of inhabitants of every sex, age and condition, except Indians not paying taxes. The obvious effect of that provision would have been to throw on the slave States the largest share of taxation, on account of their superior populousness. It was, consequently, objected to, and Mr. Chase, of Maryland, proposed to proportion taxes according to white population. But that would have laid on the North an unequal share of the taxes. The debate appears to have been both able and animated. Mr. Harrison, of Virginia, at length proposed, "as a compromise," that two slaves should be counted as one freeman. But the amendment was lost; the whole North voting against it, the whole South voting for it. Another measure of taxation was, subsequently, agreed upon, which, after trial, gave satisfaction to neither party. Congress again reverted to Mr. Harrison's proposition—which they slightly modified and recommended to the States—so to alter the Federal Articles as to proportion the quotas among the States according to the whole number of free inhabitants, and three-fifths of the slaves. The outline of the debate upon that subject, as preserved by Madison, shows that the phrase, "equilibrium of taxation," was as familiar as the probable results of that ratio, as that of an equilibrium of representation afterwards became.

The fractional basis of three-fifths being, in the first place, resorted to as a mode of distributing taxes between the sections, was, afterwards, taken up and applied to the distribution of political power between them. Strange would it have been, if it had proved applicable to subjects so opposite in their nature; taxation being a charge and disability, whilst representation was, in its nature, power and privilege, and might, if adroitly used, be made the means of exemption. As a measure of taxation, it might answer well; for there would be neither inducement nor power to overthrow it; but, as a measure of political influence, there was every conceivable motive to induce each party to conspire against it. Nor did the arrangement, so cunningly contrived, that direct taxes should be determined by representation, operate as any kind of check; for if population was, in truth, a criterion of social wealth, which was the general opinion, the capacity to pay would be enlarged as federal numbers were increased. The whole scheme failed, as we know, so soon as direct taxes ceased to be the means of collecting the revenue; but, even if that had not taken place, and the government had been confined to direct taxation, the idea embodied in the basis of representation would not the less have been disappointed. It is a subject which may well excite surprise, that the Convention, constituted as it was, should have been deceived by so superficial a resemblance.

It is proper to call attention here to the explanation which was given by Alexander Hamilton, in the New York Convention of ratification, of the fractional representation of slaves; more especially as it was repeated in the Federalist:

"The regulations complained of," said he, "was one result of the spirit of accommodation which governed the Convention; and, without this indulgence, no Union could possibly have been formed. * * * * * * The best writers on government have held that representation should be compounded of persons and property. This rule has been adopted, as far as it could be, in the constitution of New York. It will, however, by no means, be admitted, that the slaves are considered altogether as property. They are men, though degraded to the condition of slavery.* They are persons known

---

* Here is what the Federalist says, No. 54: "Let the case of the slaves be considered, as in truth it is, a peculiar one. Let the compromising expedient of the Constitution be mutually adopted, which regards them *as inhabitants, but as* debased, by servitude, below the equal level of free inhabitants, which regards the *slave* as divested of two-fifths of the *man*." He who has perused the Debates of the Convention, preserved by Mr. Madison's own pen,

to the municipal laws of the States which they inhabit, as well as to the laws of nature."

Two explanations are here offered, but inconsistent with each other. If any proposition is clear beyond controversy, it is the one that slaves were admitted in the single character of population, they being, as Gen. Pinckney called them, the black peasantry of the South. Nor were they partially excluded from representation because of their supposed inferiority to the white peasant of the North, but their partial exclusion was insisted upon by one party, and assented to by the other, because of the effect which such exclusion would produce upon the partition of power. There could not be a more conclusive argument against the exclusion of the slave, because of moral inferiority, than the fact that the free negro, wherever he might be, was admitted to the full privileges of representation.

---

may well be surprised at this extraordinary interpretation of the fractional basis. How was it ascertained that the slave was less, by two-fifths, a *man* than the free negro in America, or the wild cannibal negro in Africa?

The controversial character of the Federalist is evidenced by the contradictory grounds it sometimes assumed; and its sectional complexion is as undoubted. It was addressed to the people of the State of New York, and only particular numbers of it were republished in the South. This explanation of the sectional basis was accommodated to the temper of an anti-slavery population. It certainly was wholly the offspring of imagination.

CHAPTER IV.

VIRGINIA.

Like a stately ship
Of Tarsus, bound for th' isles
Of Javan or Gadire,
With all her bravery on, and tackle trim,
Sails fill'd, and streamers waving,
Courted by all the winds that hold them play.—SAMSON AGONISTES.

When, in 1788, the Convention of Virginia adopted the Federal Government as a part of her Constitution, they effected a greater change in our Constitution than the wildest reformer now suggests to us. To estimate the amount of that change, we must have reference to her interests and power at that day.—JOHN RANDOLPH, *of Roanoke.*

When I call this the most mighty State in the Union, do I not speak the truth? Does not Virginia surpass every State in the Union in the number of inhabitants, extent of territory, felicity of position, in affluence and wealth?—HENRY.

In Virginia, the new Constitution underwent the severest ordeal. The opposition was led by men of the most distinguished abilities, the largest knowledge, the highest dignity and the most splendid public services. Among its advocates, too, were to be found men of the first order of talent. In the Debates of the Virginia Convention of Ratification (imperfectly reported as they have been), posterity will find the principles of that instrument most thoroughly exposed, and there, as in the leaves of the Sybil, are many of those predictions found, the verification of which has been reserved until the present day. There the battle of the Constitution was fought, and there the victory won; but won by means which redound but little to the honor of the chief actors in those scenes. When the Convention assembled six States had ratified the Constitution; during its session Maryland and South Carolina* ratified, and its adoption by Virginia breathed life into the

* New Hampshire had ratified the Constitution about ten days before the adjournment of the Virginia Convention, but the information had not reached Richmond.—MADISON TO WASHINGTON OF THAT DATE.—*Correspondence of the Revolution.*

new government. Had the decision there been different, the Constitution as it is, and as it has existed for the ruin of that lordly Commonwealth, would have been rejected. It would have been committed to a new Convention, its national features would have been purged off, and the Articles of Confederation, based upon purely federal principles, but amended in those particulars wherein experience had showed amendment to be necessary, would have been presented to the people of the several States. This the simple negative of Virginia would have produced; for no federal system, however devised, could have sustained itself that did not embrace her. The contest over the Constitution stirred the popular elements from the bottom; and that we may be able more justly to appreciate the nature of that mighty conflict, it will be necessary, first to take a survey of the theatre upon which it took place.

Virginia, between the termination of the war of the Revolution and the creation of the existing central authority, has been but little sought after, and is but little known. That period is generally regarded as a dark interval in her history, either as a chaos or a waste from which little is to be gathered to reward the researches of the student or excite the attention of the curious. A deep gulf, indeed, divides it from present times—a mighty Revolution; but, yet, to that desolate waste, that unvisited region, the steps of the reader are now invited. But our trouble will not be without its reward. If I mistake not, those times, upon a closer inspection, will appear to have been the most glorious in the annals of that State, and to have rendered her, indeed, worthy of that distinguished position, which, by common consent, had been conceded to her among the confederated sovereignties of North America. From that altitude, like a stricken orb, she has slowly descended, until her loyal children, with grief and indignation, behold her ready to sink below the horizon shorn of her beams.

The limits of Virginia embraced at this time Kentucky.

Kentucky, it is true, had petitioned for an independent establishment, and her prayer had been granted, but subject to the concurrence of the federal authority. Clogged with that condition, the grant had been rejected; for the people of that province preferred the old connection rather than have its abrogation made a subject of congressional license.* Indeed, the consent to its admission into the Union appears to have been given by Congress; but, for some cause, had not been accepted or acted upon. The number of its inhabitants amounted to sixty thousand, and was from time to time receiving additions from the more populous parts of Eastern Virginia. Louisville was the principal town, indeed, the only one *laid down* on the maps of that period. But, as yet, Kentucky was embraced by the geography of Virginia; her delegates and senators resorted annually to Richmond; she received from thence her laws and her justice; she contributed an important element to the military and voting strength of the parent State; and for her loyal obedience, her distinct interests, which were strongly marked, received that vigilant attention which the concerns of an affectionate daughter merited from a fond and indulgent mother. On this, the most interesting occasion in the history of either, the delegates from Kentucky sat on the floor of the Convention, and exercised an important influence on the late deliberations of that body.

The late war had brought evil times upon Virginia. It had operated a total suspension of her foreign trade, the only source from which she derived money, as well as many of the comforts and all the elegant luxuries of life. The government had been compelled in consequence to resort to the cumbrous and expensive expedient of specific supplies, as a mode of contributing to the defence of the country. But when peace was published and the sea cleared of British cruisers, business, to some extent, revived. A gentle tide of prosperity set in, which was exhibited by the regularity with which her federal

* Madison to Washington, 9th December, 1785.

quotas were contributed, and which surpassed in amount the sum furnished during that period by the entire North. Whilst peace had restored, in some measure, prosperity to Virginia, it brought nothing but disaster to the North; as the war had brought nothing but disaster to Virginia, but had conferred upon the North equivalents and compensating advantages. It is a fact deserving attention, that the Revolution, which brought business to a dead halt in the South, should, strangely enough, have buoyed it up in the North, and that peace, which brought healing on its wings to the one, should have blighted the whole industry of the other. The North had been the principal theatre of the war, and, consequently, the principal theatre of all the disbursements of both the English and American governments. Thus it happened that those thrifty patriots were enabled, by an ingenious chemistry, to distill the materials of prosperity even out of the misfortunes of their country. It happened in this wise: During the whole contest, a brisk, lucrative and systematic traffic was kept up by the country people with the British lines. So extensive was the scale upon which it was conducted, that the General-in-chief, lamenting the wide-spread depravity, apprehended that by its means the contest would be prolonged, and the success even of the cause endangered. Every description of men were engaged in those contraband dealings—Whigs and Tories, King's-men and Patriots, Priests and Laymen. Every corporal's tent was a bazaar. They bought and they sold as in peace, and, encouraged by universal example, they scarcely drew the veil of secrecy over their proceedings.

Washington would distress the enemy by day, but the country people would supply them by night with those comforts which, in an enemy's country, an army most requires. Thus the advantages of "a home market" were first impressed upon the Northern mind. The farmer reaped the whole profit, for, dispensing with the merchant, he dealt face to face with the enemies of his country. None were found able to resist the strong appetite for British gold; the national instinct was irresistible, and the illegality of the transaction but lent to it a keener relish.

The principal exports of Virginia were tobacco, wheat and Indian corn; but tobacco, out of all comparison, held the first place. The cultivation of that plant had, however, begun to decline. This was referable to the low price to which that commodity had fallen, its producers not being able to afford those manures which had become necessary, after the virgin properties had been extracted from the earth. The condition of the tobacco market gave birth, as we shall see, to political consequences of the most important nature. To the value of tobacco, which lay at the basis of her prosperity, Virginia had always been sensitive—the commercial monopoly, to which it had been subjected by the policy of the British government, having entered prominently into the causes of the Revolution itself. No one can peruse the history of that quarrel without perceiving the anxiety of the British cabinet to retrace the false step it had taken in American affairs, and its willingness to make any concessions compatible with the dignity of the government and its general supremacy over the colonies. But all compromise was defeated by the American leaders, because the monopoly of their trade had become incompatible with the growth and prosperity of the colonies. The intolerable nature of this burden is forcibly presented in the following extract from the writings of Edmund Burke:

"These colonies were evidently founded in subservience to the commerce of Great Britain. From this principle, the whole system of our laws concerning them became a system of restriction. A double monopoly was established on the part of the parent country: 1. A monopoly of their whole import, which is to be altogether from Great Britain. 2. A monopoly of all their export, which is to be nowhere but to Great Britain, as far as it can serve any purpose here. On the same idea, it was contrived that they should send all their products to us raw, and in their first state, and that they should take every thing from us in the last stage of manufacture. Were ever a people under such circumstances, that is, a people who were to export raw, and to receive manufactured, and this, not a few luxurious articles, but all articles even to those of the grossest, most vulgar and necessary consumption—a people who were in the hands of a general monopolist—were ever such a people suspected of a possibility of becoming a just object of revenue? * * * * Are not these schemists well apprised that the colonists, particularly those of the Northern provinces, import more from Great Britain, ten times more, than they send in return to us? That a great part of their foreign balance is, and must be, remitted to London? I shall be ready to admit that the colonies ought to be taxed to the revenues of this country, when I know they are out of debt to its commerce. * * * But he tells us that 'their seas are covered with ships, and their rivers floating with commerce.' This is true. But it is with *our* ships that the seas are covered; and their rivers float with British commerce. The American merchants are our factors, all in reality, most even in name. * * * * We have all, except the *peculium;* without which, even slaves will not labor."

To break through this double monopoly, and obtain the freedom of the general market, constituted the true cause of the Revolution.* Threats of taxation served but to rouse the people. When aroused, nothing short of free commerce could

* This is not the prevalent belief as to the origin of the Revolution; but yet I was convinced that it was the true one, from perusing the works of Mr. Burke. I was well pleased to discover that this opinion was entertained by so commanding an authority as Mr. Webster. "It was easy," says Mr. Webster, "to foresee, what we know also to have happened, that the first great cause of collision and jealousy would be, under the notion of political economy then and still prevalent in Europe, an attempt on the part of the mother country to monopolize the trade of the colonies. Whoever has looked deeply into the causes which produced our Revolution has found, if I mistake not, the original principle far back in this claim on the part of England, to monopolize our trade, and a continued effort on the part of the colonies to resist or evade that monopoly."—FIRST SETTLEMENT OF NEW ENGLAND—*Works*, vol. 1, p. 24.

allay the popular ferment. But the Revolution had not borne its promised fruits, and the trade of America was in a worse condition than before the war. The commercial monopoly, though abolished in law, existed in fact; but existed under a greatly aggravated form. As the prospect of a free commerce had impelled Virginia in the paths of the Revolution, we shall presently see that the same motive induced her to propose organic reforms in the federal system.

Domestic tranquility reigned within the border of Virginia. The authority of law was every where firmly established. Lying on the Northern rim of the slave section, her internal peace stood in striking contrast with the volcanic condition of the North. This fact connected itself with the subject of its deliberations, and was strongly developed in the debates of the Convention. The advocates of the new government attempted to establish, in debate, that the condition of things in Virginia, as well as in the North, required a strong external authority. In order to maintain their position, they resorted to the case of Josiah Philips; but the case of Josiah Philips did not sustain their position. Josiah Philips had been attainted by act of the legislature, declared to be an outlaw, and was, without the ceremonies of a legal trial,* afterwards executed. This instance of irregularity in the execution of justice, in florid and exaggerated rhetoric, Gov. Randolph related. But Henry, ever the good angel of Virginia, explained the facts of this attainder. Josiah Philips was a fugitive, an outlaw, a murderer, and the chief of a band of robbers. At a time when the war was at the most perilous stage, he broke loose on the community, committing the most shocking barbarities. The case was an unusual one, and justified swift and stern measures. "A pirate, an outlaw, a common enemy to mankind, may be put to death at any time. It is justified by the law of nature and of nations."

* Howison, in his History of Virginia, gives a different account of this transaction, but, for obvious reasons, I stick to the version of it given in the Convention. I do not enter into the question of historical accuracy.

When two witnesses, like Henry and Randolph, confront each other with opposite statements, it may not be deemed unnecessary or irrelevant if the balance is cast by one, the accuracy of whose observations, and the sober verity of whose statements will command the implicit confidence of mankind. In a letter addressed to David Humphreys, two years previous to this time, after describing the distracted condition of New England, Washington thus speaks of Virginia. It is a picture of dignified repose, and I would that it were imprinted on the minds of this generation of her children. "*Peace and tranquility prevail in this State. The Assembly, by a very great majority and in very emphatic terms, have rejected an application for paper money, and spurned the idea of fixing the value of military certificates by a scale of depreciation. In some other respects, too, the present session has been marked with justice, and a strong desire of supporting the federal system.*" Did such a community require the strong hand of a national government?

All the sources of revenue were open to the Assembly; that of direct taxation, which she did not share with Congress, and the custom-house, over which she exercised exclusive control. The receipts from these sources, even in the crippled condition of her trade, were great enough to induce Virginia to undertake a system of public works on the grandest scale.

There is not to be found a surer indication of prosperity, and the healthfulness of the public mind, than that works of public utility engage the general attention. This criterion may, with advantage, be applied to Virginia at this period. A revisal and codification of her laws had been recently accomplished, and enlarged plans for internal development had been formed and begun. She had entered on a splendid career with a strong and steady march.

The war was but just ended, when Washington, with a mind ever occupied with the welfare of his country, called to his fellow-citizens, amid their rejoicings, to take counsel about the future interests of the young Commonwealth which the fortune of arms had committed to their custody. Convinced of the inestimable advantages resulting from a prosperous and independent trade, and perceiving that upon it depended the value of agriculture, that truly great statesman, whilst the sound of the bugle yet lingered on the air, exerted himself to place the commercial interests of his country on a firm and lasting foundation. His plans were comprehensive and practical. That the reservoir of commerce might be deepened and enlarged, he proposed to create new tributaries.

To this end he devised and recommended a system of internal improvement, at once comprehensive and minute, which, as it was developed, would furnish means for its own completion. Each stream was to be explored, and, as far as practicable, its navigation improved, canals were to be opened, and a spreading net-work of roads established and maintained at the public charge. But his views were not confined by the limits of the State, nor to the single and primary object of developing her internal resources. His purpose was to render Virginia the commercial empire of America—to render her the great maritime power of the Western hemisphere, and consequently its political centre. Looking beyond the Appalachian mountains, he estimated at its proper value, the contributions to commerce of that interior empire, bounded on the north and west by the Mississippi and the Lakes. He desired, whilst things were in the germ, to forestall competition, and to direct that fertilizing stream through Virginia into the waters of the Chesapeake. That one of the maritime States, which should win that inestimable prize, he clearly foresaw would contain the entrepôt, and conduct the commercial transactions of North America. Destitute of a sea front, it was clear to his mind that the great West would decide between those jealous commercial rivals. Thus convinced, Washington did not, fatigued with the exercises of war, stop to recruit his wearied virtue amid the slumbering groves of Mount Vernon; but, inured to exertion and qualified for action, he at once began to realize his profound speculations. His old, but unforgotten project, which had been thrust aside by the war, of uniting the Bay of Chesapeake, by her two great arms, the the James and Potomac rivers, with the Ohio, was revived. Extending his comprehensive plan to the Lakes, he believed it practicable to drain even their commerce into the same great basin. The fur trade* was the immediate prize at which he aimed.

Nor were events inauspicious. The western posts still retained by the British, held the activity of New York in check. Pennsylvania, torn by faction and threatened with dismemberment, was in no condition to enter into the contest for the western trade, and evidence is adduced in the writings of Washington to show that the inhabitants of the western counties of that State were all so favorable to the Virginia plan that they were ready to coerce their government to acquiesce in, if not facilitate, its execution, so far as the waters of Pennsylvania were to be employed. The Mississippi was closed by the short-sighted policy of Spain. Nor was Washington desirous that the impediments to its navigation should be removed until his own plan should open a commercial outlet on the Atlantic. Here was a happy concurrence of events, and it was only necessary for Virginia to improve the occasion and grasp the coveted prize.

To secure immediate action, he enlisted the influential characters of Maryland and Virginia in behalf of this enterprise, and his correspondence exhibits abundant proof of the vigor and perseverance with which he prosecuted his object. In Virginia alone, there were Henry, Jefferson, Grayson, the Lees, Harrison, Madison. In order to throw the full weight of his influence in favor of his work, Washington encountered the fatigue of a personal exploration. He inspected the several routes and estimated the extent of the obstacles with which

---

* Mr. Jefferson mentions in his correspondence whilst at the French court, that a French Company proposed to make Alexandria the Eastern depôt of the fur trade in which it proposed to embark.

they were beset. On his return to Mount Vernon, he addressed a letter to Gov. Harrison, in which the whole plan is unfolded in the most luminous manner, which, with the Executive sanction, was laid before the Assembly. Advised by Washington, advocated by Henry and Madison, and recommended by Harrison, the Assembly adopted it in all its parts. Nor was the action of Maryland less prompt. United to Virginia by friendship, ancient neighborhood and similarity of interests, the two governments combined their efforts in the promotion of this enterprise.

But Washington revolved even yet profounder thoughts, and aimed at political results of the highest importance to Virginia and the whole slave section. By means of those commercial connections the Western country would be united to the South in a compact of political matrimony. He said "commercial connections lead to others, and united are difficult to be broken." It was evident to his unclouded understanding that the seaboard States would necessarily be rivals, as then stood confessed, in respect to the western trade. Any union between the North and South would be purely of a political nature which temporary events and temporary sympathies might create, but which conflicting interests might at any time induce them to dissolve. Apart from their co-partnership in the recent quarrel with Great Britain, there was in good truth no better reason for a political connection between the South and the maritime States of the North, than between either of those parties and Labrador or Canada. But with the West it was very different. The probability of these combinations the matured wisdom of Washington beheld from afar. The drift of public affairs begins now to force them on the attention of his posterity, and a new union between the South and West will ere long be the absorbing question in American politics. There needs no higher illustration of the grandeur of his political speculations.

The supervision of those works, so soon as they were determined upon, was offered to Washington, and accepted by him, and he entered upon the business with characteristic energy. In a letter to Jefferson, he says: "I divide my time between the superintendence of the opening of the navigation of our rivers and attention to my private concerns."

He conceived and was allowed to begin, but he was not suffered to prosecute that noble work. An event at this time occurred, which converted his reasonable expectations into gay illusions, and deserves to be reckoned the most disastrous in the annals of Virginia. The new Constitution was adopted, and Washington was arrested forever in his useful career. In the flower of his wisdom, and with physical energy unimpaired, he was carried off to discharge other duties amid other scenes. Henceforth that great man lost his peculiar identity with Virginia—his nativity forgotten, he transferred his allegiance to another power. After him were carried off too, in a long unbroken line, generation after generation of the most gifted sons of Virginia. All that she has brought forth, that was great, wise and noble, has been swallowed up in the insatiable federal vortex. State interests forgotten, amid the rush of federal politics, her public works began to languish, and were soon abandoned. She no longer heard the cheerful voice of her Washington exciting her to laborious undertakings—to tunnel mountains, to span rivers and thread the depths of the trackless forest. Save Henry alone, who was possessed of every qualification to shine in council or debate, not one was found with enough of the double gift of wisdom and public virtue to induce them to support the expiring fortunes of their country, or to enable them to turn away from the splendid prizes of federal ambition. Parties soon came to be formed with reference exclusively to federal tests, the Assembly was neglected, or was regarded as preparatory only to federal life, and was unvisited by great men, save when they resorted thither to forge weapons for the federal conflict. Her primary interests both at home and abroad neglected, then began the depopulation and decay of that Commonwealth, then sank into poverty and contempt the pride and champion of America.

> Oh! what a fall was there, my countrymen.
> Then you and I and all of us fell down,
> And bloody treason flourished over us.

"Great men," says Burke, "are the ornaments and guides of the State," and no greater calamity can befall a State, whatever be the frame of its government, than to be deprived of the services of those kingly spirits. They are the precious elixir which, when drawn off, the body politic tends to disintegration and decay. To understand, to advance, to harmonize the important and multifarious interests of a Commonwealth like Virginia, demands the services of men of amplitude of mind, and instructed well in the school of political knowledge. This, if the Commonwealth stood alone and independent in the family of nations, in the full possession of all those rights and dignities which would appertain to her situation ; but her necessity for the vigilant patriotism of her most gifted men was re-doubled when she entered into politcal relations with an absorbing central government, under the control of a nation that has sought, and has almost produced, her downfall.

The public councils have been given up to an order of men devoted to the special and immediate interests of the localities they represent, unmindful of those greater and more enduring interests upon which the welfare of the whole depends. They are ever pulling down and building up their domestic government, as though in the very spirit of wantonness, but shrink back from reforming that external government where reform is, indeed, necessary.

A great writer has remarked, upon the generous patriotism which ennobles and inflames the mind of learned and wise statesmen, and on that steadfastness of purpose, amid political dangers, which belongs only to those skillful and practiced mariners of State, and the weak, selfish and vacillating counsels which spring from men of the common sort when they are advanced beyond the sphere of action to which nature assigned them. "Learning endueth men's minds with a true sense of the frailty of their persons, the casualty of their fortunes, and the dignity of their soul and vocation; so that it is impossible for them to esteem that any greatness of their own fortune can be a true or worthy end of their being and ordainment; and, therefore, are desirous to give their account to God, and so likewise to their masters under God, as kings and the States they serve; whereas the corrupter sort of mere politicians, that have not their thoughts established by learning in the love and apprehension of duty, nor ever look abroad into universality, do refer all things to themselves, and thrust themselves into the centre of the world, as if all lines should meet in them and their fortunes,—never caring, in all tempests, what becomes of the ship of State, so they may save themselves in the cock-boat of their own fortune; whereas men that feel the weight of duty, and know the limits of self-love, use to make good their places and duties, though with peril; and if they stand in seditious and violent alterations, it is rather the reverence which many times both adverse parts do give to honesty, than any versatile advantage of their own carriage."

Upon the conclusion of peace, the fleets and armies of Great Britain had, indeed, been withdrawn, but hostilities were not yet over; they had only assumed another and scarcely less harassing and dangerous form. Baffled in field operations, King George resorted to a subtle expedient to regain, or if that should prove impracticable, to destroy, his former subjects. It was but another manifestation of that cruel policy which had turned loose on defenceless communities the merciless Indian, and endeavored to arm the slave against the life of his master. To the war of arms succeeded "a war of imposts," the forcible language employed by Washington to describe that belligerent policy.

Before the war, the entire trade of the colonies, as described by Burke, had been centred in the British dominions. The channels through which it had flowed were worn deep, and though emancipated in law, it had not yet, to any considerable extent, found other issues. It was resolved to afflict it with grievous burdens, and by that means destroy the profits of those employments by which that commerce was sustained. In this way the body of the nation would be reached, and the measures of retaliation felt in every fibre. Oppressed with debt, and their industry in ruins, it was confidently expected that the reign of anarchy would begin, to escape from which the discredited leaders of revolt and cherishers of sedition would be compelled, by an angry and suffering people, to seek a restoration of the old connection. As a branch of this cunning and deep-laid plan, the savages were again enlisted in the service of the British Government. British agents were seen mysteriously to hover on the Western frontier, and soon the war-whoop broke the slumbers and disturbed the tranquility of the border. Thus was the necessity of public defence superadded to the embarrassments of the people.

In order to reconcile the British nation, ever sensitive to the interests of trade, to this suicidal method of warfare, Lord Sheffield published a pamphlet, in which, by the suppression of some facts, and the artful disposition of others, it was made to appear that the advantages of the American connection had been greatly overrated, and found more than an equivalent in the expenses incident to so extensive a colonial establishment. But such artifices were discovered to be unnecessary, for the temper of the nation, fierce and sullen, was well disposed to the employment of harsh and vindictive measures. "That nation hates us, their ministers hate us, and their king more than all other men," is the strong and emphatic language of Jefferson. The American party, once so influential in the British Parliament, as well from its numbers as the rank and ability of its leaders, had silently disappeared. No party now advocated a liberal and friendly policy towards the successful rebels. Even the opposition concurred with the ministry in this. The Marquis of Lansdowne, and a small knot of his friends, were well disposed to reciprocal intercourse with America; but the Marquis did not venture to express that opinion in parliament. The free trade policy, which had been recommended and in part begun by Chatham, had been wholly abandoned.

But in order to its success, it was indispensable that the principal States of the continent should acquiesce in that policy and adopt the same line of action. To create a general distrust of the stability of American affairs, false and exaggerated statements—our ministers called them lies—were diligently circulated through the British press. These stories got into the continental newspapers, and went the round of Europe. A general determination was evinced to stand aloof from engagements with a weak, vacillating and irresponsible government, whose constituents were represented to be in a condition bordering on chaos. Thus were the ports of commerce blockaded to the trade of the new-born Republic. In the meantime, King George, inexorable, was kept steady to the pursuit of his object. "If your majesty chooses, America may still be yours," was the comfortable assurance ever kept before the royal mind. The trade of America continued to be loaded with fresh exactions. This bellicose system began soon to produce the desired fruits. Popular discontents showed themselves throughout the Northern section, upon which it bore with peculiar hardship; for Great Britain had furnished markets for more than three-fourths of the exports of the eight Northern States. In that part of the Union the voice of lamentation was indeed loud. Estimating all things, whether in heaven above, or the earth beneath, or in the waters under the earth, according to the money valuation, those zealous patriots had begun to repent them of their dear-bought independence, which had brought upon the country such times as had not visited it since the landing of the Pilgrims. With bitter and unavailing regret, they now remembered the good times when their products were received without charge in the ports of England. Their ablest public man was sent to London. But nothing could be done. John Adams attempted in vain to excite the compassion and relax the severity of his old master: America had broke loose from the British empire, had sought independence, had found it, and the king was resolved she should enjoy that blessing to its fullest extent.

But it was in New England, in the commonwealth of Massachusetts, and from that centre branching into the adjoining States, that these distempers chiefly prevailed. They soon kindled into a rebellion, which, in the opinion of one of the ablest military men of that day, wanted only a leader of competent ability to be crowned with success.* As it was, the attempt to overthrow the government, and by its equal distribution to confiscate property, was only suppressed by a meditated intervention with federal troops. The force ordered by Congress was ostensibly to act against the Indians, but really to awe the insurgents of Massachusetts, and re-establish the authority of law. Shays' rebellion was produced by the severity of the commercial regulations of Great Britain, in cooperation with the exclusive policy prevalent elsewhere. Fish and the oil of fish, seventy years since, composed almost wholly the exports of that region, now the seat of opulence and power.† Anterior to the Revolution, a considerable amount of dried fish had been disposed of by the fish merchants of New England in the markets of the Mediterranean.

* "I was then in Congress, and had a proper opportunity to know the circumstances of this event. Had Shays been possessed of abilities, he might have established that favorite system of the gentleman, King, Lords and Commons. Nothing was wanting to bring about a revolution, but a great man to head the insurgents; but, fortunately, he was a worthless captain. There were thirty thousand stand of arms nearly in his power, which were defended by a pensioner of this country. It would have been sufficient had he taken this deposite. He failed in it; but even after that failure, it was in the power of a great man to have taken it. But Shays wanted design and knowledge."—Henry Lee, in the Va. Convention.

† The fisheries were the great indraught of wealth of Massachusetts, if we except the slave trade, but had engendered a wretched population. John Adams thus speaks of that class: "The condition of the laboring poor in most countries, that of the fishermen, particularly, of the Northern States, is as abject as that of slaves." Massachusetts had first planted the tree of free labor, and such was the fruit it had borne.

But when the protection of the British flag was withdrawn, the gates of that sea were closed by the Corsairs of North Africa. Expelled from those waters, they found it impossible to dispose of the commodity elsewhere.

But it was in striking the whale that those people had found their constant and most advantageous employment. Without the encouragement and support of bounties, the whale fisheries have ever been and are the poorest business into which a merchant or sailor can enter. If, instead of wages, the sailor takes part of the venture, he soon finds that it will not pay him for his labor, and the merchant that it will gradually sink the capital employed. In consequence, the nations who had tried it successively gave up the business to the fishermen of Nantucket and Cape Cod. These hardy mariners, owing to their proximity to the fishing ground, the poverty of their country, and the English bounties, had been enabled to prosecute the fisheries with success. They had formerly employed in the whale trade alone more than three hundred vessels, but of that number, such was the blasting effect of the English duties, not one remained afloat. The duty upon foreign oils, among which those from the United States were now classed, amounted to a sum equal to the price for which they were sold, and were equivalent to a prohibition. The terms upon which they were received in other countries were almost as hard. The whale fisheries perished, and with them perished, in Massachusetts, that love of independence, order and morality which had so honorably distintinguished the pioneers of Plymouth Rock. They did not rise from their ashes until, under the auspices of the present government, they were again allowed to feed off the public treasury. A dissolution of the union with England, by suspending the bounty and closing the ports of that kingdom, bereft New England of all prosperity,* and plunged her people into anarchy and civil war,

* The Eastern States have lost every thing but their country and their freedom. It is notorious that some ports to the Eastward, which used to fit

as a dissolution of the union with the South, from the operation of similar causes, will be productive of the same terrible results. Destitute of all natural resources, behold the weakness and dependence of New England! Like the misletoe, she has ever thriven off the fatness of other communities. It will be well for the South, as it was a fortunate occurrence for the mother country, to be freed from the clasping arms of that parasite.

But it was not in the Eastern States alone that those commercial restrictions were severely felt, though nowhere else were they attended by such unhappy consequences. Every part of the Union was keenly sensible of them. The flour and grain trade of the Middle States had been looking up; it was prostrated to the earth; nor did it again raise its head, until the desolating wars, which originated in the French Revolution, had destroyed the husbandry of Europe. Then the grain trade recommenced, and those articles became important in the external commerce of the country. The tobacco and rice of the Southern section likewise met with but little favor from British tariffs. Upon the first, the duty, with port charges added, was about equal to the price, and the second was so heavily taxed as to prevent it from entering into general use. The continental tariffs bore with an equal weight upon them. Thus the nations of Europe were banded in a commercial league against America.

In this gloomy state of affairs, Congress turned their attention to France, and endeavored, by negotiation and treaty, to soften the rigor of her commercial system. In that quarter, it was believed, something might be done to relieve the general distress. To divide the commerce of America with England was known to have constituted a principal motive with the French cabinet, in forming the military pact during the

---

out one hundred and fifty sail of vessels, do not now fit out thirty; that their trade of ship-building, which used to be very considerable, is now annihilated; that their fisheries are trifling, and their mariners in want of bread!—GEN. PINCKNEY *in Legislature of South Carolina*, Jan. 1788.

troubles of the Revolution. The most accomplished man in all America was chosen to conduct that delicate and important negotiation. To a conciliating address and great good temper, Mr. Jefferson united a varied knowledge and a thorough acquaintance with the public interests. His understanding was at once comprehensive and acute, and he spoke the French tongue with grace and fluency. Thus qualified, thus accomplished, thus adorned, he appeared at the court of Louis XVI. and opened negotiations with the Count de Vergennes, then at the helm of affairs. It appears to have been the general expectation in both countries, that a great trade would grow up between the late allies, to which their cordial feelings, as well as their respective wants and capabilities, afforded the strongest probability. All things invited to an extensive commerce. America offered productions in a raw, unmanufactured state. France, articles upon which industry had been exhausted, and which had received the highest finish of art. Notwithstanding these strong inducements to trade, the French cabinet had been inactive, and had entertained only a silent wish for those advantages which fortune had placed within reach. Rejected on all hands, and placed under the ban of Europe, the commerce of the United States, as far as it survived, continued to flow in the old channels. Braced by the difficulties of his situation, and encouraged by the hope of success, that accomplished diplomatist addressed himself to the task of extricating the commerce of the two nations from the embarrassments by which it was surrounded, and putting it upon a new and prosperous footing.

Some acts of a favorable nature manifested a disposition on the part of the French court to cast off its inert and sluggish policy. Boulton and Watt, at the head of the plated manufactures of Birmingham, the steam-mills of London, copying-presses, and other mechanical works, were invited to France. Wedgewood, too, was induced to come, so famous for his steel manufactures, and earthen ware in the antique style. The transfer to France of those manufactures, which contributed so much to draw American trade to England, it was believed, would tend to strengthen its connections with the one, and loosen them with the other. To rival Cowes on the other side of the channel, the indefatigable minister solicited the enfranchisement of Honfleur at the mouth of the Seine. It would be the out-post of Paris, and from it not only the northern parts of the kingdom might be supplied with the products of the United States, but it would be the entrepôt from which other countries should be furnished. Bordeaux, through the Garonne and canal of Languedoc, would, in the same way, be made the centre through which the Southern provinces would receive the unwrought productions of the New World.

But these acquisitions were, in their nature, only preliminary, and of little value, except as parts of that commercial system which he insisted upon. Unfortunately for the success of the mission, the correct principles of trade were not recognised by the government of Louis. The mutuality of commerce, which is now an elementary truth, was not regarded as necessary to its existence. On the contrary, surprise was expressed that the American merchant did not dispose of his tobacco and rice in London, and come and lay out the price in the merchandise of France. In order to lay a basis for trade, it was clearly pointed out that it would be necessary to relinquish the restrictive system, and, by low tariffs, to invite to the ports of France such articles as America was capable of producing, in exchange for which the products of the loom and vineyard would be taken. Of these articles, oil, rice and tobacco were the chief. After some delay, a reduction of duties on the first was made. But as it was to last only during the pleasure of the minister, it offered not that stability which would induce the merchant to re-build his ships. That duty had been devised to foster the French fisheries; an object which was reluctantly abandoned, and to which the government subsequently reverted.

It was agreed to receive the rice of Carolina on such terms as would enable it to compete with the rice of Italy and

Egypt; but the tobacco of Maryland and Virginia was placed on the worst possible footing, and yet tobacco was greatly the most valuable export of the United States, and the one which, if well received, would have created the strongest commercial ties. It was then a monopoly in the hands of the farmers general, for which they paid a heavy sum into the treasury.

To break through that monopoly constituted accordingly the great result to be accomplished by the diplomacy of Jefferson. In May, 1796, he writes to Pleasants: "I was engaged in endeavors to have the monopoly in tobacco suppressed. My hopes on that subject are not desperate, neither are they flattering. I consider it the most effectual means of procuring the full value of our produce and of diverting our demands for manufactures from Great Britain to this country, to a certain amount, and of thus producing some equilibrium in our commerce, which, at present, lies all in the British scale. It would cement an union with our friends and lessen the torrent of wealth which we are annually pouring into the lap of our enemies."

The farmers had been in the habit of making their purchases from London or Cowes, and had always paid in money. They continued still to resort to the same market, though they occasionally made their purchases in America. But, even then, payment was made through the medium of London remittances, and the returns were in English commodities. In either case, tobacco was lost to the commerce of the United States and France, and the benefit of the transaction inured to Great Britain. It was clear that political had not produced commercial independence to the United States, but that the old vassalage was continued, with new aggravations. Although the commercial restrictions of France were productive of such blighting consequences, it was still no easy matter to extirpate that deep-seated and inveterate evil, and have tobacco placed on the list of commerciable articles. It was shown, by the able statements of Jefferson, that not only would commerce spring up elastic if that superincumbent weight were removed, but that the revenue derived from tobacco would be increased by the extension of the circle of consumption—an object, as we shall see, of the first moment to the tobacco growers of Virginia. But all efforts to disenthrall that trade proved fruitless.

The Marquis La Fayette, in obedience to his active impulses, was ever ready to assist in promoting the joint interests of his "two countries," as he affectionately styled the United States and France.*

But his solicitations were productive of no good. The ameliorations which he obtained were properly regarded in a contrary light, inasmuch as the very enormity of the abuse might ultimately lead to its reform. The king received on that article a revenue of twenty-eight million livres, a sum so considerable as to render it impolitic, it was alleged, to tamper with it. The collection, by way of farm, was of ancient date, and it was believed to be hazardous to alter arrangements of such long standing and of such infinite combinations with the fiscal system. But the true impediment to successful negotiation appears to have been, that the farmers-general were great capitalists, who had before and might again relieve the wants of the state. Standing a great power behind the throne, and holding a sceptre of gold, no minister was safe in a contest with them.

But it would be doing injustice to the abilities, the firmness and the integrity of that great minister not to add, that the Count de Vergennes was convinced by the lucid expositions of

---

* Mr. Jefferson repeatedly acknowledges the services of the marquis, and thus sketches his character: "The Marquis de La Fayette is a most valuable auxiliary to me. His zeal is unbounded, and his weight with those in power great. His education, having been merely military, commerce was an unknown field to him. But his good sense enabling him to comprehend whatever is explained to him, his agency has been very efficacious. He has a great deal of sound genius, is well-remarked by the king, and is rising in popularity. He has nothing against him but the suspicion of republican principles. I think he will one day be of the ministry. His foible is a canine appetite for popularity and fame, but he will get above this."

Jefferson, and that he declared against the monopoly. But the phalanx of farmers proved too strong for him.

Here is a portrait of the Count de Vergennes, as depicted by the American negotiator. It is the picture of an accomplished statesman by a great artist: "The Count de Vergennes is a great minister in European affairs, but has very imperfect ideas of our institutions and no confidence in them. His devotion to the principles of pure despotism renders him unaffectionate to our governments. His fear of England makes him value us as a make-weight. He is cool, reserved in political conversations, but free and familiar on other subjects, and a very attentive, agreeable person to do business with. It is impossible to have a clearer, better organized head; but age has chilled his heart." It stands in contrast with the sketch which Mr. Jefferson gives of the count's successor in office: "Montmorin is weak, though a most worthy character. He is indolent and inattentive in the extreme." It was Montmorin who recalled the concessions which had been made to the oil trade of the United States.

Thus were the commerce and navigation of France and the United States sacrificed to the false views and timid counsels of a weak and necessitous sovereign. That false system held its ground till swept away by the Revolution, which destroyed so many of the abuses that festered under the old regime. The republic set free the wings of commerce; the returning monarchy fettered them again; nor have the genius and energy of the second empire abolished those unwise and hurtful restraints. The commerce of Virginia and France is still an empty pageant, to kindle the hopes and inflame the desires of the sanguine and visionary. These hopes have sprung from the dying embers of other hopes, not less warm or less glowing. They would have received a brilliant realization, but for the most stupendous fraud, involving the grossest political turpitude ever practised upon a free people.

Mr. Jefferson was convinced, as his correspondence declares, that nothing by negotiation and treaty could be done for the liberation of commerce. The restrictive system of Europe could only be broken down by the application of harsh measures, and these he advised his countrymen to adopt. He thus writes to Madison: "I have heard, with great pleasure, that our Assembly has come to the resolution of giving the regulation of their commerce to the federal head. I will venture to assert that there is not one of its opposers who, placed on this ground, would not see the wisdom of the measure. *The politics of Europe render it indispensably necessary.*" And to John Adams, at the court of London, as follows: "The determination of the British cabinet to make no equal treaty with us, confirms me in the opinion expressed in your letter of October 24th, that the United States must pass a navigation act against Great Britain, and *load her manufactures with duties*, so as to give a preference to those of other countries, and I hope the Assemblies will wait no longer, but transfer such power to Congress, at the sessions this fall."

The import of the United States, which our minister to France proposed to load with duties, was of the utmost consequence to Europe. Upon that import, it was proposed to lay burthens equal in degree with those imposed by foreign nations upon the American export trade.

In this conclusion, the ministers of the United States at the several courts of Europe concurred. Indeed, throughout the United States, there appears to have been great unanimity in this belief, and commercial retaliation became the universal demand. This had been attempted by the several State legislatures, but, from the want of co-operation, failure was the result. By showing the impotency of our political system, it served only to confirm the nations of Europe in their unfriendly policy. England found herself in the possession of the trade of her late colonies, and that the federal government was not possessed of sufficient powers to divert it into other channels. Thus the public mind was directed to the question of federal reform, and all the States, save one, consented so far to enlarge the powers of Congress, as to give it jurisdiction over the custom-house, for the purpose of regulating commerce with foreign nations. Free trade with all nations was the common object proposed to be obtained by this enlargement of congressional power, and Virginia took the initiative in the movement, an unrestricted liberty of trade having been from a remote period of her history a cherished object with her people.*

But in Virginia, and indeed in the slave States generally, there was not entire conformity of opinion among public men, with respect to the grant of so formidable a power. Some, whilst they were willing to grant the power, were willing to grant it only for a term of twenty-five years, to be renewed if it were used for the advantage of Southern trade; others were disposed to make an unqualified cession of it to the federal agent. An interesting account of the debate in the Virginia

---

* When, in 1650, after the dethronement of Charles I., the Parliament, claiming to be substituted to his prerogatives, assumed jurisdiction over the colonies, and passed an act for inhibiting their trade with foreign nations, Virginia strenuously resisted the revolutionary government. She was not induced to lay down her arms, and acknowledge the government of Cromwell, until a solemn convention had been entered into guaranteeing what she considered her most important rights, so little inclined was that high-spirited people to submit patiently to oppressive exercises of power. It is the first instance on record where a subordinate province exacted terms from the imperial power. Principal among the conditions demanded by the government of Virginia in 1651, as the price of her submission to the Protector, is the seventh article, which stipulates, "That the people of Virginia shall have free trade, as the people of England do enjoy, to all places and with all nations, according to the laws of that Commonwealth, and that Virginia shall enjoy all privileges equal with any English plantation in America." The eighth article provides, "That Virginia shall be free from all taxes, *customs* and impositions whatsoever, and none be imposed on them without consent of the General Assembly," &c.

This secured to Virginia the freedom of the general market for her export trade,—she might sell and buy wherever she pleased,—and her import trade was to be free from all customs and impositions whatever.

Free trade, then, is a Virginia, not a South Carolina, principle. It is Virginian in its origin and in its maturity. Virginia first took up arms in its defence, and afterwards proposed to her sister States to reform their organic laws, that its blessings might be secured.

Assembly upon this point has been preserved. Madison was a member of the Assembly, and it need not be added that he, ever an advocate of federal power in its greatest excess, contended for an unconditional surrender of the commercial jurisdiction to Congress.

The writings of Washington at this period are replete with interest upon this subject. He, too, favored a cession of that power to Congress, but proposed, at the same time, to place its exercise under such guards and checks as to make it impossible to be used by the North without the concurrence and co-operation of the South. He admitted the danger of abuse, but contended that, great as the power was, it ought to be deposited with the federal legislature under the safeguards which he proposed. In his letter to James McHenry, he says: "Let the Southern States always be represented; let them act more in union; let them declare freely and boldly what is for the interest of, and what is prejudicial to, their constituents; and there will, there must be an accommodating spirit. In the establishment of a navigation act, this in a particular manner ought, and will doubtless be attended to. If the assent of nine States, or as some propose of eleven, is necessary to give validity to a commercial system, it ensures this measure, or it cannot be obtained. Wherein then lies the danger? But if your fears are in danger of being realized, cannot certain provisos in the ordinance guard against the evil? I see no difficulty in this, if the Southern States would give their attendance in Congress, and follow the example, if it should be set them, of adhering together to counteract combinations. * * * * * * As you have asked the question, I answer, I do not know that we can enter upon a war of imposts with Great Britain or any other foreign power, but we are certain that this war has been waged against us by the former, professedly, upon a belief that we never could unite in opposition to it, and I believe there is no way of putting an end to, or at least stopping an increase of it, but to convince them of the contrary. Our trade, in all points of view, is as essential to Great

6

Britain, as hers is to us; and she will exchange it upon reciprocal and liberal terms if better cannot be had. It can hardly be supposed, I think, that the carrying business will devolve wholly on the States you have named, or remain long with them if it should, for either Great Britain will depart from her present contracted system, or the policy of the Southern States in framing the act of navigation, or by laws passed by themselves individually, will devise ways and means to encourage seamen for the transportation of the products of their respective countries.* * * * * To sum up the whole, I foresee, or I think I do, the many advantages which will arise from giving powers of this kind to Congress (if a sufficient number of States are required to exercise them), without any evil, save that which may proceed from inattention or want of wisdom in the formation of the act; whilst without them we stand in a ridiculous point of view in the eyes of the nations of the world, with whom we are attempting to enter into commercial treaties without the means of carrying them into effect, who must see and feel that the Union, or the States individually are sovereigns, as best suits their purposes; in a word, that we are one nation to-day and thirteen to-morrow."

In a subsequent letter to LaFayette, Washington touches this subject, which so frequently occupied his pen. He not only shows the impossibility of commercial retaliation by the individual action of the States, but indulges in anticipations

* The shipping of Virginia, in common with the shipping of all the other States, had been destroyed during the Revolution, and her commerce was carried on in foreign bottoms. But previous to the Revolution, as we learn from the Debates of the first session of Congress under the new Constitution, there was a large shipping interest owned by the merchants at her various ports, and this was true of every exporting State in the Union. Even after the adoption of the present government that interest again sprung up in Virginia. It is within the memory of men still living, that at the port of Alexandria that interest existed to a considerable extent, but it perished as soon as the foreign trade of the Commonwealth was transferred to the Northern cities.

of the efficacy of Congressional action: "I notice with pleasure the additional immunities and facilities in trade, which France has granted to the United States by the late royal arrêt. I flatter myself it will have the desired effect in some measure of augmenting the commercial intercourse. From the productions and wants of the two countries, their trade with each other is certainly capable of great amelioration. *Whenever we shall have an efficient government established, that government will surely impose retaliating restrictions upon the trade of Britain.* At present, or under our existing form of confederation, it would be idle to think of making commercial regulations on our part. One State passes a prohibitory law respecting some article, another State opens wide the avenue for its admission. It is in vain to hope for a remedy of these and innumerable other evils, until a general government shall be adopted."

The question was taken up by Congress, who solicited in the most pressing terms, that the power to regulate commerce with foreign nations should be intrusted to them. Mr. Monroe brought forward a resolution on this subject, which was referred to a committee, from whose report, in May 1785, the following extract is made: "The common principle upon which friendly commercial intercourse is conducted between independent nations, is that of reciprocal advantage; and if this is not obtained, it becomes the duty of the losing party to make such further regulations consistently with the faith of treaties, as will remedy the evil, and secure its interests. If, then, the commercial regulations of any foreign power contravene the interests of any particular State, if they refuse admittance into its ports, upon the same terms that the State admits its manufactures here, what course will it take to remedy the evil? If it makes similar regulations to counteract those of that power, by reciprocating the disadvantages which it feels, by impost or otherwise, will it produce the desired effect? What operation will it have upon the neighboring States? Will they enter into similar regulations and make it a common cause? On the contrary, will they not, in pursuit of the same local policy, avail themselves of this circumstance to turn it to their particular advantage? Thus, then, we behold the several States taking separate measures in pursuit of their particular interests, in opposition to the regulations of foreign powers, and separately aiding those powers to defeat the regulations of each other; for unless the States act together, there is no plan of policy into which they can separately enter, which they will not be separately interested to defeat, and of course all their measures must prove vain and abortive. * * * * * * But, if they act as a nation, the prospect is more favorable to them. *The particular interests of every State will then be brought forward and receive a Federal support.* Happily for them, no measures can be taken to promote the interests of either, which will not equally promote that of the whole. If their commerce is laid under injurious restrictions in foreign ports, by going hand in hand in confidence together, by wise and equitable regulations, they will the more easily sustain the inconvenience, or remedy the evil. If they wish to cement the Union by the strongest ties of interest and affection; if they wish to promote its strength and grandeur, founded upon that of each individual State, every consideration of local as well as federal policy urges them to adopt the following regulation." The committee goes on to propose resolutions vesting in Congress the power to regulate commerce with foreign nations, to the end that the commerce of the United States might be freed from the embarrassments of European tariffs.

There was no State in the Union which had embarked with greater zeal on the policy of commercial retaliation than Virginia. But Maryland and Pennsylvania refused to act with her, and by lower scales of duties had invited the trade of Virginia to their own ports. It was these sinister means that gave the first impulse to Baltimore, until then a collection of fishermen's huts. The merchants of Virginia clamored loudly against a system of legislation which expelled trade from the

Commonwealth. The agricultural interest joined in the cry, for both purchases and sales were subjected to a heavy commercial tribute. The table of the Assembly was covered with petitions, and the restrictive system was abandoned. An interesting allusion to this perplexing subject is contained in the correspondence of Madison with Jefferson, December 10th, 1783. The writer had just returned from Annapolis, and gives an account of an interview which he had held at Gunston with Col. Mason, on the public topics which were then uppermost—*The defence of our trade against British tariffs—the proposition to clothe Congress with the power to collect an impost for the purpose of revenue*; federal reform, and the deplorable condition of the foreign trade of the State, produced in some measure by the system of retaliation upon which the Assembly had just embarked. In respect to the latter, Mr. Madison says: "The situation of commerce of this country, as far as I can learn, is even more deplorable than I had conceived. It cannot pay less to Philadelphia and Baltimore, if one may judge from a comparison of prices here and in Europe, than 30 or 40 per cent. on all the exports and imports—a *tribute** which, if paid into the treasury of the State, would yield a surplus above all its wants. If the Assembly should take any step towards its emancipation, you will no doubt be apprised of them, as well as other proceedings from Richmond."

But this commercial rivalry between States bordering on the same rivers and bays could not long subsist, without producing irritations that might at any time lead to unpleasant results. Measures of accommodation and friendly co-operation between Maryland and Virginia were soon proposed. Commissioners to form a compact to regulate the navigation of the rivers Potomac and Pocomoke, and part of the bay of Chesa-

---

* The commercial tribute Virginia still pays, and its oppressive weight, as well as the means of escaping from it, are ably set forth in an elaborate speech of Mr. D. H. LONDON, of Richmond city, January, 1860.

peake, had been appointed by the legislatures of those States. They assembled in Alexandria in March, 1785, and whilst on a visit to Mount Vernon, it was concerted with Washington that the commissioners should propose to their respective governments the appointment of other commissioners, with power to make arrangements for the maintenance of a joint naval force in the Chesapeake; and the establishment of a tariff of duties on imports to which the laws of both States should conform.

Thus was a commercial league* between those two States set on foot by the instrumentality of no less a personage than George Washington, to which other States were to have been admitted according to the agreement of their interests with the interests of the original contracting parties. The State legislatures were then invested with unlimited power over inter-State commerce, which was habitually employed to lay it under disabilities. Had this plan, so wisely conceived by the sage of Mount Vernon, been carried into execution, the happiest results would have followed. The States were already united by a political compact which covered those particulars in which their interests lay together, and that subordinate association, that trade's, union would have exercised jurisdiction over the important concerns of commerce. The plan was based upon the possession of the custom house remaining with the State authorities, and that the federal treasury should be replenished by direct

---

* SATURDAY, NOVEMBER 25th, 1786,—"The House proceeded, according to the order of the day, by joint ballot with the Senate, to the choice of five commissioners to meet commissioners appointed, or to be appointed by the States of Maryland and Pennsylvania, to confer on the subject of *Commercial Regulations* to be adopted by this and the said States." (Jour. H. D. p. 60.) The commissioners appointed were St. George Tucker, Wm. Ronald, Robert Townsend Hooe, Thomas Pleasants and Francis Corbin.

Five days later, on the 30th of the same month, the House determined to ballot for delegates to the Federal Convention to "revise" the Constitution. We would infer from this that it was the intention of the Legislature of Virginia to reform the federal articles and yet to form a subordinate commercial association with both Maryland and Pennsylvania.

taxation alone, or from contributions. Thus the powers of self-development, to which the custom house giving jurisdiction over trade is so indispensable, would have been left with each State, nor would it have been placed in the power of Congress to sacrifice one State to another State or to have erected the prosperity of the North upon the ruins of Southern industry. There would have been harmony and perpetual union between those sections, instead of contention, hatred, disunion and war.

But things took a different turn; for when those propositions received the assent of the legislature, an additional resolution was passed, directing that which respected the duties on imports to be communicated to all the States in the Union, who were invited to send deputies to a convention. On the 21st January, 1786, soon after the passage of these resolutions, another was adopted by the Assembly of Virginia, designating "commissioners to meet such as might be appointed by the other States in the Union, at a time and place to be agreed on, to take into consideration the trade of the United States; to consider how far a uniform system in their commercial relations may be necessary to their common interest and permanent harmony; and to report to the several States such an act relative to this great object, as when unanimously ratified by them will enable the United States, in Congress assembled, effectually to provide for the same." Thus the well-considered plan of Washington miscarried in the Assembly of Virginia, who, impelled by a blind fury, rushed forward to cast their Commonwealth into the maelstrom of federal power. The Convention at Annapolis followed. Those evil genii, Hamilton and Madison, attended and guided its deliberations. The object of the Convention was circumvented, and it was converted into an instrument for calling the Federal Convention, which assembled the following year at Philadelphia.

The population of Virginia, in 1788, was computed at more than 500,000, and its military force at 50,000 militiamen. These had seen service in the late war, and composed a formidable soldiery, adequate to the defence of the Commonwealth.

Next to the numbers and military force, the constituent elements of the population of Virginia deserve attention. The cavalier or aristocratic class still existed, though the foundation of that order had been upturned by the abolition of the entail. Sullen and discontented at the ascendancy of the Democratic power, the great bulk of that interest, embracing the diseased stump of the Tory party, hailed the new Constitution with a great joy. It would erect a mighty central authority, confined by doubtful limits, which, in its development, would probably contain the substance as it was certainly impressed with the image of the British Constitution. At all events, it would deposit the highest attributes of power with a government external to, and independent of, the Democracy of Virginia, whose rude hand had swept away the insolent prerogative of primogeniture.

The direct and untrammeled intercourse which had subsisted between the parent State and the colony of Virginia, had produced a considerable commerce, which had erected flourishing towns at the head of tide-water on those rivers which, like great arteries, intersected the eastern part of that dependency. The towns-people, in consequence, wielded no inconsiderable share of the political power which, in a close struggle like the present, would exert an important influence on the result. They expected that a Constitution, full fledged with commercial powers, would usher in a commercial millennium, and, with the revival of trade, that their towns would expand into great cities. So strong was this delusion in the town of Alexandria, according to the testimony of Washington, there was not one voter opposed to ratification. But no such millennium came. Her verdant streets, her deserted wharves, her abandoned houses, her diminished population, soon afforded the strongest commentary upon the folly of that act.

But the great bulk of the voters lived in the country, and were composed of free-holders, occupying small farms. These farms, as the word originally signified, were held of landlords at an annual rent in money or in kind. This accounts for the dense white population which, in proportion to the cultivated area, exceeded that of the whole State at the present moment. The market crop was tobacco; a plant which, above all others cultivated by man, is best adapted to agriculture on a limited surface. But there was a mighty cause, in co-operation with tobacco, which produced that minute subdivision of the soil. That cause was cheap and abundant negro labor. An able-bodied negro could be purchased, at any market-town, for a hogshead of tobacco, which placed it in the power of the poorest man to embark in the agricultural development of the country.

Thus had been produced that general distribution of the land among the people which wisest men, and many of the noblest commonwealths of antiquity have considered so indispensable to the stability of republican institutions. So broad was the basis of liberty in that youthful republic! Thus, by a fortunate concurrence, had been destroyed "that fatal difference between poverty and riches." The slave population, but an incident and means of agriculture, except in the malarial districts on tide-water, was scattered with an equal hand among the freeholders. So universal was this distribution of negroes among the farmers of Virginia, that Richard Morris has declared, "to be a freeholder was to be a slaveholder."

The institution of slavery, contrary to representations often made, was deeply rooted in the affections of the people, as was verified by a signal example. A petition for its abolition had been presented to the Assembly of 1785. It could scarcely obtain a reading, and was flung with contempt back upon the petitioners. So promptly and vigorously was the kindling flame of emancipation trodden out in Virginia!

That visionary philosophy was just coming into vogue. Dr. Price, the English philosopher and philanthropist, had turned his attention to slavery in the Southern States of the American Union, and had written a pamphlet against it, which Mr. Jefferson had caused to be circulated among the students of William and Mary College. But those distempers had not penetrated and corrupted the mass of the country population, which with an absolute sway controlled the politics of the Assembly. From the nature of their occupations and their manner of life, they were exempt from those idle and pernicious theories which amuse and distract men of leisure. Their minds were cast in the practical mould, and they judged the institutions of society by their fruits. Theories with them were the growth of experience, and following that certain guide, they proved themselves on this occasion to be safe depositories of those great principles which constituted the basis of their social and political systems.

This decided bias for slavery was well founded. From the employment of negro labor they had seen the hunting grounds of the savage converted into the abode of a civilized community, both wealthy and powerful. But this was not all. During the late protracted war, which had been characterized by every feature of atrocity, the country had been invaded, the inhabitants dispersed, the cities occupied by the invader; yet during that gloomy and disastrous period, the negro had proved loyal. Notwithstanding the seductions of the enemy, no act of insurrection had been committed by him. On the contrary, the faithful slave had accompanied his master to the battle field, and after sharing with him privation and fatigue, had tenderly nursed him in sickness, and often carried home the last memento of the dying soldier; or engaged in the useful and necessary work of the plantation, had supported, whilst he protected, the family of his absent master. If we may credit the evidence that has come down to us, no part of the population of the South took a deeper interest in the fortunes of the Revolution, than did the bulk of the slave population. Such was the confidence that was inspired by those stormy times in the fidelity of the negro, that by leading statesmen, in different parts of the Union, it was believed that it would be expedient to place arms in his hands, that he might aid in expelling the British army, and it is well known that the Assembly of Virginia at one time took steps to embody a regiment of negroes.

Negroes had been sometimes employed in the capacity of spies,* as the correspondence of Washington shows, and whilst they would be freely admitted within the British lines, there is no instance recorded in which they betrayed the cause of their American masters.

The American armies, when acting in the South, were accompanied by great numbers of slaves, who, if they did not shoulder the musket, yet by many laborious services in the camp and field,—transporting baggage, carrying artillery, throwing up fortifications,—supplied the place of soldiers, and in this way increased the ranks of the army.†

The benefits of education were universally diffused among the tenant population. Every neighborhood was thickly settled with families in independent circumstances, and every neighborhood had its schoolmaster. The education was necessarily plain, and consisted of the rudiments of knowledge; but it was sufficient to enable the farmer and his family to read the Bible, to become conversant with the history and politics of his country, and to transact, with intelligence, the business appertaining to his sphere of life. There is nothing which speaks more eloquently or more sadly of the retrograde of Virginia, than the ruins of those humble temples of knowledge. The Old Field schools, where so many of the shining lights of Virginia first tasted of the crystal fountains of learning, was to Virginia what the Free school is to Massachusetts;

---

* THURSDAY, NOVEMBER 30th, 1786.—"A petition of James, a negro slave, the property of William Armisted, of the county of New Kent, was presented to the House, and read; setting forth that during the year 1781, he frequently, at the request of the Marquis de La Fayette, went into the British camp for the purpose of getting information, which he immediately communicated to him, and rendered him other essential services; and praying that he may be emancipated, and a reasonable sum paid to the said Armisted, for the loss he will sustain thereby." (Journal Ho. Del., 1786, p. 68.) I need not add that Jim's petition was granted.

† Consult correspondence of Madison, and that of Hamilton, Debates Federal Convention, and the Debates of the 1st Congress, particularly the speech of Smith, S. C., Annals Congress, vol. ii., p. 1457.

differing, however, in the source from which it emanated, and differing, too, in the fact that it did not propagate in the minds of the people the seeds of that moral contagion which has played so important a part in corrupting the whole free-soil section.

This tenant population was what Mr. Henry denominated "the great middling class," and constituted, in truth, the back bone of the State. Their opinions were deeply tinctured with republicanism, and were ennobled and strengthened by a proud spirit of personal independence. These were the men who, as long as colonial institutions conduced to their happiness and prosperity, regarded the British crown with unfeigned veneration and love; these were the men who had proved themselves, on the field of battle, ready to conquer the wilderness from the Indian, and restrain the encroachments of French ambition in America; these were the men who, after lingering long on the threshold of Independence, resolutely passed that Rubicon undismayed by the stormy scenes which opened upon them. These constituted the yeomanry of Virginia, whose glory is so closely connected with all the great victories of the Revolution.

The martial instincts of this class were strong.* So soon as appeal was made to the sword, the contingent of Virginia was ever in active service; and for patience, fortitude and courage, they stood in the first rank of the Patriot army. Washington, in the perilous hour of battle, never felt so safe as when surrounded by his brave and ever faithful Virginians. In the language of James Monroe, himself a soldier of the

* The yeoman population was not confined to Virginia, but constituted the rural class throughout the South. They are represented by Washington as having a great aptitude for war. Here is an extract from his reply to an address from the people of South Carolina, after he became President. Works, vol. 12, p. 187. "Seconded by such a body of yeomen as repaired to the standard of liberty, fighting in their own native land, fighting for all that freemen hold dear, and whose docility soon supplied the place of discipline, it was scarcely in human nature, in its worst character, to abandon them in their misfortunes."

Revolution, "Virginia braved all dangers. From Quebec to Boston, from Boston to Savannah, she shed the blood of her sons." When the theatre of war was transferred to her own soil, the triumph which closed the bloody drama was achieved by her sons, aided by the chivalry of France!

But it was upon the conclusion of the war that the higher qualities of the Southern soldiery were displayed, and these qualities were the immediate fruits of their social system. When the federal army was disbanded, and the Northern soldiers cast loose upon society, they, in some parts of the country, contributed to create a rebellion against that government for which they had fought. But, at the South, the behavior of the warrior class was very different. "The tempest of war," says Washington, "having at length been succeeded by the sunshine of peace, our citizen soldiers impressed a useful lesson of patriotism on mankind by nobly returning with impaired constitutions and unsatisfied claims, after such long sufferings and severe disappointments to their former occupations." So glorious is the history of the tenant farmer of Virginia.

The general diffusion of slavery, through the country population, exerted a marked influence upon the political tendencies of the people, in contrast with the political tendencies of the North. It gave to the former a strong bias to republicanism; the absence of it left the latter a prey to those wandering fancies which lead to despotism. Washington observed this. He says the North "was much more productive of monarchical ideas than was the case in the Southern States." Vol. 9, p. 247. Deeply impressed with the love of personal and political liberty, the yeomanry were the guardians of the republic.

During the colonial period, Virginia in her government, but more in her social elements, bore a resemblance to England, and the resemblance is closer, if we take England before the abolition of villeinage. This order, or estate, if I may employ a word used to describe the feudal divisions of society, constituted the commons of Virginia.

It will not be out of place here, and will illustrate an important period of Virginian history, if we make a digression and search into the origin of the rural population of Virginia. The inquiry will carry us far back in English annals, but it will prove, if I mistake not, not the least instructive portion of history.

The yeomen of Virginia were descended from the yeomen* of England. Uprooted in the land of their nativity, and scorning the condition of the peasant, great numbers of them, with that spirit of adventure which appears to have been inherent in the race, migrated to the colony of Virginia, where, under other auspices and other skies, they rebuilt their homes. They were of the hardy Saxon breed, and it is probable that not a drop of Norman blood coursed through their veins. An hereditary preference for independent free-hold possessions, cultivated by servile labor, they brought with them. Thus a partiality for domestic slavery was inherent in the Virginian character. The yeoman population of England was the fruit of the feudal system as there developed.† By its prevailing

---

* The language in current use in Virginia, among people of little education, indicates their ancestry. Many words at present deemed vulgar, and excluded from polite use, when traced back, are discovered to be old English words, at one time employed by poets and princes. Several examples occur to me. Queen Elizabeth said: "My Lord *mought* have done well to have built his almshouse," &c. I hear that word every day, yet it would scarcely be considered as graceful and proper on the lips of Victoria. So *afeared*, although now condemned as an impropriety of speech, is found in the page of Shakspeare. *Farmer*, in its proper and English sense, means one who cultivates leased land. The word retained that signification after its introduction into Virginia, but when the tenant system gave way, it changed its sense and slid into a very different meaning. So of proverbs and vulgar metaphors. When Cranmer suggested to Henry to consult the foreign Universities touching the legality of his marriage with Catherine, the king was delighted, and exclaimed, "*Cranmer has got the right sow by the ear.*" Thus evidence of their lineage is deeply embedded in the language of the people.

† The landed system of England, as it sprung out of the institutions imposed at the Conquest, together with the subordination of classes dependent upon it, is explained with brevity and precision by Lord Bacon in his essay on "The use of the Law." He who desires to look into those antiquities, may examine that author, vol. 2d, pp. 256, 257.

policy the soil was cut up into small tenancies, which were occupied by freemen and cultivated by slaves. It was not until it began to give way under a new order of society, and the servile class to assume the form of day laborers, that its existence was seriously threatened. It was a powerful interest, and struck deep into the national sympathy, and a system of legislation was devised for its preservation, and persisted in during a long series of years.

But decay was at hand, and the means selected proved in the end an insufficient barrier to the advancing march of society and the instincts of individual interest. The purposes for which the feudal system had been devised had ceased to exist, and nothing could have preserved the divisions of property which it instituted, but accomodating them to the new interests which had sprung into existence, and linking them with the new powers which had risen up to govern the world. But this the statesmen of that age did not perceive, and it is left for posterity to remark and avoid their errors. Nor was the sympathy excited by the jeopardy of that class without good reason. The yeomanry had composed the principal strength of the English armies, whilst the military system of the Middle Ages retained its vigor unimpaired. It was that martial element which enabled England to win the great victories of the Middle Ages, which had shed such undying lustre upon her arms; it was those invincible bands which had overturned the throne of France and rendered the name of England terrible in Europe. That rude and untitled chivalry had taught French tacticians that it was a dangerous thing to meet the soldiers of England in a pitched battle, and that it was safe to prolong the war by sieges. Henry VII. in a speech from the throne to parliament urging a war with France, said: "At the battles of Cressy, Poictiers, Agincourt, we were of ourselves. France hath much people, but few soldiers. *They have no stable bands of foot.*"

In the decline of agriculture is to be discovered the primary cause which imperilled this class. Indications of this declension attracted the attention of government, soon after the termination of the civil war which, during the fifteenth century, for a period of thirty years, scourged that unhappy kingdom, in the course of which, says Hume, almost the whole of the ancient nobility were destroyed. To that great catastrophe must in the first place be ascribed, though other causes soon co-operated, the fate which threatened to overwhelm the whole tenant population, and not to a rude and unskillful agriculture as suggested by the author just named.

The pacification of the kingdom by an union of the hostile factions, found every department of industry in ruins, as needs must have been after so long a train of disasters. That inveterate and inextinguishable feud had broken into many parts, and had raged with unexampled violence among the great families who, with their retainers, embraced the entire realm. Thus was that destructive war carried to every door sill. None were too low, and none too high, to escape that fatal storm. A single extract from the illustrious historian of that period, will exhibit, in striking colors, the blight which those evil times had produced. After the victory which set the crown upon his head, "the King set forward, by easy journeys, to the city of London, receiving the acclamations and applauses of the people as he went, which, indeed, were true and unfeigned, as might well appear in the very demonstrations and fullness of the cry. For they thought generally, that he was a prince, as ordained and sent down from heaven, to unite and put an end to the long dissensions of the two Houses." So absolute was the wretchedness of the people at this period, that the attempt to collect a subsidy, more than once during this reign, produced insurrection. On one occasion, "the people, upon a sudden, grew into a great mutiny, and said openly that they had endured, of late years, a thousand miseries, and neither would nor could pay the subsidy.* When the root of national industry had decayed, it followed,

---

* Bacon's History of Henry VII.

as an inseparable consequence, that its branches should wither. With the destruction of agriculture, the prosperity of the towns disappeared.

Thus it was that England, at the union of the Roses, presented so worn and dilapidated a scene. In truth, those violent disorders had broken up old foundations, and the country, as if emerging from a chaos, was preparing, under other social conditions, to enter upon the new era which then opened upon Europe. Landed proprietors had begun to consolidate their farms by converting arable into pasture lands, and a general disruption of the tenant system impended. Great flocks of sheep had begun to overspread the country, and to usurp the homes of the people. Ruined tenements and abandoned dwellings greeted the eye on every side. So destructive was that evil, that Sir Thomas More, in a subsequent reign, forcibly said: "A sheep in England had become a more ravenous animal than a lion or wolf, and had devoured whole villages, cities and provinces." A cry of distress went up from every part of the kingdom, and popular risings threatened the public peace.* Appeals were made to government, and Parliament interfered to avert the threatened calamity. Laws were enacted, the most conspicuous of which were the Enclosure Acts, the expediency of which has excited great diversity of opinion. Whilst Hume condemns, Bacon approves their sound policy.

In recapitulating "the good Commonwealth's laws," enacted in the fourth year of Henry VII., so early in the reign of this monarch was this policy begun, Bacon recites these statutes, and, in his own condensed and luminous manner, enumerates the causes that had led to their adoption. "Another statute was made, of singular policy, for the population, apparently, and, if it be thoroughly considered, for the soldiery and military forces of the kingdom. Enclosures, at that time, began to be more frequent, whereby arable land, which could not be

* See Burnet's History of the Reformation.

manured * without people and families, was turned into pasture—which was easy to be rid by a few herdsmen; and tenancies for years, lives, and at will, whereupon much of the yeomanry lived, were turned into demesne. This bred a decay of the towns, churches, tythes, and the like. The king, likewise, knew full well, and in no wise forgot, that there ensued withal, upon this, a decay and diminution of subsidies and taxes; for the more gentlemen, ever the lower book of subsidies. In remedying this inconvenience, the king's wisdom was admirable, and the parliament's at that time." Enclosures they did not forbid, but framed an ordinance, that by indirect means, sought to attain that object. It was enacted, "that all houses of husbandry that were used with twenty acres of ground and upwards, should be maintained and kept forever; together with a competent provision of land to be used and occupied with them." The act was put under the sanction of exemplary penalties.

The avowed object of the Enclosure Act and its auxiliary enactments, was to preserve from threatened annihilation the tenant or yeoman population. Hume, as already stated, strongly reprobates them as an unwise and oppressive interference with the rights of private property; but full compensation, I think, has been furnished by Bacon, who in a masterly way explains and defends their policy. I could not select from the whole body of his works, a more admirable example of the penetration of that profound and universal genius. The Virginian of the present day will observe with satisfaction, that, in the following extract, his lordship points out the inestimable advantages which Virginia afterwards experienced from a social system constructed on that noble model:

"By this means the houses being kept up, did of necessity enforce a dweller; and the proportion of land for occupation being kept up, did of necessity enforce that dweller not to be

---

* Bacon employs the word in its primitive sense. It is a modern notion that lands can be "manured" without human labor.

a beggar or cottager, but a man of some substance, that might keep hinds and servants, and set the plough on going. This did wonderfully concern the might and manorhood of the kingdom, to have farms, as it were, of a standard sufficient to maintain an able body out of penury, and did in effect amortise a great part of the lands of the kingdom unto the hold and occupation of the yeomanry or middle people, of a condition between gentlemen and cottagers or peasants. Now, how much this did advance the military power of the kingdom is apparent by the true principles of war and the examples of other kingdoms. For it hath been held by the general opinion of men of best judgment in the wars, howsoever some few have varied, and that it may receive some distinction of case, that the principal strength of an army consisteth in the infantry or foot. And to make good infantry, it requireth men bred, not in the servile or indigent fashion, but in some free and plentiful manner. Therefore, if a State run most to noblemen and gentlemen, and that the husbandmen and ploughmen be but their work folks and laborers, or else mere cottagers, which are but housed beggars, you may have a good cavalry, but never good stable bands of foot; like to coppice woods, that if you leave in them staddles too thick, they will run to bushes and briers, and have little clean underwood. And this is to be seen in France and Italy, and some other parts abroad, where in effect all is noblesse or peasantry (I speak of people out of towns), and no middle people, and therefore no good forces of foot; insomuch that they are enforced to employ mercenary bands of Switzers, and the like, for their battalions of foot. Whereby, also, it comes to pass, that those nations have much people and few soldiers. Whereas, the king saw, that contrariwise it would follow, that England, though much less in territory, yet would have infinitely more soldiers of their native forces than those other nations have. Thus did the king secretly sow Hydra's teeth; whereupon, according to the poet's fiction, should rise up armed men for the service of this kingdom."

It is to be inferred from the language of Bacon, who composed his history in the reign of James I., that the Enclosure Acts of Henry VII., amended and perfected in subsequent reigns, had provided a stable bulwark for the protection of the yeomanry of England against the powerful causes which threatened their existence. This doubtless, to some extent, was true, inasmuch as the policy of those laws was persisted in for more than a century and a half. But complaints of encroachments on the plough were continually heard, until emigration relieved the plethora of population.

During the minority of Edward VI., discontents emanating from this source rose so high as to produce a rebellion, serious enough to embarrass the government of the Protector. Boards of Commission, invested with discretionary authority to inquire into all controversies originating in that cause, were dispatched to every part of the kingdom. Such prompt and summary, not to say violent and arbitrary, measures, doubtless, for a time, arrested the evil and restored the tenant population to their farms and their homes.

But the root of this evil lay deeper, and was not reached by the Enclosure Acts, and that root was, as already suggested, an unproductive agriculture. The reason that the profits of agriculture were poor, in comparison with the profits of pasturage, and why agriculture alone did not revive after the general prostration superinduced by the civil wars, appears to be referable to an injudicious regulation of trade by royal authority, together with the sudden expansion of manufactures and commerce, which, at that time, occurred both in England and on the continent. The exportation of breadstuffs was prohibited by an executive edict, from which the produce of pasturage was exempted. The policy upon which the king proceeded was the encouragement of the English woollen manufactures, a cherished object, as is evidenced by the statute law of England. So far did government proceed in pursuit of this object, that Parliament enacted a law requiring the dead to be buried in woollens.* It was by this means that the profits of agriculture were sacrificed to the creation of a new interest, and, consequently, was sacrificed that landed system by which the yeomanry of England were sustained. We shall see hereafter that the yeomanry of Virginia were destroyed, by Congress employing kindred means, and in pursuit of a similar object. The English monarch, by an order in council, prohibited the exports of the farm, and the legislators of the United States taxed the imports for which the agricultural exports of Virginia had been exchanged. The interference of government in either case injuriously affected the farmer.

Another cause which co-operated in the discouragement of English agriculture was the demand for wool on the continent, particularly in the low countries, then the seat of industry and the arts in the north of Europe. The extent of English commerce with the low countries at that period was exhibited by the great inconvenience produced by a suspension of trade, which occurred in consequence of the countenance and protection afforded to Perkin Warbeck by Margaret of Burgundy. So great was it, that, by particular agreement, commercial intercourse was exempted from the operation of wars that might thereafter occur between those parties. But those restraints upon the exportation of grain were long persisted in, and agriculture did not begin to flourish until after those restraints had been removed,—so inseparable is the connection in all ages, and under all governments, between commerce and agriculture. They spring, indeed, from the same root, and are imbedded in the same soil.

But, in the fullness of time, great events occurred, and a new theatre was prepared for the yeomanry of England. The settlements in Virginia had been established, and into them the living current was poured, precipitated and enlarged by the domestic troubles engendered by the tyranny of the

---

* See Hallam's Constitutional History of England.

Stuarts, the like of which had loosened that order of society from its first holdings. The yeomanry of England, torn from their parent soil, were elected to the high destiny of founding a new empire of a type of civilization, before unknown among men, which, after many vicissitudes, was destined to stand alone, as the one under which republican liberty can be reconciled with social order, and with the highest forms of moral and industrial development. In the posterity of those who fought at Cressy, Agincourt and Poictiers, the trust was not committed to unworthy hands. In war and in peace, in the council and the field, through good report and through evil report, they and their descendants have been faithful to their high trust; and at the present hour, when the billows of fanaticism threaten to overwhelm it, they constitute the firmest barrier of that peculiar civilization—a civilization derived from the blended elements of liberty and slavery—the twisted cord of white and black, out of which the destiny of the South has been woven.

A considerable portion of the yeomanry of Virginia espoused the cause of the new government, deceived by men who were themselves deceived into the general belief, that the transfer from the legislatures of the States to the legislature of the Union of "the power to regulate commerce," for which the new Constitution made provision, would be the means of lifting the heavy weights from the trade of the State. But this motive operated not upon the great majority of that class. They turned a deaf ear to the seductive voice of interest. They sternly opposed a constitution which, in its development, they were convinced would destroy their recent and dear-bought independence. But the voice of the majority was not always heard in the councils of the State. The political organization was so framed, as to enable a minority of the voting population to impose laws, constitutions and systems on the contrary wishes of the people. Had the people been provided with organs for the expression of their will, the new Constitution would have been discarded by a great majority, and the Articles of Confederation amended, to which they were strongly attached. As it was, the heart and mind of Virginia did not ratify the Constitution; but Virginia, by mixed fraud and violence, was dragged hand-cuffed into the new Union.

I should very imperfectly discharge the unpleasing task of recounting the wrongs and misfortunes of my country, if I did not here give some account of the means by which that fatal result was accomplished; a free and high-spirited people enslaved; the riches and pre-eminence of the Commonwealth destroyed; her dignity and respectability lost.

The two pillars upon which rests the edifice of a democratic republic are suffrage and representation. In both particulars the Constitution of Virginia was so defective, as scarcely to deserve the name of a popular government. The two are indeed but one—representation being to the community, what suffrage is to the individual. In its two-fold application of that fundamental principle of free government, the Constitution had indeed deviated from the correct rule; but in apology for that aberration it has been urged by one who was himself schooled in sound principles, that "the Constitution was formed when we were raw and unexperienced in the science of government, and it is no wonder that time and trial should have discovered very capital defects in it." It may be added, that it was struck out at a single heat by the genius of one man, was framed in a season of public anxiety, and almost amid the tumult of arms, and was after all but an imperfect adaptation of her colonial institutions to the altered condition of Virginia.

Only freeholders by that Constitution were allowed to vote. That qualification excluded from the exercise of the franchise those adult male citizens who were possessed only of a chattel interest in lands, a class that was growing to be more numerous on account of the gradual change which had begun in lease tenures. The white laborer laboring for wages was then not known in Virginia, he being a recent and unnatural growth in a slave holding community. Complaints had already been heard of the exclusion from the ballot box produced by that requirement; but still, for the following reasons, I am strongly inclined to the belief that the freeholders embraced the great body of male citizens who had attained majority.

1. Every democratic government, from its nature, must, in the vital particular of suffrage, reflect the image of the community and be a correct test of the general condition. Of this important truth the constitutional history of Virginia affords ample proof. At the period when the freehold qualification was first adopted into the political system of Virginia, it excluded nobody, the object of that test being, not exclusion, but to offer an inducement to the young men to brave the wilderness and widen the area of the settlements. The great landholders gladly co-operated in this policy by granting life terms, and thus that standard of qualification came to be moulded into the political fabric and adopted among the political ideas of Virginia. But when, owing to causes hereafter to be considered, the land system was disrupted by a consolidation of farms, and heirs ousted of their freeholds, the freehold suffrage was abolished and a lower property test substituted. To accomplish that reform a new constitution was fabricated. After the lapse of twenty years the number of non-property holders had greatly multiplied, for Virginia had reached a a further stage of decline. Even that lower test had become exclusive, and additional modifications had become necessary. Thus it is the constitutional reflects the social history of Virginia.

2. At the period when the first Constitution was made, it was amid violent heats and conflicts of opinion, and it was of great moment to conciliate the democratic elements in society. It is hardly probable that so politic a statesman as George Mason would have proposed, or the Convention have adopted, a scale of suffrage that would have shut out from the honors of that liberty, which they were invited to defend, the very men who were to bear the burden of the contest.

3d. Gov. Randolph, in the Convention of '88, declared that

Virginia had begun the Revolution under a Constitution as democratic as that of Athens. It is highly improbable that, once in possession of the privilege of voting, the non-freeholder would have voluntarily relinquished it, and that at the outbreak and during the course of a revolution, when old foundations were loosened and broken up, that men, in the first transports of freedom, should, at the fiat of a revolutionary committee, submit to be despoiled of the proudest ornament and noblest prerogative of freemen.

4. It is, to say the least, scarcely to be received as reasonable that the leaders of the Opposition in the Convention of 1788, who strongly inveighed against the abuse of the representative system, should have spared this the greatest abuse of all.

But the greatest imperfection in the Constitution, and which operated to the virtual disfranchisement of great numbers, even of the qualified voters, was the mode of representation which it ordained. Against that deep-seated malady, every just and wise man lifted up his voice, more particularly when it was taken from beyond its original application and used to force, upon a reluctant and indignant people, a hated government. The Constitution ordained an equal representation to the several counties of the State, without respect to their size, the amount of taxation, population in gross, or the number of qualified voters. That the enormity of that abuse may be exhibited, I transfer to this page a table prepared by Mr. Jefferson, together with his judicious observations upon it: "Among those who share the representation, the shares are very unequal. Thus the county of Warwick, with only one hundred fighting men, has an equal representation with the county of Loudoun, which has 1746. So that every man in Warwick has as much influence in the government as seventeen men in Loudoun. But lest it should be thought that an equal interspersion of small among large counties, through the whole State, may prevent any danger to particular parts of it, we will divide it into districts, and show the proportions of land, of fighting men, and of representation in each:

	Square Miles.	Fighting Men.	Delegates.	Senators.
Between the sea-coast and falls of the rivers, - - -	11,205	19,012	71	12
Between the falls of the rivers and the Blue Ridge mountains, - - - - -	18,759	18,828	46	8
Between the Blue Ridge mountains and the Alleghany, -	11,911	7,673	16	2
Between the Alleghany and the Ohio, - - - - -	79,650	4,458	16	2
	121,525	49,971	149	24

"An inspection of this table," continues Mr. Jefferson, "will supply the place of commentaries on it. It will appear at once that nineteen thousand men, living below the falls of the rivers, possess half the Senate, and want four members of possessing a majority of the House of Delegates, a want more than supplied by their vicinity to the seat of government. These nineteen thousand, therefore, living in one part of the country, give law to upwards of thirty thousand living in another, and appoint all their chief officers, executive and judiciary."

Counties, not population, being represented under that method, it so chanced that the counties of tide-water, where the cavalier or aristocratic interest chiefly prevailed, composed likewise that section which embraced all the small counties. And it was to them that the popularity of the proposed government was, in a great measure, confined. In the midland and western counties, the strength of the Opposition was intrenched. It is stated in the correspondence of Washington, that in the country contained within the upper James river and the Carolina border, the seat of a dense population, the people were almost unanimous against it. In confirmation, I will quote here an uncontradicted statement made by Mr. Henry, on the floor of the Convention, which will throw a flood of light upon the effects produced by that vicious and anti-republican method of representation. Speaking of the Constitution, he says: "*The great body of the yeomanry are in decided opposition to it. I may say with confidence that, for* NINETEEN COUNTIES *adjacent to each other, nine-tenths of the people are opposed to it.*"

Had representation been according to any just standard, and more especially had it been in accordance with that now established, the Philadelphia scheme of government would have been tossed back upon the North—its birth-place, its natural patroness, and its proper home. But why was not the majority of the people, or at least a majority of the qualified voters, represented on that truly momentous occasion, when, in the language of Henry, "a revolution was proposed, as radical as that which separated us from England?" We, who have inherited their places, and, with their places, the political thraldom of that undone and outraged people, have now the right, inalienable to the soil of Virginia, to demand, why the dregs of a corrupted and broken-down aristocracy, under the guidance of political aspirants, were suffered to immolate, upon the federal altar, the genius of Virginian liberty?

It was competent for the legislature to provide, as it was unquestionably its duty, a mode of representation by which the wishes of a majority of the voting population of the State should have been ascertained, with respect to so vital a change in their government as was proposed by the plan concocted at Philadelphia. The legislature, notwithstanding the shadow, which they called a constitution, but which sprung from no higher authority than the legislature, was indeed in possession of powers as boundless as those claimed by a British Parliament.* It could alter, amend or abolish the ordinance which

---

* It will be seen below that the Assembly did determine the very questions of representation and suffrage in that case:

"*October 25th*, 1787.—The House, according to the order of the day, resolved itself into a committee of the whole house, on the report of the Federal

some have pleased to denominate a Constitution, at pleasure, as on previous, as well as subsequent occasions, they had altered and amended it. To prove how completely that instrument was in the plastic hands of the Assembly, they changed the basis of representation in the Senate, an exercise of the very power in question. Of the tyranny produced by county representation, Mr. Baldwin, in 1829, says, "that it was a system which enabled one-third of the qualified voters to govern the whole; which places the smallest county on an equal footing, as regards political power, with others ten times superior in population, territory and wealth."

The Federal Convention had refused to have that work of

Convention lately held in Philadelphia; and, after some time spent therein, Mr. Speaker resumed the chair, and Mr. Matthews reported, that the committee had, according to order, had the said report under their consideration, and had gone through the same, and come to several resolutions thereupon, &c., and are as followeth:

"*Resolved, &c.* That the proceedings of the Federal Convention, as transmitted to the General Assembly through the medium of Congress, ought to be submitted to a convention of the people, for their full and free investigation and discussion.

"*Resolved, &c.* That every citizen, being a freeholder in this Commonwealth, ought to be eligible to a seat in the Convention; and that the people thereof ought not to be restrained in their choice of delegates by any of those legal and constitutional restrictions which confine them in their choice of members to the legislature.

"*Resolved, &c.* That it be recommended to each county to elect two delegates, and to each city, town or corporation entitled, or who may be entitled, by law to representation in the legislature, to elect one delegate to the said Convention.

"*Resolved, &c.* That the qualifications of the electors be the same with those now established by law.

"*Resolved, &c.* That the election for delegates shall be held in the month of March next, on the first day of the court to be held for each county, city or corporation respectively; and that the persons so chosen shall assemble at the State-house in the city of Richmond, on the fourth Monday in May next.

"*Resolved, &c.* That 2,000 copies of these resolutions be forthwith printed, and dispersed by the members of the General Assembly among their constituents; and that the Executive transmit a copy of them to Congress, and to the legislature and executive of the respective States."

These resolutions were embodied in an act of Assembly.

their hands submitted to the State Assemblies for ratification or rejection, preferring instead to appeal for a confirmation and ratification of that instrument to the people of the several States. Why was not that appeal made? or does "a third" of their number constitute the PEOPLE?

The Opposition, composed of these popular elements, regarded the ratification of the new Constitution as equivalent to a total subversion of the independence of the State, and a wanton sacrifice of her best interests: It was a subtle and elaborate contrivance by which the South was to be reduced to the dominion of the North, and its present and prospective wealth exposed to the avarice of that indigent section. Gov. Harrison, soon after the Constitution was published, expressed that general opinion to Washington, in a letter, in which he said: "If that Constitution is adopted, the South will become the mere appendage of the North." But just escaped from the vassalage of England, the people of Virginia were in no mood to contract under other forms a similar, but more burdensome relation with another power. They were not ready to make a tender of their bloody purchase to their Northern confederates. The fruits of the Revolution were too precious, they deemed, thus to be cast away.

The publication of the Philadelphia plan found the popular mind in profound repose; but soon that calm was broken by no gentle breeze.* A storm burst that shook the commonwealth to its centre. It reminded men of '76. New parties were soon formed, with new names to designate their respective principles. For the first time in the nomenclature of

* "A year before the meeting of the late Federal Convention at Philadelphia, a general peace and tranquility prevailed in this country; but since that period, the people are exceedingly uneasy and disquieted. When I wished for an appointment to this Convention, my mind was extremely agitated for the situation of public affairs. I conceive the Republic to be in extreme danger. It arises from this fatal system, it arises from the proposal to change our government. * * * * Difference of opinion has gone to a degree of inflammatory resentment in different parts of the country, which has been occasioned by this perilous innovation."—HENRY.

American politics the name of "Democrat" was heard; for the first time as a party description was heard the name of "Federalist." In such stormy times were those parties cradled, which, through all vicissitudes, have divided the people of the United States. Then occurred that schism which now so deeply separates the minority from the great majority of the people of Virginia. Those ranged and hostile powers, under veteran and accomplished leaders, took the field, and, for near a twelve-month, the fierce debate continued. As save once before, such profound emotions had never stirred the hearts of the people, so never but once again will they madden the hearts of their posterity—*when the work of that day comes to be undone.*

Among the leaders of the Opposition, proudly eminent stood Patrick Henry. He had been the man of '76, and was again the great figure of '88. He was without a peer. Sprung from the middling order, he was the idol of the people. They loved him for his virtues, admired him for his eminent abilities, and trusted him for that courage and fidelity, which had been approved in the fires of the Revolution. They had followed him when threatened with the tyranny of Britain, and they now looked up to him to preserve them from the imminent peril that threatened to ingulf their liberties. Nor was their confidence bestowed without good reason. He was the ablest debater in the country, had collected ample stores of knowledge with which to illustrate and adorn whatever he touched, and withal was endowed with a sublime and matchless eloquence. So deeply penetrated were they with admiration for his talents and spotless virtue, that at this day, among their descendants, the name of Patrick Henry is pronounced not without veneration and love. An incident is related by Mr. Grigsby, which strikingly illustrates the temper of those times. At Charlotte Court House, upon the court green, previous to his attendance upon the Convention, an old hunter laid his hand on Mr. Henry's shoulder, and in allusion, I presume, to a reported defection among the Opposition leaders, said to him: "Old fellow, stick to the people; if you take the back track we are ruined."

But the champions of the Constitution did not confine themselves to public and private discussion, but appealed to those other weapons of political controversy which are only resorted to by bold and unscrupulous men in a high and inflamed state of parties. So soon as the banner of Federalism was unfurled, and the inclination of leading characters had become known, every avenue to the popular mind was choked with slander. The very atmosphere was impregnated by its foul breath. Patriotism and a demand for reasonable securities for the public liberty were tortured into sedition, and a well grounded apprehension of that vast accumulation of power at the centre, for which the new Constitution provided, was treated as incontestible proof of ambition for local distinction, and a secret and unavowed desire to split the Union into independent and perhaps hostile communities. He who would indulge in the luxury of defamation, may gratify that horrid appetite by consulting the memorials of that period.

In the general aspersion of motives, Mr. Henry did not escape. How could the Federal archer forego that shining mark? More than once in debate he complained of the malignant slanders fulminated against him because he would not desert what he believed to be the true interests of his country, and be dragged along in the Federal movement.* It reminded him of the only parallel which his life had afforded, when he contended with the same adversary under other names and

* The malignant weapons employed by the Federalists in that contest, may be judged of by the letters of "Decius" published in the autumn of 1788, in the "Virginia Independent Chronicle," the numbers of which covering the period may be found in the State Library. The assaults were directed against the Democratic leaders generally, but against Henry in chief. Breaking through the barriers that protect private life, his political enemies attacked and misrepresented his private transactions. But those unscrupulous partizans called defenders into the field, who, by evidence derived from the highest sources, exonerated Henry from their aspersions. (See answers to letters of Decius. *Ibid.*

with other professions. "Suspicions," said he, "have gone forth—suspicions of my integrity. It is publicly stated that my professions are not real. Twenty-three years ago I was supposed a traitor to my country; I was then thought to be the bane of sedition, because I supported the cause of my country. I trust that there are many now that think my professions for the public good to be real." Once, during the session of the Convention, allusion more definite and personal was thrown out against him. Henry haughtily demanded a specification of the charge, or an absolute retraction of it. The allusion was promptly disclaimed. On such high principles was that great character framed! of such an ethereal temper was that gifted man!

Mr. Henry had been appointed among the delegates to attend the Convention at Philadelphia; and his name, as showing the place he occupied in the general estimation, stands next to the name of Washington. But he declined the appointment, that he might stand uncommitted, as he conceived, to that work. In this he was betrayed, as I believe, into a grave error. This is not the place to present his idea of a general government and the extent to which he deemed reform to be necessary; but it differed essentially from the Constitution as framed. Had he been present at its construction, the weight of his talents and character, added to his sway at home, would have enabled him to confine the Convention within the limits of its appointment. There was a State-rights party in that body which repeatedly manifested a strong opposition to the centralizing tendencies there prevalent, but it contained no man in its ranks who could compete with Madison and Wilson, the great debaters in the Convention. It is true George Mason and Luther Martin were there, and that the mind of the one was still as hard and as bright as diamond, and that the other was still strong in his maturity; but old age, with its chilling effects, was creeping on Mason; his energies had lost somewhat of their elastic vigor; and the intemperate zeal of Luther Martin, coupled with the double connection or Maryland with the slave States of the South and the small States of the North, inducing vacillation, disqualified her representative for the post of leader of the State-rights men. Had Henry been there, the great Tribune of the people, whom no threatened dissolution could appal and no sophistry delude, he would, beyond doubt, have controlled the action of that body. The State-rights party would have gathered around him, and federalism, discountenanced, would have been driven out of doors. Amendments would have been made to the Articles of Confederation, and he would have been able to stem the tide of innovation which swept everything before it.

The Convention to ratify or reject the Constitution convened at Richmond on the 3d day of June, 1788. It was the most brilliant assemblage, whether for talent, for reputation or for learning, ever convoked in the Western world. The principal debaters on the part of the Opposition were Henry, Mason, Monroe and William Grayson. Next in reputation to Henry, George Mason deserves to be ranked. He was more remarkable for sagacity and an ironical wit than for the power of speech; but yet such was the high estimation in which he was held by the people at large, that his simple opposition to the Constitution carried with it great weight.

But William Grayson, if we may judge by those fragments of his speeches that have been preserved, deserves to be enumerated among the most gifted sons of Virginia. His powers of reasoning were remarkable, and in that important debate he contended with Madison upon no unequal terms. He was a ripe scholar, and had studied history with the discriminating eye of a statesman. With the politics of the mother country he was familiar, and from a continued service in the Congress of the Confederation, he was thoroughly acquainted with the character of the people inhabiting every State, and was thoroughly versed in the interests of the country. He had been employed, in company with Mason, in arranging the delicate and irritating questions of boundary that had existed between his own State and Maryland. The correspondence of Washington exhibits the high estimation in which he held the abilities and public virtues of Grayson. He appears to have understood more perfectly than any of his cotemporaries, if we except Henry, the character of the Constitution, which he so vehemently opposed. He refused to debate the Constitution in its secondary character, as a compact between States, but he contended throughout, that it was sectional in its grand features. He did not partake of the debate in its earlier stages, but when he broke silence, it was evident that a great light had risen. Grayson and Richard Henry Lee, himself distinguished for his opposition to ratification, were the two first Senators elected from Virginia, but in the ripeness of his wisdom his career was cut short by death. Who now hears of Grayson? Henry has his statue, Madison lives in marble, but Grayson is almost forgotten. With so partial a hand do posterity distribute their honors among the dead!

The leading speakers, on behalf of the Constitution, were Madison, Gov. Randolph, John Marshall, George Nicholas and Edmund Pendleton. To this list must be added the name of Innes, then a young man of rising reputation. He was attorney general, and was pronounced by Patrick Henry and other competent judges, to have been one of the most eloquent orators in Virginia. He did not speak often, but when he did, he spoke with effect. His view of the Constitution will be particularly referred to hereafter. He subsequently moved to Kentucky, and rose to judicial honors.

Of this distinguished group, Madison, confessedly, stood first. Chief architect of the Constitution in its fundamental parts, he was its great advocate in the Convention. Above all others, its ratification by that body was referable to his exertions. Be his the glory, if there be glory, and his the grave responsibility of that act. He was, indeed, a Hercules in debate, and possessed in as great perfection as any man of his time, perhaps greater, if we except his illustrious rival,

Henry, the simple power of ratiocination. But it was not combined with the higher and rarer gift of wisdom, which, discerning in causes the results to which they tend, reaches conclusions by an intuitive perception of truth. He who is possessed of this faculty, so elevated, indeed, so divine, often marches many leagues in advance of his contemporaries, and foretells events to an unbelieving generation. It is only when this faculty is associated with eloquence and logic, and is ennobled and strengthened by knowledge and political experience, as in the rich and fine-strung intellect of Patrick Henry, that it is able to move the hearts of men and stamp its conclusions on the living age. Evidences are thickly strewn along the public career of Mr. Madison to show that he was possessed of the first, but not of the second quality of mind, and no part of his career is more replete with such evidence than that now about to pass under review. If the faculty of argument had been able to fly up on waxen wings to the eternal fountains of light, and, exploring the mysteries of truth, had revealed to that great master of logic consequences, which it did not and could not reveal, but which Henry clearly foresaw and, in no mystic terms, foretold, that Federal pyramid, which now casts its cold shadow over Virginia, had not been reared.

From the best analysis I have been able to make of the Debates in the Virginia Convention, the objections against the Constitution, as already indicated, may be classed under two heads. From them all others were derived. 1. That the magnitude of the powers intrusted to the federal agent would, in their development, produce a consolidation of the States into one empire. 2. That the powers thus accumulated at the centre, were so distributed between the North and the South that, by the trick of a minority representation, the latter would be brought under the political vassalage of the former.

In the outset, Mr. Henry requested the speakers on the other side to gratify his "political curiosity" by informing him by what authority the Federal Constitution had used the phrase "we, the people," instead of "we, the States." He regarded the employment of those words as tantamount to a fusion of the States into a single community. Madison promptly, and I think satisfactorily, responded, that those words were employed to pass by the immediate agency of the State legislatures, and procure for the new government a popular recognition; and that the mode of its ratification unquestionably established that fact.

It does not fall within my object here to attend further to the discussion on this point, for I am convinced that the battle over the Constitution was fought on other grounds. Though, in its nature, it was a substantive objection to that instrument, yet it was considered as preliminary to those sectional objections upon which the decision ultimately turned. Before leaving this portion of the Debates, it will not be out of place to advert to a very remarkable opinion advanced by Mr. Madison in respect to the nature and structure of the proposed Constitution. It is in manifest contradiction to interpretations of that enigmatical instrument afterwards insisted upon by him, and in contradiction, too, to many things which he subsequently uttered in the Convention. It will throw, if I mistake not, a strong light on the intellectual, if not on the moral, character of that distinguished man. It proves, beyond doubt, that he came to the Convention, not for candid discussion—that he was not there as a searcher after truth, but to play the part of a juggling sophist.

He presented to the Convention what Henry happily termed a piece of "political anatomy." "I can say, notwithstanding what the honorable gentleman has alleged, that this government is not completely consolidated, nor is it entirely federal. * * * * * * * The members to the national House of Representatives are to be chosen by the people at large, in proportion to the numbers in the respective districts. When we come to the Senate, its members are elected by the States in their equal and political capacity; but, had the government been completely consolidated, the Senate would have been chosen by the people in their individual capacity, in the same manner as the members of the other house. Thus it is of a complicated nature, and this complication, I trust, will be found to exclude the evils of absolute consolidation, as well as of a mere confederacy."

It will be remembered, that whilst the Federal Convention was employed in the perplexing task of organizing the legislative department, four distinct interests aspired to its control: 1. The small States, on the ground that an equality of representation was necessary to defend them from encroachments from the large States. 2. The large and populous States, because it was just, they contended, that political influence should be measured by riches, extent and population. 3. The free-soil; and 4. The slaveholding interests. It was a struggle for power, and each interest strove for its possession.

It will be remembered furthermore, that, amid those jarring pretensions, the legislature was so framed as, in part, to accommodate all—wholly, none; that the large States of the North, and the slave States of the South, compounded their differences by a fractional representation of slaves; and that the controversy between the large States and the small was adjusted by giving to the small States an equal vote in the Senate.

There is no evidence that the popular basis was insisted on for the purpose of consolidating the government in that feature. Certainly no evidence to that effect is contained in the report of the debates from Mr. Madison's own pen. In the first or popular branch of Congress, the large States and the slave States are represented; in the second branch, the small States and, as was believed, the free States; but in both, the States. Mr. Madison, after applying the fractional basis to one house of the legislature, attempted, if we may credit his own account of that transaction, to have it applied to the other; not for the purpose of making the government wholly consolidated, but for the purpose of engrafting the sectional equilibrium upon the Senate too. The different modes of representation finally resorted to, were for the understood object of representing different interests. But, in his attempt to apply the fractional basis to the Senate, he was deserted by his late allies, who went off under the lead of Gouverneur Morris, who was apprehensive that a Southern preponderance in every department would arise out of the slave basis.

The executive office is rested, likewise, on a popular basis. In its origin, it bears a strong similitude to the popular branch of Congress; the College of Electors being nothing more than a box in which the ballots are deposited. Is that department but another feature in which is exhibited the consolidated character of the government? In the Senate alone are the federal properties of the government to be found? If this be true, our debt of gratitude to Mr. Madison is much diminished. This redeeming principle of the Constitution we owe, then, to Mr. Morris, who loved power in all its forms. We owe to him that we are not confounded in a general *hotch-pot* with Massachusetts, and that we are not of the blood and bone of the little pedlar of Rhode Island.

If there is no evidence to be found in the history of the Constitution to give countenance to this bold asseveration, still less will be found in the manner in which it is constituted. In the organization of the Senate, confessedly federal, the people of the several States exercise control by means of their State legislatures. But, in the case of the House of Representatives, no such instrumentality is employed. In the one, the State Assemblies are the links of connection between the States and the central power; in the other, the people exercise power immediately. The individuality of the States is the point of distinction between a consolidated and a federal government, and that is preserved equally in both cases. If the appeal to the people for their sanction of the Constitution, through their State Conventions, did not consolidate the government, as Mr. Madison has assured us it did not, it is extremely difficult to understand how the direct intervention of the people in a federal election could be productive of that consequence.

But this doctrine of political amalgamation will be found to be as little comformable to the subsequent, as to the previous opinions of Mr. Madison. In the Resolutions and Report of '98 and '99, he bluntly declares that it "is a compact to which the States alone are parties." But this was after he had been "disgorged of his Federalism," if I may again quote the language of Henry, and had turned Democrat, when, under the inspiration of Jefferson, or rather under the inspiration of his own insatiable ambition, he was using his wonderful powers of argument to break through the federalist chain of succession to Presidential honors.

But it is not necessary to wait until 1798, in order to convict Madison of inconsistency on this important point. In the following year, in the first Congress which assembled under the new Constitution, not a twelve-month from the period of his collision with Henry, he declared that the government of the United States was a compact between sovereign States.

In order to present a general idea of the views of the Democratic leaders, I will venture upon an outline of the principal points of objection which they advanced in their speeches. It was argued against the act of Ratification, that the Constitution was not made in accordance with the instructions which Virginia had given to her delegates to the Federal Convention; that they had been strictly enjoined to amend, not to abolish, the Federal Articles. Instead of which, the principle of Confederation had been abandoned, and that of Consolidation taken. In that cardinal and wanton breach of trust, the proposed government had been cradled. That it had provided a mighty consolidated system was undeniable, when the extensive range of the federal jurisdiction was considered in connection with the doubtful, nay invisible, limitations put upon those powers.

The Constitution, it is true, was, on its face, an instrument of granted powers; but was there any security, by the aid of artful construction, that it would not be made to draw every subject within its ample jurisdiction? What was to prevent the federal government from silently absorbing the States? Why was there not, insisted Mr. Monroe, some impassible barrier, an equilibrium, established between the Federal and State powers? No such barrier had been pointed out—it was clear that none existed. The only protection which the States would have against the central power would be paper securities, which it would be in the power of the former to violate at pleasure. Look at the money power of the new government, and the power to create offices and appoint salaries; they were possessed without limit. The patronage from hence would be immense and overwhelming, when put in the scale against the State governments. The result would be, that whilst the new government would grow in influence, the States would be reduced to mere corporations, whose humble office it would be "to repair highways and bridges, and take care of the poor."* It had been admitted by the principal champion of the Constitution on that floor, that an absolute money power would, in effect, render any government despotic, and it was perfectly clear that the instrument, the subject of their deliberations, would place in the hands of Congress a revenue, for the expenditure of which they would not be responsible to the tax payers.

The new government, insisted Mr. Henry, if adopted, would

---

* It is a curious and interesting coincidence, that these very words, used by Mr. Henry to describe the humble occupation of the State governments under the new Constitution, should have been employed by Hume to describe the jurisdiction of the English Parliament during the reign of Elizabeth. Mr. Henry, like Chatham, to whom the English compare him, was a profound student of history: did he unwittingly employ the language of the historian, because his own mind silently traced the parallel between the new government and the despotic queen, and the State Assemblies and her subservient Parliament? The history of the house of Tudor had been published in 1759, and must be presumed to have found a place in the well-stored library at Red Hill.

prove to be an ambuscade against the public liberty. It had been conceded that the proposed Constitution had provided a government that was consolidated in its popular features. Did any man believe that a consolidated government would suit the condition of so extensive a country as the United States, inhabited by communities of such opposite characteristics and interests? What occasion had Virginia for a mighty government like that provided for? The adopting States might indeed stand in need of a strong external power, but such was not the case with Virginia. She was then the foremost State in the Union, but if such a vast cession of power was made, she might be destroyed; it was impossible to see how she could be benefitted. Indeed, urged Mr. Grayson, it was to be apprehended, that by entering into so intimate an union with the North, a country now on the verge of bankruptcy, that the Northern States would get her wealth and give back their poverty in exchange. The opponents of the proposed Constitution had been charged with a desire to break up the Union, but the charge was wholly destitute of truth. Whilst they believed that Virginia, stretching back to the Ohio and the Mississippi, would be able to maintain an independent establishment, they still desired a union with the North, but a union based on strictly federal principles. How monstrous a proposition was this! to sacrifice the great State of Virginia, that they might create a vast central authority, according to the ideal of the politicians congregated at Philadelphia.

But if the new plan were regarded in the light of a compact between the North and the South, out of which a government was to arise, its defects would be more conspicuous. The people of the North had manifested a decided inclination towards manufactures and navigation,* to which they would

* "There is a striking difference and a great contrariety of interests between the States. They are naturally divided into carrying and productive States. This is an actual existing distinction, which cannot be altered. The

be compelled to resort for a living; whereas the people of the South, invited by pleasant skies and a fruitful soil, were inclined to the cultivation of the earth. This inclination would probably continue until population and redundant capital should qualify them for other pursuits. Out of that diversity of occupation there would necessarily spring a diversity of interests, upon which a national government would bear with unequal pressure; and thus the one would be sacrificed to the other. The true plan in constructing a general government was, to give it not even a colorable jurisdiction over such opposing material interests, but to leave each State to govern itself in those particulars. But there were diversities of a moral nature, not less important, which ought to be attended to in the construction of a government for the two sections. These engendered contrary political and social tendencies, which had not been attended to in the distribution of federal power.

The American States, insisted Henry, are dissimilar in their structure, but this government will assimilate them. States dissimilar in their structure may unite in a confederacy, and from that very dissimilarity their confederated government may derive a greater stability. The union among the States of Switzerland proves this. That union, notwithstanding that some of the States are aristocratic, others democratic in their frames, some Catholic, others Protestant, has for centuries existed amidst the changeful and stormy politics of Europe. The diversities among us are not less striking. Whilst they would be preserved and tolerated by a Republic resting on the federal idea, it is manifest that a mighty national government

---

former are more numerous and must prevail. What, then, will be the consequences of their contending interests, if the taxation of America is to go on in thirteen different shapes? *This government subjects everything to the Northern majority. Is there not a settled purpose to check the Southern interest?* We thus put unbounded power over our property in hands not having a common interest with us. How can the Southern members prevent the adoption of the most oppressive mode of taxation in the Southern States, as there is a Northern majority in favor of the Northern States?"—HENRY—*Elliott*, vol. iii, p. 311.

like this, will destroy them. There will be brought about a uniformity, and when we see that power is deposited in Northern hands, we need be at no loss to determine that the conformity will be to the Northern model.

Examine the taxing power, so delicate and important that, by the friends of the Constitution, it had been called its vitals, though, with better reason, it might be called the vitals of the people; had that power been put under such restraints that it could not be abused to the injury of the South? Every source of taxation had been thrown open, and if the North, operating upon Congress, should determine to collect the public dues from taxes on the foreign trade, would not the South, the importing and consuming section, contribute the principal part of the revenue? This result, in the event supposed, it had been conceded, would follow; and that it would follow, it was certain, when it was remembered that the North, the controlling power in the new government, would be interested in this mode of collection. It was worthy of remark, in showing the unskillful manner in which the Constitution had been put together, that it contained an express prohibition against taxing exports. Why had this prohibition been made? Taxes on exports were a legitimate source of revenue sometimes resorted to by the governments of Europe. They were excepted in this case, for the avowed reason that they would operate with severity upon the South. Why had not some equivalent security been provided in the case of imports? The import and export of a country are vitally connected, being but different members of the same body, and protection from unjust taxation was as necessary in the one case as in the other. The only difference was, that a tax on the import was a more adroit way of reaching the pockets of the farmer and planter, and less palpable to the common eye. By an improper use of that power, it was perfectly evident that the commerce of the South might be crippled, and her whole industry paralysed. To obviate the force of this objection, an assurance had been given, that on account of this very inequality, the import trade of the country would be lightly taxed, and the public income principally derived from direct taxation; that, out of those elements, the fiscal system would be compounded. But it was evident that the only ground for that assurance, or rather the sole origin of that hope, was the forbearance and equitable disposition of the Northern people—a people who, by proverb, valued money above all things else. "With respect," said My. Grayson, "to the citizens of the Eastern and Middle States, perhaps the best and surest means of discovering their general dispositions, may be by having recourse to their interests. .This seemed to be the pole star by which the policy of nations is directed." It was quite impossible for any one to know what course things would take, or to foretell what use would be made of power. "When you grant titles of nobility," exclaimed Henry, quoting the language of Montesquieu, "you know what you do; but when you grant power, you know not what you do." "We are wandering," continued the prophetic orator, "on the great ocean of human events, without chart or compass, and exposed to the mercy of every storm."

But conceding, contrary to every human probability, that the federal revenue would principally be collected by direct taxation, was that power so guarded that it could not be employed to the disadvantage of the slaveholding States? A slight examination would show, that if the expectations, or rather the hopes, of the Federalists were realized in this particular, that the South would be rescued from one danger, to be precipitated on another. A fixed ratio between direct taxes and representation had been established in the proposed government. Upon this part of their work, its makers appear to value themselves highly. But in that very precaution, they manifest a suspicion of Northern integrity, and have provided for the South a seeming security against oppression. Thus it was that the symmetry and soundness of one part displayed the deformity and rottenness of other parts of their work. If it had been deemed important to protect the South against an unjust exercise of the power of direct taxation, why had not some expedient been resorted to, to compel an equitable assessment of taxes, to be collected by other modes, between the North and the South?

But was the security against an abusive exercise of the power of direct taxation of any real value? After the quota of taxation for each State had been ascertained by the standard of its representation, the Northern majority in Congress would doubtless so lay the taxes as to produce the least inconvenience to their constituents: the ballot box would be a sufficient security for that. But what security would the people of the slave or minority section have? The Northern delegates would in no degree be responsible to them. That constituted a fatal defect in the government, and violated the fundamental principle of all republics, which required that the governors should be elected by and responsible to the governed. This point was urgently put, by both Mason and Grayson.* In this connection, Mr. Henry said: "It will destroy every principle of responsibility. We shall be taxed by those who bear no part in the taxes themselves, and who, consequently, will be regardless of our interests in imposing them. The efforts of our men will avail very little, when opposed by the Northern majority." The Northern people had shown a great dislike to African slavery; some of the States had already abolished it, and others were getting ready to follow their example; what would prevent a Northern majority from throwing the whole of Virginia's quota upon her slaves? Would not that lead to speedy emancipation? It was certain that no slaveholder would hold his slaves if they were exposed to the vindictive taxation of Congress. "He deplored," said Mr. Mason, "the existence of that species of property," but he would not consent to put it without the protection of its friends and at the mercy of its enemies. However it might have been in the beginning, it is certain that, now, "the people of Virginia

---

* Elliot's Debates, volume iii. p. 275.

could not do without their slaves." The danger of popular resistance had been suggested by Mr. Madison as a sufficient security *against* this abusive exercise of the taxing power. But that did not meet the argument. The question was concerning constitutional, not revolutionary remedies. Fortunate it was for the South, that if they would not give the first, the Philadelphia Convention could not deprive them of the second of these remedies. The true purposes of a Constitution had been misconceived, which were, to provide peaceful and legal remedies against bad laws, in order to obviate that very appeal to force, which had been pointed to.

But the advocates of the new government, who appeared to be possessed of the power to loose and to bind, when pressed on this point, answered all argument with another assurance, but of a wholly different nature from the last, and contradictory to it, viz. that commerce would be made to support the government, and that direct taxes would be reserved "for extraordinary occasions, such as war," and then be used only as a source of credit. Into such glaring contradictions were the champions of the new Constitution driven—to such desperate shifts were they compelled to resort.* Were such, the leaders of the Opposition inquired, to be the fruits of the Revolution? Were the people of Virginia, after all, to lie at the mercy of a master, and to be taxed without their own consent? the only consolation being, that the extorted treasure would go into Northern, instead of English pockets.

The expenditures of the government would certainly be wasteful in the extreme; for where there was no responsibility

---

* Compare, and, if you can, reconcile the passage in which Mr. Madison says, that "direct taxes will only be received for great purposes, as for war," &c., (*Elliot*, vol. iii. p. 116,) with the one in a subsequent speech, in which he defends the propriety of vesting the government with the power to collect direct taxes, because of the disproportionate burthens which a revenue from imports would throw on the Southern States. It is in this speech that he speaks of the "mixed" revenue system, referred to in the text. The latter passage, however, will be fully extracted, further on, in another connection.

in the collection, there could be no enonomy in the disbursement of the revenue. But mere extravagance was not the only, nor the greatest evil to be apprehended. The disbursement of great sums, running through an indefinite period of time, was almost as important as the collection of them. What security did the Constitution afford that the Northern majority, which had been deliberately enthroned in the new government, would not spend upon their own country, and for their own advantage, the vast treasures collected from the South? They never would consent, they said, to a government, the revenues of which would be collected from one section, and expended on another. But, if it was looked at from another point of view, it would be found, in effect, to destroy that ratable contribution, by the North and South, provided for when the taxes should be paid by a direct appeal to the pockets of the people; for, by means of the patronage of the government, the Northern tax payer would be reimbursed the amount of revenue collected from him. Thus that very inequality, so justly to be dreaded when the public dues are derived from duties on imports, would be produced by direct taxation.

What security, they asked, would the South have against such abuses and oppressions? A minority representation, wearing the hated badge of a section. That was the only barrier provided by the wisdom of the new Constitution to preserve the rich and populous South from pillage and oppression by the half-starved and avaricious North. Could it for a moment be believed that the political characters of the South would, in emergencies, be true to their constituents, and prove unassailable by "Federal allurements." On the contrary, the Southern politician would be found a supple and subservient tool of Northern avarice, and be but too ready to countenance that legislative policy which would best commend them to those who would have the wealth and honors of the government to bestow. What good, they inquired, could be expected from a political system which places the virtue and the personal interests of our public men at variance? Such a yoke would be more galling than the yoke of Great Britain, and rather than submit to it, it would be far better for the people of Virginia again to buckle on the sword and appeal to the God of Battles.

But if the Philadelphia Constitution, they continued, be examined as a work of art, and be tried by received tests, it would be found to be as defective in theory, as in experiment it would prove unequal and disastrous. It was a task of no little difficulty, even under the most favorable circumstances, to frame a representative system, suited to the wants of a large community, which, whilst it was provided with a full measure of authority, would yet be so tempered by restraints that it would not be perverted to the public injury; but in the case before them, the difficulty had been infinitely magnified by clashing interests, dissimilar, if not opposing, social systems and opposite political tendencies in the two grand divisions of the federal community. The existence of these deep-seated and ineradicable differences was not denied—but yet that new plan of government contained no provision for them whatever. Wisest men had taught, and their teachings had been enforced by the best lessons of history, that the selfish principle was the only rock on which a stable representative government could be founded, and that in every structure of that kind opposing interests and tendencies must be balanced by opposing powers. Otherwise, that a portion of the community, if armed with power, would consult its particular interests, to the sacrifice of the particular interests of other parts of the country.

A numerical majority was, therefore, to be looked upon as a dangerous power, and, in a country like the United States, would prove fatal to the prosperity of the minority. A majority partaking, as in this case, of a sectional character, would have all the infirmities of individuals, and like them would require all the restraints which ingenuity and prudence could devise. A minority, in such a case, would wear the livery and be characterized by all the badges of political servitude. Had the framers of the new Constitution paid the least attention to those fixed and invariable principles of government? Had they introduced in their work securities correspondent to the peculiar interests to be found in the country? On the contrary, they had invoked the terrible numerical majority, as the presiding genius of their government, and in the most reckless manner had turned it loose, under every provocation, to abuse power, to lord it over the Constitution and the country. Its champions and advocates, it was true, talked of balances and checks, but none could be pointed out worthy of the name.* Paper checks and paper balances there might be, but paper checks and paper balances would be found to be inadequate to restrain an inflamed, malignant, and, perhaps, corrupt majority. Nothing but the iron curb of an absolute negative would do that. But those gentlemen, driven to every subterfuge, had at length been driven to rely on the federal judiciary, as a security worthy of the confidence of prudent men. But it must be remembered, that only a small number of cases could be brought before that bar of judgment; but over corrupt abuses of power the court would have no jurisdiction whatever. At the best, however, the federal courts could only be relied on as long as the judges should be disinterested, wise and virtuous; but was it probable that they would continue long to possess those high attributes? A little attention to the mode of their appointment would dispel that illusion, for the judges themselves were but an emanation of the numerical majority, made absolute monarch of the whole system; and yet to that department of the govern-

* My honorable friend went on a supposition that the American rulers, like all others, will depart from their duty without bars and checks. No government can be safe without checks. Then he told us they had no temptation, to violate their duty, and that it would be their interest to perform it. Could not the same be said of all rulers? Does he think you can trust men who cannot have a separate interest from the people?—HENRY—*Elliot's Debates*, vol. iii, p. 310.

ment would be confided the power to declare the meaning of the Constitution, and define the extent of federal authority. That was, in its nature, a boundless power, and the judiciary, instead of being looked to to restrain the excesses of the more active branches of the government, would itself, above all others, stand in need of control.

They conceded, they said, that the Constitution contained a set of congressional checks, but that did not reach the evil apprehended. Those checks had been framed on the model of the English legislature, but the resemblance was wholly superficial. Representation in the English Parliament was founded on the three estates into which the English nation was divided; by that means an equilibrium or balance of power had been introduced in the government, which, above all other causes, had preserved it from decay, and made it, notwithstanding admitted defects, the great temple of freedom in the world.*

But no such divisions of society existed in the United States, and so far from interweaving the healing principle of an equilibrium, the sages of Philadelphia had subjected the federal machine, so complicated, to the control of that very despot, Numbers, against which the English Constitution had so carefully guarded. Why did not these fabricators of constitutions imitate the interior structure as well as the outward form of that venerable establishment? Why attempt to deceive us with an outward similitude? Why did they take only the rind—why did they snatch the flower and neglect the precious fruit? If they compared, Mr. Grayson contended, the proposed government, in its essential principle, with the admired constitution of England, or with the models of Montesquieu and Tacitus, its glaring defects would stand revealed to

* "To me, it appears there is no check in that government. The President, Senators and Representatives, all, mediately or immediately, are the choice of the people. Tell me not of checks on paper, but tell me of checks founded on self-love. The English government is founded on self-love. This powerful, irresistible stimulus of self-love has saved that Government."—HENRY—*Elliot's Debates*, vol. iii, p. 174.

every eye. He did not propose, he said, to transplant any of those governments to America. They would not suit the genius of the people, nor the circumstances of the country; but why not take the great principle common to them all, which was capable of universal application and would operate as well in the modern as in the ancient world—in America as well as in Italy, Greece or Great Britain?

But, after all, they concluded, good republics are the children of time and the creatures of gradual reform, and are never the product of human genius. The only safe course for the people to follow in respect to that momentous business, was to adhere firmly to the existing system, which was sound in its first principles, and from time to time, as defects might be manifested, to correct them, taking good care to provide safeguards against abuse. In that way, the government, gradually developed, would be adapted to the real wants of the people, and in process of time would attain a high degree of perfection. "Too much suspicion," argued Henry, "may be corrected. If you give too little power to-day you may give more to-morrow; but the reverse of the proposition will not hold. If you give too much power to-day, you cannot take it back to-morrow. To-morrow will never come for that purpose. If you have the fate of other nations, you will never see it. It is easier to supply deficiencies of power than to take back excess of power." In every case, it would be the act of prudence to pursue this course, but most of all, in this country, where new and powerful agencies were at work, and things were too much in the germ for any man to know what government would suit best.

In pursuance of this argument, Mr. Grayson continued, "Keep on so, till the American character is marked with some certain features. We are yet too young to know what we are fit for. The continual migration of the people from Europe, and the settlement of new countries on our western frontiers, are strong arguments against making new experiments now in government. We ought to consider, as Montesquieu says, whether the construction of the government be suitable to the genius and disposition of the people." *

The people of Virginia had resolved to follow this prudent course, and the Convention at Annapolis had been the first step in that direction, but that wise design had been frustrated by the rash and unauthorized conduct of individuals. The Convention which assembled at Philadelphia, had no doubt done their best, but it was impossible for any set of men, however enlightened, to lock themselves up for three months, and in that brief space pull down one political edifice and build up another in its place on entirely new foundations. The task which they had so rashly undertaken was, indeed, too great for human hands, and it had surprised no one, but the architects themselves, that their labors had proved abortive. In the same headlong spirit, and "with wild precipitation," they had come home to rush things through, and bring the States into a precipitate adoption of their work. But there was no need for haste. There was full time for deliberation: the country was at peace, the States disposed to union, and above all, a powerful majority of the people of Virginia, were known to be opposed to the proposed change of government. Let another Convention then be called, and let the people themselves be consulted that the delegates might go instructed as to their wishes. The adoption of the new government by seven States had been urged as a reason why they should adopt likewise, but, declared Mr. Henry, that if twelve States or twelve and a-half were to adopt it, "with a manly firmness, and in spite of an erring world, I would reject it." That Constitution, proposed for the adoption of the Convention, was not worthy of a free people. Let it be struck from the list of republics and classed with those of an arbitrary nature, to which it properly belonged.

I will not attempt to give a summary of the arguments used by the Federalists. That would be an arduous, if not an impos-

* Elliot's Debates, vol. iii. p. 270,

sible task. No two of them agreed as to the extent of the powers, or as to the true theory of the Constitution. But, according to the feeling of the House and the pressure of the debate, would they start new theories and suggest new explanations. In the outset, Mr. Madison and Gov. Randolph, as well from the superiority of their abilities, as from their attendance at Philadelphia, stepped into the arena of debate. They assumed high ground, but they were soon compelled to relinquish it, and to take other positions, from which again they were compelled to retreat. They were sorely harrassed, and complained with good reason of "the bolts" which Henry threw with such strength and skill, as well as of the mocking scorn and satirical wit of George Mason. Never before was a party so torn and riddled by the projectiles of debate. They were beaten from post to pillow, and from pillow back to post. No candid reader can peruse that debate, even in the fragmentary form in which it has been handed down to us, a medium all insufficient to convey the subtle wit, the withering scorn and the electric eloquence which burst from the ranks of the Opposition, without being convinced that the defenders and advocates of the Constitution, able and accomplished as they were, were driven back on every serious issue, and that the contest was, on their part, at best, but a running and desultory fight. In the outset the admission was frankly made, that the Federal Articles had been found to be so very defective as to set reformation at defiance, and, therefore, a government *de novo* had been created; thus stultifying the opinion of the whole country,* and the wisest and best men in the country, that the Confederation needed only some additional powers to be adapted to the wants of the people. That plea, in extenua-

* "How were the sentiments of the people before the meeting of the Convention at Philadelphia? They had only one object in view. Their ideas reached no farther than to give the general government the five percentum impost, and the regulation of trade. When it was agitated in Congress, in committee of the whole, this was all it asked, or was deemed necessary.—GRAYSON—*Elliot's Debates*, vol. iii. p. 268.

tion of the conduct of the Virginia delegates, had been made by Randolph; but Madison, as we shall see, took quite another view. It has not been forgotten, that Madison, in his anatomy of the Constitution, had pronounced the government in its nature to be partly national and partly federal. I suspect that that notion of a partial consolidation did not please, for consolidation, as Grayson declared, was abhorrent to the people of Virginia. But how could that amorphous beast, that nondescript monster, create less than horror? Tortured by the fiery javelines which Henry ever showered upon his head, Madison was compelled to abandon that loose and precarious raft, and embark the fortunes of the party of which he was head, on another bottom. With a fertility of imagination, truly wonderful, he invented a new ideal of the Constitution, to meet the present emergency. This is highly important, not because it shows the suppleness of Mr. Madison's constitutional theories, but because it displays the temper of the Convention. It proves beyond controversy, that if the true nature of that Constitution had been understood by its friends, had they known it as we know it, it would have been an object of general execration: even Madison would not have had the hardihood to recommend its adoption.

This new theory of the Constitution is contained in the following extract from one of his speeches: "Is it supposed that the influence of the general government will facilitate a combination between the members? Is it supposed that it will preponderate against that of the State governments? *The means of influence consist in having the disposal of gifts and employments, and in the number of persons employed by, and dependent upon, a government.* * * * * *I may say, with truth, that there never was a more economical government in any age or country, one which will require fewer hands, or give less influence.* * * * * *The powers of the general government relate to external objects, and are but few, but the power of the States relate to those great objects which immediately concern the prosperity of the people. Let us observe,* *also, that the powers of the general government are those which will be exercised mostly in time of war, while those of the State governments will be exercised in time of peace. But I hope the time of war will be little compared to that of peace.* I should not complete the view which ought to be taken of this subject, without making this additional remark, that the powers vested in the proposed government are not so much an augmentation of the powers of the general government, as a change rendered necessary for the purpose of giving efficacy to those which were vested in it before. It cannot escape any gentleman, that this power (the taxing power), in theory, is in the Confederation as fully as in this Constitution. The only difference is this, that now they tax the States, and by this plan they will tax individuals. *There is no theoretic difference between the two.*" Pages 253, 254, vol. iii.

Such was the view of the Constitution presented by him who has been proudly styled its father, whilst it depended for ratification! A mere war establishment! A vast power to slumber during peace, but at the first bugle note to spring up like an armed giant for the defence of the country! An economical government! the most economical government in any age or country! a government that would move without hands, not having at its disposal those rich gifts and emoluments in which the means of influence consist! Wise Mr. Madison! far-sighted Mr. Madison! sagacious Mr. Madison! or shall we, changing style, say, ingenuous Mr. Madison? Oh! that you could have penetrated the future but seventy years, a shorter term than was allotted to yourself, and have seen the last budget of the Secretary of the Treasury, and the multitudes of flocking vultures that crowd the avenues of the Federal City!

Such was that political architect's conception of the properties of his own work, such his ideal of the Federal Constitution, whilst it lay inert, awaiting the Promethean touch, to start into powerful life. Away, thou dreamer! Thy reveries, dressed in the sweetness and majesty of chaste rhetoric, borrowing the semblance of reality from the very mould of thy thoughts, and uttered, too, in the confident and solemn tones of an oracle, passed in thy day for wisdom. Yes! thy visions, they peopled men's minds! Thy fantasies, they governed men's acts. Virginia rose up and crowned thee with honors, and took thee to be among her household deities. Alas, for the predictions of men! Alas, for the false gods which they ignorantly worship!. Time! thou breaker of images, when thou enterest the temple of the hero gods, thy march is silent and slow. The misty curtain at length rises, and conjecture is turned into knowledge. That future, which teemed with bright illusions, or was shadowed with dark prognostications, is explored and laid bare by the searching hand of experience. Lo! the prophet's gown falleth away, and his staff from thy hand. Madison, thou must stand amid the monumental heroes of Virginia, the deceiver of thy country—perhaps, thyself deceived.

But time, if it detects the false, reveals the true, and we turn, with a stronger faith, to kneel at the altar of true greatness. Reverence, then, the prophetic warnings of George Mason, who, amid the snows of age, was animated by the fires of his lustrous genius; of Monroe, of Harrison, of Tyler, of William Grayson, but chiefly of him, that bright paragon, to whom, amid the rank and fetid corruptions of the present hour, the people look back, as the faultless impersonation of all that was eloquent, wise, patriotic and most truly noble among the sons of men. Listen to their voices, uniting in solemn chorus as they come swelling along the galleries of time, warning their beloved countrymen not to enter into the deadly toils spread for their feet.

If the general government was, in truth, designed only for the purposes of war, why, it was asked, was there so much power bestowed upon it, applicable only to peace? Why had they not provided only "war taxes?" But, instead, a discretion unlimited in point of fact, because no power of control had been deposited with the minority, had been conferred to collect and disburse taxes, together with an unlimited power to pledge the public credit. It was perfectly evident that there was no foundation in the Constitution for the unplausible theory that had just been enunciated; it would turn out, assuredly, that a gradual consolidation, or a violent dislocation of the Union between the sections, would follow.

In respect to the supposed economy of the proposed government, Mr. Mason was unable to agree with Mr. Madison. On the contrary, he thought, "after the government was set in motion, all restraint would be gone. They would appoint what number of officers they pleased. They would send ambassadors to every part of Europe. Here was, he thought, as wide a door for corruption as in any government in Europe. There is the same inducement for corruption, there is the same room for it in this government, which they have in the British government." (Vol. iii. p. 237.) Mr. Henry, addressing himself to the constitutional theory propounded by Madison, said, "that he (Mr. Madison) thought that the State governments will possess greater advantages than the general government, and will consequently prevail. His opinion and mine are diametrically opposite. Bring forth the federal allurements, and compare them with the poor contemptible things that the State legislatures can bring forth. On the part of the State legislatures, there are justices of the peace and militia officers, and the like. On the other hand, there are rich, fat emoluments—your rich, snug, fine, fat federal offices. The number of collectors of taxes and excises will out-number anything from the States. There are none in this country who can cope with this class of men alone. But, sir, is this the only danger? Would to Heaven that it were! If we are to ask which will last the longest, the State or the general government, you must take an army and a navy into the account. Lay these things together, and add to the enumeration, *the superior abilities of those who manage the general government.*" (P. 307.) "A change of government," urged Mr. Henry, "will not pay money. If, from the probable amount of imports, you take the enormous and extravagant expenses which will certainly attend the support of this great consolidated government, I believe you will find no reduction of the public burdens by this new system. *The splendid maintenance of the President and of the members of both houses, and the salaries and fees of the swarms of officers and dependents of the government, will cost immense sums.* Double sets of collectors will double the expense. To these are to be added oppressive excisemen and custom-house officers. Sir, the people have an hereditary hatred to custom-house officers. The experience of the mother country leads me to detest them. They have introduced their baneful influence into the administration, and destroyed one of the most beautiful systems that the world ever saw."

It has been averred, that the real ground on which the contest took place over the Constitution was the sectional character of that instrument. Evidence of this has been adduced; but I cannot, in justice to the subject, or in justice to that great political prophet, omit a passage from the leading speech of Mr. Grayson, applicable to this point, so replete is it with wisdom. After declaring that it was a struggle between the North and South for empire, he proceeded to inquire, "Are not all defects and corruptions founded on an inequality of representation and want of responsibility? My greatest objection is, that it will, in its operation, be found unequal, grievous and oppressive. If it have any efficacy at all, it must be by a faction—a faction of one part of the Union against another. If it be called into action by a combination of seven States, it will be terrible indeed. We must be at no loss to determine how this combination will be formed. There is a great difference of circumstances between the States. The interests of the carrying States are strikingly different from that of the productive States. I mean not to give offence to any part of America, but mankind are governed by interest. The carrying States will assuredly unite, and our situation will then be wretched indeed. Let ill-fated Ireland be ever present to our view. We ought to be wise enough to guard against the abuse of such a government. Republics, in fact, oppress more than monarchies. If we advert to the page of history, we will find this disposition too often manifested in republican governments. The Romans in ancient, and the Dutch in modern times, oppressed their provinces in a remarkable degree. I hope that my fears are groundless; but I believe it, as I do my creed, that this government will operate, as a faction of seven States, to oppress the rest of the Union.* But it may be said, that we are represented, and cannot, therefore, be injured. A poor representation it will be! The British would have been glad to take America in, like the Scotch, by giving us a small representation.† The Irish might be indulged with the same favor by asking for it. Will that lessen our misfortunes? A small representation gives a pretence to injure and destroy. * * * * The greatest defect in the new Constitution is the opposition of the component parts to the interest of the whole. For, let gentlemen ascribe its defects to as many causes as their imaginations may suggest, that is the principal and radical one. I have urged, that to remedy the evils, which must result from this government, an equal representation in the legislature and proper checks against abuse were indispensably necessary. (Pp. 273, 274.) In this connection, Henry said, "Sure I am that the dangers of this system are real, when those who have no similar interests with the people of this country are to legislate for us—when our dearest interests are to be left in the

* This anticipation was literally fulfilled by the Convention of the Northern States, from which every slave State was excluded, to frame the tariff bill, which was afterwards adopted by Congress. That was the tariff of 1828, so justly styled "the bill of abominations." The history of this convention of Northern manufacturers is given by Mr. Giles, in an extract from one of his speeches, hereafter quoted in the text.

† Mr. Grayson alludes to the proposition, which had received the approbation of the ministers of the crown, made by Galloway and others, that the difficulty with the colonies should be obviated, by allowing them representation in the British Parliament. The colonies would have been allotted *one-third* of the representatives. But the proposition met with no favor from Congress. They claimed an *equal* vote.—*Madison Papers*, p. 833.

power of those whose advantage it will be to infringe them." (P. 289.)

The theory, as already stated, which confined the action of the new government to the exercise of its war power, affords sufficient evidence of the general opposition, in the Convention, to a strong central authority; but there were individuals who concurred with Mr. Madison, in his preference for a government of that nature. This preference was avowed by Col. Henry Lee, whose experience, as a soldier, had given him a strong bias for an energetic government; but I have searched in vain for any sentiment uttered, by even the most bigoted Federalist of them all, which implied a willingness, through the agency of a constitutional compact, to place the South, for any duration of time, under the dominion of a Northern majority. All were opposed to that. Even Madison did not venture to reconcile them to that idea. Looked at in that light, the arguments of the Opposition, based on the absence of the necessary "bars and checks," were overwhelming against the Constitution. The Federalists admitted, that the Constitution was a struggle for power, but managed to convince the Convention, that the South would have the best of the bargain, and would preponderate, at least, in those departments of the government where power was immediately derived from the people. The means by which that result was to be produced, and power taken out of the hands of the North and given to the South, will be presently brought to the attention of the reader.

But, first, as an act of justice to the men who officiated on that occasion, and who were chiefly instrumental in sacrificing their country and fixing upon her the heavy yoke of the Northern despotism, I will insert in these pages the abhorrence which they expressed of an event so much dreaded by the Democrats. The evidence will leave no doubt upon any mind, that, had they been as deeply versed in the philosophy of government as the leaders of the Opposition, they would have united with that patriot band to reject the political edifice so hastily constructed at Philadelphia. But, as it was, the event afforded but another proof of how little wisdom governs the world.

"Of all things in the world," profoundly remarked John Randolph, of Roanoke, "a government, whether ready made to suit casual customers, or made per order, is the very last that operates as its framers intended. Governments are like revolutions: you may put them in motion, but I defy you to control them after they are in motion."

"On a candid examination of history, we shall find that turbulence, violence and abuse of power, *by the majority trampling on the rights of the minority, have produced factions and commotions, which, in republics, have, more frequently than any other cause, produced despotism.* If we go over the whole history of ancient and modern republics, we shall find their destruction to have generally resulted from that cause. If we consider the peculiar situation of the United States, and *what are the sources of that diversity of sentiments which pervades its inhabitants, we shall find great danger to fear that the same causes may terminate here, in the same fatal effects, which they produced in those republics. This danger ought to be wisely guarded against.* Perhaps, in the progress of this discussion, it will appear, that the only possible remedy for those evils, and means of preserving and protecting the principles of republicanism, will be found in that very system which is now exclaimed against as the parent of oppression." (! !)—(MADISON—*Elliot*, vol. iii., p. 109.)

The speaker does not explicitly state that slavery was the source of diversity between the two classes of States, but the allusion is perfectly clear from his speech in the Federal Convention, in which he proposed an equilibrium between the North and the South. On that occasion he said, it will be remembered, that "the real difference between the States was in having or in not having slaves." The speeches, taken together warrant the following conclusions: 1. That majorities are, in their nature, tyrannous, and, from the peculiar situation of the United States, growing out of the diversity in respect to slavery, would be productive of the same fatal effects here that had been experienced in the ancient and modern republics. 2. That the adoption of that Constitution would be found to be the only possible remedy against the occurrence of that evil.

This ought to vindicate the motives of Mr. Madison from the intention to place his country in a situation to be plundered and oppressed by the Northern majority, which at that time he so much deprecated. Were it not for his course subsequent to the adoption of the government, it would hush the voice of blame, when it would lay upon his memory responsibility for his headlong and precipitate action.

"The evils that are most complained of in such governments (and with justice) are faction, dissension and consequent subjection of the minority to the caprice and arbitrary decision of the majority, who, *instead of consulting the interest of the whole community collectively*, attend sometimes to partial and local advantages. To avoid this evil is, perhaps, the great *desiderata* of republican wisdom; it may well be termed the philosopher's stone. Yes, sir, *this evil will be avoided by this Constitution.* * * * * It is impossible that this government, which will make us one people, will have a tendency to assimilate our situations. It is admirably calculated to produce harmony, and can never admit of an oppressive combination of one part of the Union against the other."—CORBIN—*Elliott*, vol. iii, p. 126.

"The taxing power is the lungs of the Constitution. If it be sick, the whole system is consumptive, and must soon decay; and this power can never be dangerous, if the principles of *equal* and free representation be fully attended to. While the right of suffrage is secured, we have little to fear. The government, sir, fully secures us this noble privilege, *on the purest and simplest principles of equality.*"—CORBIN—*Ibid*, p. 128.

"As long as the privilege of *representation* is well secured, our liberties cannot be well endangered. I conceive it to be secured in this country more fully than any other."—LEE—*Ibid*, p. 191.

"But I observe, with regret, that there is a general spirit of jealousy with respect to our *Northern brethren.* Had we this political jealousy in 1775? * * * * Did we then expect that, in case of success, we should be armed against one another? *I would have submitted to British tyranny, rather than to Northern tyranny*, had what we have been told been true, that they had no part of that philanthropic spirit which cherishes fraternal affection, unites friends, enables them to achieve the most gallant exploits, and renders them formidable to other nations. Gentlemen say that the States have not similar interests, that what will accommodate their in-ests will be incompatible with ours; and *that the Northern oppression will fetter and manacle the hands of the Southern people.* Wherein does the dissimilarity consist? Does not our existence as a nation depend on our union? Is it to be supposed that their principles will be so corrupted, and that they will be so blind to their own true interests, as to alienate the affections of the Southern States, and adopt measures which will produce discontents, and terminate in a dissolution of an union as necessary to their happiness as to ours? Will not brotherly affection rather be cultivated? Will not the great principles of reciprocal friendship and mutual amity be constantly inculcated, so as conciliate all parts of the Union? This will be inevitably necessary, from the unity of their interests with ours. To suppose that they would act contrary to these principles, would be to suppose them to be not only destitute of honor and probity, but void of reason; not only bad, but mad men.

"The question is as important as the revolution which separated us from the British empire. It rests now to be determined whether America has, in reality, gained by that change which has been thought so glorious, and whether those hecatombs of American heroes, whose blood was so freely shed at the shrines of liberty, fell in vain, or whether we shall establish such a government as shall render America respectable and happy. * * * * We are told that the *New Englanders mean to take our trade from us, and make us hewers of wood and drawers of water, and the next moment that they will emancipate our slaves.* How inconsistent is this? * * * * Let us try it; experience is the best test. It will bear equally on all the States, from New Hampshire to Georgia; and *as it will operate equally on all*, they will all call for amendments; and whatever the spirit of America calls for, must, doubtless, take place immediately."—INNES.

"But the influence of New England and other Northern States is dreaded; there are apprehensions of their combining against us. Not to advert to the improbability and illiberality of this idea, it must be supposed, that our population will, in a short period, exceed theirs, as their country is well settled, and we have very extensive uncultivated tracts. We shall soon outnumber them in as great a degree as they do us at this time; therefore this government, which, I trust, will last to the remotest ages, will be, very shortly, in our favor." —GEORGE NICHOLAS, (pp. 121, 122.)

But it is unnecessary to multiply evidence of the belief of the Federal party of the Convention of 1788, that the result of the proposed experiment in federal politics, would not be to subject the South to a Northern majority in the new government. It was true, that there was an actual Northern majority in the popular branch of Congress, but that majority was small, and it was believed that the next census would redress the inequality.

It is known that distribution of power was made with reference to a flow of population, which at that time had begun, from the sterile regions of the North, to the rich but uncultivated plains of the South, and that Mr. Madison and those who acted with him relied confidently upon that transfer of population, which they made but another name for political power, from the one section to the other—that shifting of weights from the Northern to the Southern scale, either to create a Southern preponderance or to produce the desired balance. It is known, likewise, that the Constitution was agreed to in view of that actual emigration, and we shall afterwards ascertain whether it was not made with reference to it. But it is proposed, at present, to show that it was ratified, by Virginia at least, under the full belief that that tide of emigration would continue. The opinion that it would continue was universal, and Mr. Mason reluctantly acquiesced in it. He said: "The same gentleman assured us that though the Northern States had a most decided majority against us, yet the increase of population among us would, in the course of a few years, change it in our favor. A very sound argument, indeed, that we should cheerfully burn ourselves to death in the hope of a joyful and happy resurrection." (Pp. 260, 261.)

"The people of New England have purchased great quantities of lands (in Kentucky), great numbers of them have moved thither."—NICHOLAS, (p. 238.)

"The increasing population of the Southern States is far greater than that of New England: consequently, in a short time, they will be far more numerous than the people of that country."

But the vigilant and unsleeping leaders of the Opposition were not satisfied with the assurance held out by the Federalists. They said that the Northern majority could not be trusted, even for a short time, with power in such a government as that which had been just created, and that they would interfere with the natural course of events, and take away the inducements to Southern immigration, and thus retain control of the government. It was impossible, they said, to know in advance what device they would adopt to attain that result, but there was room to apprehend that the right to navigate the Mississippi would be given up to Spain, according to the demands of her diplomacy. The effect of such a cession would be to destroy the value of agriculture in the west and south-west, and put a sudden stop to Northern emigration. This fear, they said, was not idle, for a recent attempt had been made by the Northern interest in Congress to achieve that very result, although it involved a gross and flagitious violation of the Federal Articles. Upon that issue the vote of Kentucky depended, and, by the agreement of all parties, the Convention went into committee of the whole on

The Mississippi Question.

Owning the mouth of the Mississippi, as well as being one of its riparian proprietors, Spain contended for the right to close the outlet of that river. Great Britain, and afterwards the United States, contended, that by the public law the dwellers on the upper waters of a great highway like the Mississippi, were possessed of the right of free navigation, and even the right to establish upon its banks a place of deposite for merchandise. Upon the establishment of that claim depended the value of that western country, to which, as we have observed, migration was tending. It was an old question, and had vexed the diplomacy of the United States from the time that they took their position among independent nations. It was a question of great delicacy on the part of the United States; for if that right, which the western settlers claimed, freely to navigate that river, were surrendered, they had, by unmistakable evidence, manifested their intention to tear themselves from the American Union, and assert their pretensions at all hazards. An inveterate feud already existed between the borderers on the Spanish dominions and the Spanish authorities. It had given birth to bands of desperate adventurers, who often made sanguinary forays. The aggressions were generally from the American side, and Virginia had enacted severe laws to punish them. During the late war, when the American cause was most depressed, it was, when resistance was prostrated in South Carolina and Georgia, and Virginia had stripped herself of troops for their defence, that a proposition had been submitted in Congress, by Virginia and other States of the South, to accede to the Spanish pretension, as the price of a military alliance with the Spanish crown. The cause of the Revolution seemed almost desperate and the South was ready to sacrifice that great object to its success.

But the relinquishment was opposed by the North, and particularly by the New England States, who were actuated in this by motives of self-interest. They apprehended, if it were once begun to yield claims of that nature, that the claims which they had set up to the fisheries, so important to their existence, might, in turn, be sacrificed to the same policy. But as soon as the war terminated and New England was no longer apprehensive on the score of the fisheries, its policy, as well as the policy of the other Northern States, underwent an important change. The Southern States, so soon as the pressure of public necessity had been removed, reverted to their old position in respect to their claim to the free navigation of the Mississippi.* Not population, but the number of States,

---

* WEDNESDAY, NOVEMBER 29, 1786.—*Resolved,* That a copy of the memorial of sundry inhabitants of the western country, ought to be forthwith transmitted to the delegates representing this State in Congress.

Resolved, That the common right of navigating the river Mississippi, and of communicating with other nations through that channel, ought to be considered as the bountiful gift of Nature to the United States, as proprietors of the territories watered by the said river and its eastern branches, and as moreover secured to them by the late Revolution.

Resolved, That the Confederacy, having been formed on the broad basis of equal right in every part thereof to the protection and guardianship of the whole, a sacrifice of the rights of any one part to the supposed or real interest of another part, would be a flagrant violation of justice, a direct contravention of the end for which the Federal Government was instituted, and an alarming innovation on the system of the Union:

Resolved, therefore, That the delegates representing this State in Congress, ought to be instructed, in the most decided terms, to oppose any attempt that may be made in Congress *to barter* or surrender to any nation whatever, the right of the United States to the free and common use of the river Mississippi; and to protest against the same as a *dishonorable* departure from that *comprehensive and benevolent policy which constitutes the vital principle of the Confederacy;* as provoking the just resentments and reproaches of our western brethren, whose essential rights and interests would be thereby sacrificed and *sold;* as destroying that confidence in the wisdom, justice and liberality of the Federal Councils, which is so necessary, at this crisis, to a proper enlarge-

was the source of political power under the Articles of Confederation. But as population composed States, and it was a struggle with the North or free-soil States to obtain control of the federal agent, the statesmen of the North were desirous, by the means already referred to, to stop the flow of population to the west and south-west, and drive it back upon the unoccupied lands of Maine, then a province of Massachusetts. In pursuit of this policy, Massachusetts had reduced the price of land in Maine to one dollar per acre. But that inducement was not sufficient to make the emigrant prefer the inhospitable region of the Penobscot to the fertile and undulating prairie lands of Kentucky or the fruitful vales of Frankland, a name then given to the western district of North Carolina. It was necessary that the navigation of the Mississippi should be relinquished, in order to realize their hopes, but the North could not command the requisite number of votes in Congress to authorize a treaty, without the concurrence of some slave State. But no slave State would agree to lend a helping hand to that business, and so matters were brought to a stand.

But Northern statesmen, true to their national instincts, were nothing dismayed by constitutional obstacles. They sought to obtain that object by a fraudulent device unparalleled for its immorality in the history of American legislation. The plan was this: To obtain from Congress instructions to the Secretary of State, Mr. Jay, to negotiate a treaty with Spain, upon the basis, that the claims of the United States to the Mississippi should not be conceded, and then to have that part of the instruction which concerned that condition revoked, which they

---

ment of their authority; and finally, as tending to undermine our repose, our prosperity and the *Union* itself; and that the said delegates ought to be further instructed to urge the proper negotiations with Spain, for obtaining her concurrence in such regulations touching the mutual and common use of the said river, as may secure the permanent harmony and affection of the two nations, &c."—*Journal House Delegates.*

Patrick Henry and Grayson were both in the House of Delegates when these resolutions were adopted, and it is easy to detect in them the handiwork of those illustrious patriots and statesmen.

contended might be done by a simple vote of the majority in Congress, which was composed of Northern men. But would the Secretary of State prostitute his office to that base object? In this they met with no difficulty whatever, for Mr. Jay proved to be a supple instrument* in their hands. The benefit to be derived by the North from this act of treachery was a free commerce with the Spanish dominions, both in Europe and America,

---

* "As to the American Secretary, the goodness of his private character is not doubted. It is his public conduct which we are to inspect. The public conduct of this Secretary goes against the express authority of nine States. Although he may be endowed with the most brilliant talents, I have a right to consider his politics abandoned."—HENRY—*Elliot's Debates*, vol. iii, p. 383.

About the existence of this intrigue, and the culpable agency of Jay, there is no room for doubt. Independent of the positive evidence of Monroe, Grayson and Henry, we have that of Madison himself, notwithstanding the different colors in which he sought, the following year, to invest the transaction. Here is what he writes from Congress, 19th March, 1787, to his confidential friend, Jefferson: "The Spanish project sleeps. A perusal of the attempt of seven States to make a new treaty, by repealing an essential condition of the old, satisfied me that Jay's caution would revolt at so irregular a sanction. A late accidental conversation with Gardoqui proved to me, that the negotiation is arrested. It may appear strange that a member of Congress should be indebted to a foreign minister for such information, yet, such is the footing on which the intemperance of party has put the matter, that it rests wholly with Jay how far he will communicate with Congress, as well as how far he will negotiate with Gardoqui. *But it appears that the intended sacrifice of the Mississippi will not be made; the consequences of the intention and the attempt are likely to be very serious.* I have already made known to you, the light in which the subject was taken up by Virginia. Mr. Henry's disgust exceeds all measure, and I am not singular in ascribing his refusal to attend the Convention to the policy of keeping himself free to combat or espouse the result of it, according to the result of the Mississippi business, among other circumstances." Consult his letter to Randolph, 25th March; but his letter to Jefferson, in April, is direct on this point: "This Spanish negotiation is in a very ticklish situation. You have been already apprised of the votes of seven States, last fall, for ceding the Mississippi for a term of years. *From sundry circumstances it was inferred, that Jay was proceeding under this usurped authority. A late instruction to him to lay the state of the negotiation before Congress, has discovered that he has adjusted with Gardoqui an article for suspending the use of the Mississippi by the citizens of the United States.* The report, however, leaves it somewhat doubtful how far the United States are committed by this step, &c." That was the school in which the clear-sighted Grayson acquired his estimate of Northern character, but its lessons fell unheeded upon the cold and insusceptible nature of Madison.

affording a profitable market for the grain and flour of the Middle States, and for the oils, fish and lumber of New England. Gardoqui was on the ground, with instructions to conclude a treaty with the United States on those terms. But this scheme, so cleverly contrived, miscarried in its execution; for when the proposition was made in Congress to repeal that part of the Secretary's instruction which related to the Mississippi, and the Northern members impudently contended that it lay within the power of a mere majority, it raised so great a tempest, that the conspirators were frightened from their purpose. There is no doubt that, had they possessed the hardihood to have acted upon their plans, it would have produced a violent dissolution of the Union between the two sections.

The question for the committee of the whole was, under which Constitution the claims of the South to the Mississippi were safest from spoliation by the federal government. All admitted that constitutional securities were necessary. The Democrats contended that the Articles of Confederation afforded the best guaranty; the Federalists, that the best protection would be found under the new government. The weight of the argument, undoubtedly, was on the side of the latter. By the terms of the Confederation it required nine States to authorize a treaty, and which, as things stood, armed the South with a veto upon the improper use of that power. But the admission of other States, sympathizing in interest with the North, would destroy the value of this check; and the danger was imminent, that other States of that character would soon be admitted into the Union. Vermont was already an applicant for admission. At any time a sufficient number of settlers might be huddled together into the province of Maine to give it an independent establishment.

But the danger did not stop here. As early as 1784, a committee of Congress had reported a proposition to divide the north-west territory ceded by Virginia to the United States, into ten States, each State to be admitted into the Union on a footing of equality with the other States so soon as its population should be equal to that of the smallest State of the Confederation. Against that scheme of sectional aggrandizement the Federal Articles offered no security.

But by the proposed government, a designated proportion of votes, instead of a definite number of States, was required to wield the power of making treaties. This promised a permanent veto to those States interested in the navigation of the river. But the agency of the President in the negotiation of treaties afforded, in the opinion of the Federalists, the most positive check. Mr. Nicholas said: "But, says he, the concurrence of the President, in the formation of treaties, will be no security. Why so? Will he not injure himself, if he injures the States, by concurring in an injudicious treaty? How is he to be elected? Where will the majority of the people be? He told you that the great weight of population will be in the Southern part of the United States. Their numbers will weigh in choosing the President, as he is to be elected by Electors, chosen by the people in proportion to their numbers. If the Southern States be interested in having the Mississippi, and have weight in choosing the President, will he not be a great check in favor of this right?"

The fallacy of Mr. Nicholas' argument is very apparent. It is based on the retention of the Mississippi until the migration from North to South should give those interested in its navigation the power of self-protection. But the argument of the Opposition was, that the claim in question would be relinquished to Spain before the anticipated event could come to pass, and before the power to elect the President would pass from the hands of the Northern into those of the Southern people.

Mr. Grayson closed the debate on the Mississippi question, with the following forcible remarks:

"Mr. Chairman, I conceive the investigation of this subject, which materially concerns the welfare of this country, ought not to wound the feelings of any gentleman. *I look upon this as a contest for empire. Our country is equally af-*

fected with Kentucky. The Southern States are deeply interested in this subject. If the Mississippi be shut up, emigration will be stopped entirely. There will be no new States formed on the western waters. This will be a government of seven States. The contest of the Mississippi involves this great national contest, that is, whether one part of the continent shall govern the other. The Northern States have the majority, and will endeavor to retain it. This is, therefore, a contest for dominion, for empire. I apprehend that God and nature have intended, from the extent of territory and fertility of soil, that the weight of population should be on this side of the continent. At present, for various reasons, it is on the other side. This dispute concerns every part of Kentucky."

The citations from the debates, contained in the previous pages, show clearly enough the opinion of the Federalists, that agencies were in operation which would give the weight of population to the South, and consequently, if the proposed Constitution were ratified, that the South would be the seat of empire. This result Mr. Madison himself prognosticated, though there were others of his party who, with Gov. Randolph, believed that something like a balance of power would be established in the course of a short period. But the speakers in favor of ratification preferred to hold out the hope of ultimate dominion as more probable, or, at least, more palatable to those whose votes they sought to influence.

The ratification ultimately turned on the question of previous or subsequent amendments. The latter prevailed by a majority of eight votes. After that course was determined upon, the Constitution was adopted as a matter of course. But before this vote was taken, Mr. Henry declared: "I shall have nothing to do with it, if subsequent amendments be determined upon. Oppressions will be carried on by the majority, when adjustments and accommodations will be held up. I say, I conceive it to be my duty, if this government is adopted before it is amended, to go home. I shall act as my duty requires." But for reasons, afterwards to be explained, he did not pursue this course. Party feeling, towards the close of the session, became very embittered. If Mr. Henry had stuck to the resolution to withdraw from the Convention, in the event that subsequent amendments were resolved upon, there is but little room to doubt that a ratification by that body would have been disregarded by the people. He resolved on another course, but that course involved him in a labyrinth of intrigue, in which he proved to be no match for his accomplished opponent. But before the fatal step of ratification had been taken, and impressed with the solemnity of the occasion, he uttered these memorable words: "The voice of tradition, I trust, will inform posterity of our struggles for freedom. If our descendants be worthy of the name of Americans, they will preserve and hand down to the latest posterity, the transactions of the present times; and though I confess my explanations are not worth the hearing, they will see I have done my utmost to preserve their liberty."

Tyler echoed that sentiment: "I wish to hand down to posterity my opposition to that system. British tyranny would have been more tolerable."

So soon as the Constitution was ratified, a committee was appointed, of which Mr. Wythe was chairman, to report a Bill of Rights and such amendments to the Constitution as the Convention deemed to be necessary and proper. These had been already drafted and proposed by Henry, and may, therefore, be considered as indicative of the opinions of the Democrats as to the particulars in which that instrument was considered most defective. No exception was taken to any part of the report, except the third article of the proposed amendments. But that article was of the highest importance, and was regarded by the Federalists as of such force as, if adopted, greatly to modify the nature of the new system, and to impair the strength of that federal giant which they had just called into existence. It was expressed in these words: "When Congress shall lay direct taxes or excises, they shall immediately inform the executive power of each State of the quota of such State, according to the census herein directed, which is proposed to be thereby raised, and if the legislature of any State shall pass a law which shall be effectual for the raising of such quota, at the time required by Congress, the taxes and excises laid by Congress shall not be collected in such States."

The motion to strike out that article from the amendments was lost by a majority of 20 votes, and exhibits how little popularity the Constitution possessed in that body. For when the taxing power conferred on the new government was under examination, the absence of such a provision was greatly insisted upon by the Opposition speakers. The vote then, on that amendment, was a substantial victory over the Constitution as it is.

But it is important in another respect. Mr. Madison had been compelled to admit the unequal distribution of taxes which would be collected through the custom house, and that the inequality would be to the injury of the South. He had succeeded in convincing a majority in the Convention that, on account of that very inequality, the revenues would, for the most part, be collected by having a direct recourse to the property of the people. As the power of direct taxation is now never recurred to by Congress, that amendment, to which such great value was attached, would have been rendered wholly nugatory; but the Convention voted, believing that it would provide a certain protection for the slaveholding section against the burden of unequal taxation.

The opinion which a majority of that body entertained of the efficacy of subsequent amendments, shows the wonderful hallucination under which they acted. In vain were they warned that their amendments would be disregarded. They would listen to nothing but their own idle and extravagant hopes. The influence of Madison and Randolph, and Nicholas and Pendleton, was in the ascendant, and that influence was thrown on the side of an immediate ratification.

The delegates furnish evidence that the long list of amendments was regarded by both parties in the Convention in the light of a condition subsequent, with which they confidently believed the great influence of Virginia in the Union would ensure a literal compliance. But in this they greatly erred, as events soon proved; for that temple of liberty, which they vainly imagined the new Constitution to be, was resolutely converted into the barred and bolted prison in which the independence of Virginia has been incarcerated. That such was the general understanding, we have the explicit evidence of the great Federalist leader himself. On the eighth of June, the following year, he brought forward the Virginia amendments to the notice of Congress. On that occasion he used the following language: "I considered myself bound *in honor and in duty* to do what I have done on this subject, to proceed to bring the amendments before you as soon as possible and *advocate them* until they shall be finally adopted or rejected by a constitutional majority of this house." Why bound in honor and in duty to propose amendments, against one of which, and that the most important of the series, he had voted—why bound to advocate them, unless for the reason before stated? Some of the States had joyfully adopted the Constitution without any condition whatever. This was the fact in regard to Connecticut, and Delaware had ratified by an unanimous vote.

The language used by Mr. Gerry in Congress, on the 8th of June, shows the importance attached to subsequent amendments by the States which had proposed them. "The ratification of the Constitution in several States would never have taken place, had they not been assured that the objections would have been duly attended to by Congress. And I believe many members of those Conventions would never have voted for it if they had not been persuaded that Congress would notice them with that candor and attention which their importance requires."

When the amendments were first introduced by Mr. Madison, the government had not been organized, and no revenue had been provided to meet public expenditures. The Congress would not listen to the propositions until the government should be firmly seated in the federal throne. Then Mr. Vining, alluding to the principal amendments proposed by Virginia, boldly declared, "There were many things mentioned by some of the State Conventions which he would never agree to on any conditions whatever; they changed the principles of the government, and were, therefore, obnoxious to its friends."

Congress treated, as Mr. Henry had foreseen and predicted, the Virginia Amendments with contempt; but the legislature, at that time the vigilant guardian of the rights of Virginia, took the matter up, and, on the 14th November, 1788, determined to transmit a remonstrance and an application to Congress, in the words following. It was presented, not by Mr. Madison, whose course had lost him the confidence of the Assembly, but by Mr. Bland, another of the delegates from Virginia:

"VIRGINIA, to wit:—In General Assembly, Nov. 14, 1788:

"*Resolved*, That an application be made, in the name and on behalf of the legislature of this Commonwealth, to the Congress of the United States, in the words following, to wit:

"The good people of this Commonwealth, in Convention assembled, having ratified the Constitution submitted to their consideration, this legislature has, in conformity to that act, and the resolutions of the United States in Congress assembled, to them transmitted, thought proper to make the arrangements that were necessary for carrying it into effect. Having thus shown themselves obedient to the call of their constituents, all America will find that, so far as it is dependent on them, the plan of government will be carried into immediate operation.

"But the sense of the people of Virginia would be but in part complied with, and but little regarded, if we went no farther. *In the very moment of adoption, and coeval with the ratification of the new plan of government, the general voice of the Convention* of this State pointed to objects no less interesting to the people we represent, and equally entitled to our attention. At the same time that, from motives of affection to our sister States, the Convention yielded their assent to the ratification, they gave the most unequivocal proofs that they dreaded its operation under its present form.

"In acceding to the government, under this impression, painful must have been the prospects, had they not derived consolation from a full expectation of its imperfections being speedily amended. In this recourse, therefore, they placed their confidence—a confidence that will continue to support them, whilst they have reason to believe that they have not calculated upon it in vain.

"In making known to you the objections of the people of this Commonwealth to the new plan of government, we deem it unnecessary to enter into a particular detail of its defects, which they consider as involving all the great and unalienable rights of freemen. For their sense on this subject we beg leave to refer you to the proceedings of their late Convention, and the sense of the House of Delegates, as expressed in their resolutions of the thirtieth day of October, one thousand seven hundred and eighty-eight.*

"We think proper, however, to declare that, in our opinion, as those objections were not founded in speculative theory, but deduced from principles which have been established by the melancholy example of other nations in different ages, so they will never be removed, until the cause itself shall cease to exist. The sooner, therefore, the public apprehensions are quieted, and the government is possessed of the confidence of the people, the more salutary will be its operations, and the longer its duration.

"The cause of amendments, we consider as a common cause; and, since concessions have been made from political motives, which, we conceive, may endanger the republic, we trust that a commendable zeal will be shown for obtaining those provisions, which experience has taught us are necessary to secure from danger the unalienable rights of human nature.

---

* See Appendix I.

"The anxiety with which our countrymen press for the accomplishment of this important end, will ill admit of delay. The slow forms of congressional discussion and recommendation, if, indeed, they should ever agree to any change, would, we fear, be less certain of success. Happily for their wishes, the Constitution hath presented an alternative, by admitting the submission to a convention of the States. To this, therefore, we resort as the source from whence they are to derive relief from their present apprehensions.

"We do, therefore, in behalf of our constituents, in the most earnest and solemn manner, make this application to Congress, that a convention be immediately called, of deputies from the several States, with full power to take into their consideration the defects of this Constitution that have been suggested by the State Conventions, and report such amendments thereto as they shall find best suited to promote our common interests, and to secure to ourselves, and our latest posterity, the great and unalienable rights of mankind.

"JOHN JONES, Speaker Senate,
"THOS. MATHEWS, Speaker Ho. Del."

This application, when taken in connection with evidence already adduced, leaves no doubt that the Constitution was ratified in Virginia under the belief that the amendments, which she might propose, would be adopted as a part of the instrument, and that, but for that conviction, it would have been rejected. No serious attention was paid to that remonstrance by the body to whom it was addressed; they had Virginia in the federal yoke, and they meant to keep her there.

It is a fact worthy the attention of those who eulogize the memory of Madison, that, although he declared himself to be bound in honor and in duty to present and advocate the amendments proposed by the Virginia Convention, that he only presented and advocated a portion of them, and that portion, those of a secondary importance. His excuse for that partial performance of his obligation was that, from the temper of

Congress, it would be useless to propose any that would radically affect the power of the new government.

I will now bring to the knowledge of the present generation a fact, in the secret history of Ratification, which, until this time, has escaped notice. It is the darkest chapter in the history of the Federalist party of 1788, and will consign to merited reproach those who participated in that transaction.

With a popular majority, according to the computation of Henry, as great as three-fourths of the voting population of Virginia, against the Constitution, it may well excite surprise, that the Convention, notwithstanding the partial mode of representation which prevailed, was not impressed with the same opinions. A majority of delegates opposed to a ratification was elected, but it was lost before the close of the session, and, by mismanagement and intrigue, shifted to the Federal scale. This assertion rests upon evidence of the most unquestionable character.

The Constitution of the committee of elections, and the favorable reception of its reports by the Convention, notwithstanding the many irregularities in the conduct of the elections, determines the political character of that body. That committee was composed of a majority of Democrats, and at its head was placed Gov. Harrison, who was distinguished, even in those heated times, for his determined and unwearied opposition to the new government. There were contested elections from five counties, and, in every instance, the seats were adjudged to the sitting members, who, with a single exception, voted with Henry and Mason. There is not the slightest evidence that the decision, in each case, was not warranted by law ; yet, from the unscrupulous means to which the Federalists were ever ready to resort, negative proof is afforded that they were not in the ascendant in the early stages of the Convention.

It gives me pain to relate, that chief among the turn-coats was Gov. Randolph. He was then chief magistrate of the

State, and, after attending at Philadelphia, had, along with his colleague, Col. Mason, refused to sign the Constitution, and had justified that refusal in a letter to the speaker of the House of Delegates. On the strength of that letter, and without solicitation, as he informs us, he had been elected to the Convention by the freeholders of Henrico county. Even before the Convention assembled, suspicions had got abroad that the unexpected popularity of the Constitution had wrought a change in Randolph, and had abated the strength of his opposition to it. Washington informs La Fayette: "*The Governor, if he opposes it at all, will do it feebly.*" That information was given in a letter written about the end of April. But when the Convention met, irresolution had passed, and his Excellency openly left his party, and took a position in the ranks of their opponents, where he was distinguished as the staunchest Federalist of them all.

The elections had been held in the month of March. The Convention was to have deliberated in May, but, by an adroit movement of those able tacticians, the Federal leaders, they contrived to get the session postponed until June, in the hope that its deliberations might be influenced by the example of other States. But, for that postponement, it is agreed that a ratification was hopeless. Randolph himself admits that, but for that event, he should have voted against the adoption of the new government. That his constituents were opposed to the Constitution is an undoubted fact, established by the testimony of John Marshall, his colleague. Marshall was a Federalist, and declares that he owed his election from a Democratic county solely to his personal popularity. Randolph addressed a letter to his constituents, in which he sought to vindicate, or, at least, excuse the step which he had taken. But why did not he resign his commission, and, in his new character, seek a renewal of the trust? The contagion spread. Others followed in the footsteps of Randolph,—countenanced, influenced, perhaps determined, by his example. The defection of that distinguished public man, with its effect upon the final vote, is established by the clearest and strongest evidence. In no terms of discourtesy, it was alluded to by Henry in debate, yet the allusion produced a violent collision with Randolph. His outburst of temper and muttered threats disclosed a mind ill at ease.

Washington, though at Mount Vernon, was kept informed of the progress of things in Richmond, and it is from his correspondence that the following facts are derived.

On the 4th of June, Madison wrote to him, as follows: "Yesterday little else was done than settling some questions of form, &c. To-day, the discussions commenced in committee of the whole. *The Governor has declared the day of previous amendments over, and thrown himself into the Federal scale. The Federalists are a good deal elated at the existing prospect. I dare not speak with certainty of it.*" Here, not only is the fact of Randolph's change of sides related, as important intelligence,* but that, previous to that time, Randolph had demanded previous amendments, as a condition of his adhesion to the Constitution—the ground upon which the Opposition stood in the Convention. The letter likewise reveals the fact, that that defection from the Democratic ranks had elated the Federalists with sudden prospects of success, but that the writer still doubted the event. Is it not a fair inference from it, too, that the original majority was opposed to the views of the Federalists?

A few days later, Bushrod Washington wrote to his uncle a letter, which confirms the evidence contained in Madison's letter. The writer says, "Mr. Henry, on Thursday, called upon the friends of the proposed plan to point out the objections to the present Constitution. This challenge, which was

---

* In giving Jefferson an account of the actors in the Convention, one of his correspondents writes: "The G——r exhibited a curious spectacle to view. *Having refused to sign the paper, every body supposed him against it;* but he afterwards had written a letter, and, having taking a part which might be called rather vehement than active, he was constantly laboring to show that his present conduct was consistent with that letter, and that letter with his refusal to sign."—JEFFERSON TO SHORT, Sept. 20th, 1788.

11

given with the appearance of confidence, drew from the Governor yesterday a very able and elegant reply for two hours and a half; *for I suppose you have been informed of Mr. Randolph's determination to vote for the proposed government.*"

So important and unexpected an accession to their party would naturally excite interest among the advocates of the new Constitution residing in other States. We accordingly find, that soon after the reception of those letters, and in consequence of the information they contained, Washington writes to Jay: "*That Randolph's declaration will have considerable effect with those who had been hitherto wavering.*" It appears to have been decisive; for Bushrod Washington, in continuation, informs the General: "*However, I am not so sanguine as to trust to appearances, or even to flatter myself that he made many converts. A few, I have been confidently informed, he did influence, who were decidedly in the Opposition.*" This proves, beyond doubt, that the hopes of a ratification rested upon conversions to be made from the other side. What effect the conversion of *a few* at that critical moment produced on the result, we are at no loss to determine. On the 18th of June, Washington again writes to La Fayette, as to the chances of the Constitution in Virginia: "So nicely," says he, "*does it appear to be balanced, that each side asserts that it has a preponderance in its favor.*" On the test vote it will be remembered that ratification prevailed by a majority only of *eight* votes. Four men, in consequence, held the balance between the parties, of whom Randolph was one. Whether the language of Bushrod Washington will embrace *three* men, must be left to the determination of the reader. Who were the "wavering" members, who at so late a day halted between two opinions on a question which had agitated the popular mind to its lowest depth? The correspondence of Washington does not disclose their names. But this we know, they represented no wavering constituencies. The question was far too important for any portion of the people of Virginia to maintain a neutrality in respect to it. The people never hesitate, never doubt on occasions of such moment, and it is certain that no delegate left his constituents uninformed with respect to their wishes on so vital a question. That such was the fact in that case, is proved by the letter of Washington to Wilson, April 4th: "*Some judgment*," says the General, "*may be formed, when the members chosen by the several counties are known; as their sentiments will be decided and their choice determined by their attachment or opposition to the proposed system.*"

Those waverers were all Democrats. It is no where intimated that any of the Federalists betrayed their constituents, or that the Opposition recruited their ranks from among the friends of the new system. The conversions were all from the other side. Upon this point Washington is again conclusive. On the 8th June, he replies to Madison, who without doubt made good use of that letter in the dark intrigue of which the Convention was the scene, "*What I mostly apprehend, is that the insidious arts of its opposers, may have produced instructions to the delegates, that would shut the door against argument and be a bar to reason.*" But the apprehension was without good reason, for the delegate who violates instructions given at the polls, will take little heed of any other expression of the popular will. Thus were the freeholders of Virginia disfranchised and the foundations of representative government torn up.*

Of the political character of this transaction, I presume only to speak. Its morality I leave to the consciences of good men and the judgment of mankind. With the acts, not the motives of men, it is my province here to deal; and "since this is the first law of history, that it should neither dare to utter a falsehood, nor in the next place want the courage to speak the truth, I have taken sincere pains to bring up the

---

* See Appendix II.

truth, which oftentimes lay deeply buried under the passions of the quarrelling parties." *

In the fullness of time the tree bore its appointed fruit; for the chief actors in that drama lived to enjoy the highest emoluments and honors of the new government. But it is ours, amid the degeneracy and decay of Virginia, to drink deep of the bitter waters which have thence issued. Upon one of them only was the hand of retributive justice laid. His shield was reversed, his good name ravished away, and the lustre of a great and shining character dimmed forever by that government which he had forced upon his countrymen, and by that stern man for whom he had prepared that seat of power. So terrible are the punishments of God! †

There is a show of right in superior power to which men submit, there is a native majesty in force, to which the weak bow down; but the Federalists, unable to command that, evoked a subtle and wicked fiend for their service—Fraud—and well did he serve his masters. It was by that diabolical agency that the Constitution was riveted on the free people of Virginia; it was thus that the cunning circumvented the wise, and the feeble overpowered the strong.

That men less established in wisdom and the sense of duty should have been blinded by selfishness, and entangled in the meshes of expediency, does not excite my surprise; but that Washington should have lent his countenance to the bad faith towards the constituent body, does excite both my grief and wonder.

---

* De Thou's History of his Own Time—Dedication.

† I feel little inclined to credit accusations against a Southern man coming from *the Northern phalanx.* Washington was not perfectly suited to the juggling scenes around him, and those characters soon acquired an undue influence over his administration. They drove Jefferson from the Cabinet, poisoned the heart of Washington against him, and pursued his successor, even in retirement, with prosecutions, slanders and confiscations. The league was so compact, as to make Madison desert his first love. But they crowned all when they made one of their own set, ever conspicuous for malignant hatred of the South, the next President. Was not that desecration?

Surprise is not diminished when we learn his own impartial estimate of the merits and defects of the new Constitution. On the 18th September, 1787, when the ink with which the Constitution was written was scarcely dry, he thus writes to La Fayette concerning it: "*It is now a child of fortune, to be fostered by some and buffeted by others. What will be the general opinion on the reception of it, is not for me to decide; nor shall I say anything for or against it. If it be good, I suppose it will work its way; if bad, it will recoil on its framers.*" In another place he says: "*There are some things in the new form, I will readily acknowledge, which never did, and I am persuaded never will, obtain my cordial approbation.*" He was not specific as to the particular parts of the new plan which had excited his objection, but it may well be inferred that the objections were of no trivial nature. When the letter to La Fayette was penned, the civil war by which society in New England had been rent, was scarcely extinguished, and the public mind, consequently, of the entire North was agitated and inflamed. Notwithstanding the unsettled condition of the North, Washington had determined to leave the new Constitution to its fate. But in June, 1788, that section of the country had settled down to the pursuits of peace, and was enjoying that new spring which industry had received. This change in the General's course, in respect to this important matter, is referable in some degree to the ambitious and able men who had gathered around him, all of whom were strenuous advocates of the proposed change. Party spirit, too, had begun to flame high, and of that spirit, it is known, the nature of Washington was strongly susceptible.

Governor Randolph, conscious that his action in the Convention of 1788 would be reviewed by posterity, has left his vindication of it. He was justly numbered among the intellectual lights of a period fruitful in great men, when Patrick Henry, William Grayson, Richard Henry Lee, Thomas Jefferson, George Mason, and Madison shone with unsurpassed splendor. It is no pleasing task to visit with blame a man like Randolph, but great and gifted as he was, this event of his life must not escape that condemnation which it so justly merited. He voted for the new government, he said, to save the Union—a wretched plea, which in our own day has been been made to cloak the venal motives of interested politicians. But the true motive, gathered from his own justification, was the unexpected favor with which the proposed change was received. "The genius of America" was nothing more than the genius of popularity, and popularity and success have a powerful charm for the judgments of men. They soften the obstinate, they illuminate the dull, they fix the inconstant, they bridge chasms, and break down mighty barriers, and open a passage broad and level as the Appian way.

It is incomprehensible what connection the spirit of America could have with the adoption or rejection of the Constitution by Virginia. Its merits or defects were alone involved, and whether it was politic for Virginia to enter into the new league. The North had adopted it; some of the States with a joyful precipitation, others with a show of deliberation. But as the Constitution was itself a compact, to which the North and the South were the parties, it was irrational for Virginia to be swept away by the tide of popularity which set in from the North. In fact, the very existence of popularity in that quarter was in itself enough to put Virginia on her guard. Then was the time, if there ever was a time, when her public sentinels were called upon to exercise vigilance and courage. It was true, South Carolina, Maryland and Georgia had ratified the Constitution, but the two former had not ratified until after Randolph had passed over to the enemy.* He

* The Constitution was ratified by South Carolina, May 23, 1788, by *a majority of seventy-six votes.* "Doubts were entertained of the acceptance of the Constitution by Virginia. To gain time till the determination of that leading State was known, a motion for postponement was brought forward. This, after an animated debate, was overruled by a *majority of forty-six.* The rejection of it was considered as decisive in favor of the Constitution. When the result of the vote was announced, an event unexampled in the

had certainly declared, when he returned from Philadelphia, that the Constitution had provided a bad government, and that Virginia ought not to adopt it until it had been amended. Can any man see how the ratification of a bad government by nine States could remove any of its defects? In order to provide Gov. Randolph with a justification for the course which he had pursued, he was appointed to draft the Act of Ratification, where it is broadly stated that the adoption of the new Constitution was necessary to the preservation of the Union; a question which will be presently examined.

The Democratic leaders contended that, if amendments were the object of Virginia, it would be folly first to adopt the Constitution; and that the obvious course for her to pursue was, to stand outside of the Union, along with North Carolina, and make her amendments the price of accession to it. Such was her moral and geographical position among the States, that she was enabled to dictate such terms as she might deem necessary. This course, so politic and safe, was not only advocated by the Democratic leaders in the Convention, but had been advised by Jefferson, and was, at one time, approved by Washington. On the 28th April, 1788, he writes to La Fayette: "The opinion of Mr. Jefferson and yourself is certainly a wise one, that the Constitution ought, by all means, to be accepted by nine States, before any attempt should be made to procure amendments."

But nothing could restrain the precipitancy of the Convention of 1788. It appears to have been possessed by a judicial madness. They followed the cunning example of Massachusetts, of adopting first, with the hope of amending afterwards. The result, as predicted, has been, that the adoption was accepted, but the conditions upon which Virginia was willing to

---

annals of Carolina took place. *Strong and involuntary expressions of applause and joy burst forth from the numerous, transported spectators.*"—Ramsay's Hist. of South Carolina, vol. ii., p. 452

This does not look, Col. Memminger, as though "South Carolina always thought the Constitution *a hard bargain.*"

enter into this more perfect union, were flung behind the fire by the insolent central power.

Having tasted of the folly of our predecessors, and proved the utter futility of subsequent amendments, it remains for Virginia now, in co-operation with the rest of the Southern States, to recur to the rejected counsels of the opponents of the present Constitution. Yes, let us buckle on our armor, and resolutely withdraw from this treacherous association—unless another Constitution is made, or the present one so amended as to be compatible with the prosperity, expansion and safety of the whole slave section. It requires only unity and courage, in the Southern counsels, to accomplish, in 1860, that result which, by similar means, the Democratic leaders sought to accomplish in 1788.

There may, undoubtedly, exist in the affairs of a people, a crisis so hazardous as to admit of no delay, and to justify, nay to compel, those who find themselves in the possession of power, to make a discretionary use of it. Did such a crisis, such a great national emergency, exist in the month of June, 1788? Randolph habitually represented the country to be almost in a state of anarchy; but that assertion was always denied by his political opponents. The peaceful and comparatively prosperous condition of the State of Virginia has been exhibited by the most authoritative evidence; and it is to be inferred, from the following extract from the correspondence of Washington, that the condition of the United States was not quite so desperate as Randolph would have us believe. He writes thus to La Fayette:

"*I expect that many blessings will be attributed to our new government, which are now taking their rise from that industry and frugality, into the practice of which the people have been forced from necessity. I really believe that there never was so much labor and economy to be found before in the country, as at the present moment. If they persist in the habits they are acquiring, the good effects will soon be distinguishable. When the people shall find themselves secure under an ener-*

getic government, when foreign nations shall be disposed to give us equal advantages in commerce, from dread of retaliation, when the burdens of war shall be, in a manner, done away by the sale of western lands, when the seeds of happiness, which are sown here, shall begin to expand themselves, and when every one, under his own vine and fig tree, shall begin to taste the sweets of freedom, then all these blessings (for all these blessings will come) will be referred to the fostering influence of the new government; whereas many causes will have conspired to produce them."

This is not the picture of a country rent by factions and civil wars. During the twelve-month which had just passed a new condition of things was arising in the Northern States. Emigration to the southward and westward, as already observed, had begun to draw off the diseased social elements, both from New England and Pennsylvania. The States of that section had begun to discharge their federal obligations, by paying in their quotas with regularity, and the only power indispensable to the efficient action of Congress, was a jurisdiction over foreign trade, in order, from the dread of retaliation, to be able to counteract the policy of foreign nations. There cannot be found, in all history, after such recent disasters, so pleasing a picture. Yet that portrait was drawn by the pencil of Washington, whilst still the Confederation existed. There never was so fortunate an epoch for a people to deliberate on public affairs. But "the recoil upon its framers," which would have resulted from a rejection of the Constitution by the Virginia Convention, gives the true solution of the desperate means resorted to to procure its adoption. Madison, in that event, would never have been the sage and idol of parties; and, above all, he would never have been President of the United States. But their political opponents, both in Virginia and elsewhere, would have been the master-spirits of a new Convention, or even the guiding minds under the Philadelphia Constitution, after it had been modified in essential particulars. The politicians, who had assisted at

Philadelphia, abashed and discredited by defeat, would have retired into private life, it might have been forever. This, all knew; but Washington alone had the candor to commit it to writing.

It will strike every reader of the Debates of the Virginia Convention, how much of their importance the reasonings and declamations of the Federalists derived from the disastrous effects of the war upon the people, and the embarrassments which it brought upon government. All the embarrassments, and many of the disasters, they boldly and directly attributed to the imperfections of the Confederation. There is a strong tendency in the human mind to refer all public calamities to the government. That string, the leaders of the Federal party touched with great skill. There are vast evils, inseparable from war, to feeble colonies, divided among themselves upon the question out of which the war had arisen. The war destroyed the commerce of the country—the sole source from which money was derived. It dried up, then, the very fountains of prosperity. No government could have robbed war of its terrors; no government could have made money plenty; for no government could have restored the foreign trade of the country. Jefferson was of opinion that, but for the scarcity of money, * every State would have discharged her federal obligations. In that cause alone, originated the expedients of paper money and specific supplies.

The Federalists, too, advocated a theoretic government, and who can contend against a government to which all theoretic perfections might be attributed? The Democrats, on the contrary, were called on to defend a system but imperfectly developed; a Constitution having defects, which they, themselves, admitted, and were anxious to reform. Here was an immense advantage. We have seen the skillful use which Madison and his friends made of it.

* "On the commencement of the late Revolution, Congress had no money. The external commerce of the States being suppressed, the farmer could not sell his produce, and, of course, could not pay his tax. Congress had no resource, then, but paper money."—Jefferson.

In addition to the positive evidence already produced, that the ratification of the Constitution by Virginia was due to the infidelity of certain Democratic delegates to the representative connection, there is another circumstance looking in the same direction, worthy of our attention. The members of the Assembly were elected by a county representation, by the same voters who had elected the delegates to the Convention. The Assembly was Democratic* by a vast majority of votes, as was exhibited at the ensuing session by the election of William Grayson and Richard Henry Lee to the Senate of the United States, over Mr. Madison. (See Appendix, III.) The State legislatures are always taken as the correct exponent of the politics of the people. So strong was the Democratic spirit in the Virginia legislature of 1788, that they addressed to Congress the energetic remonstrance already laid before the reader, demanding another Federal Convention to construct a new Constitution for the United States.

When a ratification was about to be procured by such reprehensible means, it is not difficult to understand why Mr. Henry should declare his determination to withdraw from the Convention. But it is difficult to understand why he did not execute that purpose. His whole life had proved that courage and promptitude of action were striking traits of his character, and that he was not in the habit of uttering vain and impotent threats. The reason that he did not pursue that course was, that Mason, the most influential leader of the anti-Federalists, next to himself, refused to unite in that course of action, but preferred another less decided. Mason preferred to allow ratification to take place without producing a disruption of the Convention, and then, by management, to prevent an organization of the new government. The plan appears to have been to combine the Opposition in all the States, and by their

---

* As to the politics of the legislature of '88–'89, Mr. Jefferson writes to Short: "A vast majority of anti-Federalists have got into the Assembly of Virginia, so that Henry is omnipotent there."

joint counsels, to produce that result. The enemies of the new government met, from every direction, at Richmond, but the whole scheme miscarried. Whilst the Constitution was still depending for ratification, an attempt had been made by the anti-Federalists of Virginia, to unite the Southern States against it, and so procure another Convention and another Constitution. But South Carolina was infatuated with the new government, and Georgia had gone mad with Federalism. North Carolina alone was true. The ratification of the Constitution by South Carolina, more than any other cause, operated to produce a similar result in Virginia. But she has lived to deplore, in sack-cloth and ashes, the folly of that day's work. She has been plundered, insulted, menaced, by the Federal tyrant, and comes now to Virginia proposing that very combination of Southern power which she once rejected.

It had been determined by the Federal Convention, that the government which they had framed should be ratified by conventions of the people, rather than by the State legislatures, to the end, as they pretended, that the government should derive its authority from the highest sources. Why then was it not submitted to the people directly? Why introduce the medium of a convention? I think the proceedings in Richmond afford a satisfactory answer to this question.

Madison appears to have been, not only the ablest debater of his party on the floor of the Convention, but to have been the honored instrument by which the delegates, pledged against the Constitution, were induced to vote for it. My reason for preferring that charge against him is, that Patrick Henry, in the succeeding Assembly, pronounced against him his celebrated philippic. Following immediately on the heels of ratification, it had been doubtless provoked by the objectionable means which had been resorted to by that accomplished tactician to produce that result. No part of that celebrated speech has been preserved. It is an irreparable loss to our forensic literature. A splendid tradition is all that remains of it. The speech would unfold, in ample detail, the network of treachery that, to the eternal shame of the Federal party, was woven in 1788.

It is apart from my purpose to follow the great orator beyond those interesting scenes, but an examination of the correspondence of Washington discloses the breakers which, on every side, threatened his administration. It shows that those dangers had a sectional origin, and that the President, that he might disperse them, besought Mr. Henry to enter his cabinet as Secretary of State. But Henry responded, "I am a Democrat," and he could not unite himself to a government administered by Federalists. It was not until a later period, when he thought that it was proposed to precipitate the United States into the quarrels of France—to lash her to that fire-ship—that he quitted his retirement once more to take part in public affairs. But the Angel of Death interposed, and closed forever the mortal career of Patrick Henry.

On the 25th June, 1788, the deliberations of the Convention were brought to a close. Governor Randolph humbly supplicated one parting word: "The suffrage which I will give in favor of the Constitution will be ascribed, by malice, to motives unknown to my breast. But, although for every other act of my life, I shall seek refuge in the mercy of God—for this, I request his *justice* only. Lest, however, some future annalist should, in the spirit of party vengeance, deign to mention my name, let him recite these truths—*that I went to the Federal Convention* with the strongest affection for the Union; that I acted there in full conformity with this affection; *that I refused to subscribe, because I had, as I still have, objections to the Constitution,* and wished a free inquiry into its merits, and that the accession of eight States reduced our *deliberations* to the single question of *Union or no Union.*"

On the same day, an engrossed form of ratification was agreed to. The next day, amendments were considered and adopted, and the Convention adjourned, having been in session twenty-four days.

It had all along been understood, that Washington was to be the first President of the United States. Soon the hunt after Federal office began. It was arranged among them that Madison should go to Congress. Defeated for the Senate by a Democratic majority, he contented himself with the secondary honors of the federal legislature. But it was necessary to take care of Gov. Randolph, for he, above all other men, had conferred the greatest benefit upon the party now in power. But for him, there would have been no House of Representatives, no Senate, no spoils-distributing President, no image of the British monarchy. Randolph was the first attorney-general, an office which he filled with distinguished ability and reputation. He afterwards became head of the State department, and the diplomatic correspondence of the government proves that he was as successful in discussing questions of diplomacy, as he had been in discussing questions before the courts.

The party, which had so strenuously, yet so unsuccessfully, opposed the adoption of the Constitution, stood aloof, ready, so soon as the occasion should arise, to become a formidable power in opposition to that policy which the Federalists subsequently introduced. They wanted only a leader, to exhibit their determination to defend the doctrine of State Rights, under the Constitution, as they had just exhibited it in opposing its ratification. When Jefferson withdrew from the cabinet of Washington, to organize an Opposition party, he found one ready formed. It was only necessary to place himself at the head of it. This is the origin of the Great Democratic Party in the United States.

CHAPTER V.

DECLINE OF VIRGINIA.

Oh! by what plots, by what forswearings, betrayings; and under what reasons of state and politic subtlety!—SIR WALTER RALEIGH.

Take heed of small beginnings, and meet with them even at the first, as well touching the breaking and altering of laws, as of other rules which concern the continuance of every several state. For the disease and alteration of a commonwealth doth not happen all at once, but groweth by degrees, which every common wit cannot discern, but men expert in policy.—SIR WALTER RALEIGH.

The favorite notion that has been advanced by the enemies of African slavery has been, that it produced the decline of Virginia, and that, in consequence, its continuance is incompatible with her material prosperity. In proof of that bold assertion, they point to the unexampled progress in the last seventy-five years made by the Northern or free-soil States, in the acquisition and development of wealth. They point to the manufactures of New England, the mineral wealth of Pennsylvania, and to the splendid commerce of New York, in contrast with the tattered and sluggish condition of Maryland and Virginia. They ask, where is that commerce which, at one time, constituted the Chesapeake the chosen resort of the trader? They inquire, where is that prosperous agriculture which made Virginia the foremost of the British colonies? In the most illogical manner in the world, they attribute these astonishing results to the presence of negro slavery in Virginia, and the employment of free or hireling labor in the North. They do not stop to inquire, whether the negro has not worked as a slave, in Virginia, since the first successful experiment of society on her shores. They do not stop to consider that it was at a former period, compatible with that very pre-eminence in wealth which they now say slavery has caused her to lose. Whilst they direct attention to the results of free labor in the North, they do not direct attention to the results of slave labor in those States of the Union to the southward of Virginia, where it is made the agent of the richest agriculture to be found in any part of the world. They do not direct attention to Cuba, nor to Brazil, nor do they direct attention to the Island of Jamaica, whose wealth and prosperity have been struck down by an abolition of that very slave system which they say has destroyed Virginia.

It is not the kind of labor which you employ, nor the name by which you distinguish the laborer, nor the continent from which he is imported, that renders a country prosperous, or the reverse; but the profitable or unprofitable nature of the employments in which the laborer is engaged. The history of Virginia agriculture establishes this fact. Before the Revolution, whilst the tobacco planters of Virginia were admitted to trade without restriction to British ports, the agriculture of Virginia flourished, and the labor of slaves was valuable. No one talked about abolition then—no one hinted that slavery was inconsistent with the creation of social wealth. But when, as we have seen, the tobacco of Virginia and Maryland was so heavily taxed upon its admission into the custom-houses of Europe, as greatly to impair the profits arising from its cultivation, the husbandry of Virginia declined, and with it the value of its agencies.

We have seen that those bad times had induced Virginia to move in the question of Federal reform, for the purpose expressed and understood, of investing Congress with the power to regulate the foreign trade of the country. We have seen that those classes more immediately interested in trade, advocated the new Constitution because it contained that power, as it was the argument ever in the mouths of the Federalists.*

---

* There could not be stronger evidence of the inducements held up to the people to ratify the new Constitution, than are to be found in the pages of "The Federalist." In the eleventh number of that series, this is what is said in respect to the commercial blessings to be conferred by Ratification, that demon in the garb of an angel:

"The importance of the Union, in a commercial light, is one of those

Mr. Corbin and Gov. Randolph, in the Convention, described the disastrous condition of trade growing out of the unfriendly policy of European governments towards it, as well as the hopes of those better times which the new Constitution would bring. The former said: "Let him visit the sea coast, go to our posts and inlets. In these ports, sir, where we had every reason to see the fleets of all nations, he will behold a few trifling little boats,—he will everywhere see commerce lauguish, the disconsolate merchant with his arms folded, ruminating in despair on the wretched ruins of his fortune, and deploring the impossibility of repairing it. The West Indies blocked up against us. Not the British only, but other nations, exclude us from their islands, our fur trade gone to Canada." "But," urged Gov. Randolph, "if you adopt this Constitution, giving to Congress the power to regulate our foreign trade, credit will be restored and confidence diffused in the country. Merchants and men of wealth will be induced to come among us, and commerce will flourish." This was the argument which enabled the Federalist leaders to collect a party for that Constitution, notwithstanding that men trembled whilst they favored its adoption.

Upon tobacco rested the whole system of Virginia. With the exception of a little wheat and Indian corn, it constituted the bulk of her foreign trade. It was the principal source

---

points about which there is least room to entertain a difference of opinion, and which has in fact commanded the most general assent of men, who have any acquaintance with the subject. *By prohibitory regulations, extending at the same time throughout the States, we may oblige foreign countries to bid against each other, for the privileges of our market. This assertion will not appear chimerical to those who are able to appreciate the importance, to any manufacturing nation, of the markets of three millions of people, increasing in rapid progression; for the most part, exclusively addicted to agriculture, and likely, from local circumstances, to remain in this disposition. Suppose, for instance, we had a government in America, capable of excluding Great Britain from all our ports; what would be the probable operation of this step upon her politics? Would it not enable us to negotiate, with the fairest prospect of success, for commercial privileges of the most valuable and extensive kind, in the dominions of that kingdom?" &c.*

from which the people derived money, wherewith to discharge their federal quotas, to support their State government, and to maintain their local institutions. It was the power that was to construct that great internal improvement system, the conception of Washington, which they had but just undertaken. It was the power, too, that had built thriving towns on her principal rivers and inlets; it was the power which promised to make those towns cities; and, above all, it was the power, in combination with cheap negroes, that had subdivided the territory among the rural population of the Commonwealth; it was the power* which made the agriculture of Virginia prosperous, and which rendered her the foremost State in the Union, in all those particulars which constitute a great and influential community.

We have seen that the Congress of the Confederation solicited the States to be entrusted with jurisdiction over the foreign trade of the United States, covenanting that "the particular interests of every State will then be brought forward and receive a federal support, and that their commerce laid under injurious restrictions in foreign ports, will, by wise and equitable regulations," be liberated.

Was the general expectation, that the export trade of Virginia would be liberated from the oppressive burdens, which weighed it down, realised by the new government? Were the covenants of the Congress of the Confederation complied with, to whose debts and obligations, by the terms of the Constitution, the new government had succeeded? We know, without reference to the proceedings of the Congress, that the pledge, so far as the tobacco trade of Virginia is concerned, has been wantonly violated, and that, so far from the exactions and monopolies of foreign governments being removed, or at least moderated, by the promised retaliation of the federal legisla-

* As late as 1786 the government of Virginia received, by special act, Tobacco, even in payment of taxes, and paid a portion of the troops which had been sent to fight in South Carolina, in the same article, instead of money.—*Jour. H. Del.*, 1786.

ture, they have been accumulated, and are at this day more oppressive than they have been at any former period.* Such is the faith that the central power has kept with Virginia and Maryland. When, at a recent session of Congress, the subject of the tobacco duties was brought to the attention of that body, by the Honorable T. F. Bowie of Maryland, instead of enacting counteracting duties, the question was referred to the diplomatic action of the government, thus remitting Virginia

---

* By a comparison of the following tables, it will be seen to how great a degree the tobacco interests of Virginia and Maryland have been injured under that federal reform which, under so many flattering hopes, was devised in 1787, and ratified in 1788. The tobacco trade, instead of being unfettered by the energetic interposition of the new government, has been loaded down under its eyes with additional weights.

The tobacco trade in 1793, the date of Jefferson's Report on the Commerce of the United States in Foreign Countries, was valued at four millions three hundred and forty-nine thousand five hundred and sixty-seven dollars. By Spain, the introduction of tobacco and indigo was prohibited. By Portugal, tobacco and rice were prohibited. In France, under the kingly government, America tobacco was under a monopoly, but paid no duties. The first National Assembly emancipated tobacco from its monopoly, but subjected it to duties of 18 livres, 15 sous the quintal. In Great Britain, tobacco, for their own consumption, paid one shilling three pence sterling the pound, custom and excise, besides heavy expenses of collection. In Denmark, heavy duties were laid on tobacco and rice, but the exact amount not known.

The duties on the importation of tobacco exacted, at the present day, by the principal nations of Europe, appear from a Report on the Commercial Relations of the United States with all Foreign Nations (34th Congress, 1st session) as follows:

By Russia, six rubles, or $4 50 per 110 lbs.; by Austria, $12 12½ per 110 lbs., but allowed to be imported only with permission of the government. Besides the import duty, an extra due for the grant of the license must be paid, amounting to ninety-seven cents per lb. for unmanufactured; $1 21½ per lb. for manufactured. The Zollverein, five dollars fifty-two cents per one hundred and ten lbs. In Sardinia, tobacco is a government monoply. In the two Sicilies it is prohibited. In Spain it is prohibited. Tobacco, in France, is either prohibited or is a government monopoly. There are particular relaxations, but they are of no account to the trade. The British government exacts upon the importation of tobacco, unmanufactured, 72 cts. per lb. and five per cent. additional. On manufactured or cigars, $2 16 cts. per lb. and five per cent. additional. On snuff, $1 44 cts. per lb. and 5 per cent. additional. The reader here sees how greatly the tobacco tariffs of Europe have been magnified since the new government went into operation.

back to that condition in which she stood anterior to the formation of the new government. Here are the resolutions introduced by the gentleman above named:

"*Resolved by the Senate and House of Representatives of the United States of America in Congress assembled*, That the trade in tobacco with Great Britain, France, Spain, Portugal, Austria, Brazil and all other foreign nations, is clogged with restrictions and limitations, wholly inconsistent with that fair and reciprocal condition of commerce which ought to exist between the United States and those nations respectively, and is, therefore, unsatisfactory to the States of Virginia, Kentucky, Maryland, North Carolina, Missouri, Tennessee, Ohio and Connecticut, in which the article of tobacco is an important if not the chief staple of agricultural production.

"SEC. 2. *Be it further resolved*, That it is the duty of the Federal Government to use its utmost power, by negotiation or other constitutional means, to obtain a modification or reduction on the part of said foreign nations, of the duties and restrictions imposed by them on the importation of American tobacco, and to this end to employ all the diplomatic and commercial powers which the Constitution has confided to it, in producing a more just and equal reciprocity in a trade so deeply involving the value of that portion of the agricultural labor of the country in which at least one-fourth of the confederacy is concerned.

"SEC. 3. *Be it further resolved*, That the treaties of the United States with China and Japan present a fair and fitting occasion for the enlargement and extension of the tobacco trade of the United States, and it is the duty of the government of the United States to use all their exertions within the limits of constitutional power, to foster and encourage the introduction of American tobacco as an article of use among the people of those nations.

"SEC. 4. *Be it further resolved*, That diplomatic negotiations with England, France, Spain and Austria, as well as with China and Japan, ought to be commenced as soon as practicable, by the government of the United States, with the view of obtaining a modification of the existing systems of revenue and taxation of those nations, in respect to American tobacco; and for this purpose instructions ought to be given to our foreign ministers, consuls, and commercial agents in those nations by the Executive of the United States, to use all their constitutional and legitimate functions in producing so desirable a result."

Soon after the organization of Congress, that question was brought to its attention by Mr. Madison. He contended that "agriculture was the great staple of the United States, and that it was the duty of the government to foster and protect it by every power with which it was armed by the Constitution. Retaliation was the only means by which that object could be accomplished, and that it was the main inducement that led to federal reform. He said, "We shall soon be in a condition, we are now in a condition, to wage a commercial warfare with Great Britain. The produce of this country is more necessary to the world, than that of other countries is to America. If we were disposed to hazard the experiment of interdicting the intercourse between us and the powers not in alliance, we should have overtures of the most advantageous kind tendered by those nations. If we have the disposition, we have abundantly the power to vindicate our cause. Let us show the world that we know justly how to consider our commercial friends and commercial adversaries. * * * * I will not enlarge on this subject; but it must be apparent to every gentleman, that we possess natural advantages that no other nation does; we can, therefore, with justice, stipulate for a reciprocity in commerce. The way to obtain this is by discrimination."

Mr. Baldwin observed, "That the question immediately before the committee was of less importance than the one which had been argued by the gentleman from Virginia (Mr. Madison) and the gentleman from New York (Mr. Lawrence). He was glad to have this question discussed, and thought the gentleman had very properly called in the public sentiment, as an argument in favor of his motion for discrimination; but the gentleman over the way wants evidence of what the public sentiment is. I think, said he, we have a strong proof of what the public sentiment is, in the very existence of the House. This sentiment he believed to be the cause of the revolution, under which we are about to act. The commercial restrictions which Great Britain, in pursuing her selfish policy, imposed, gave rise to an unavailing clamor, and excited the feeble attempt which several of the State legislatures made to counteract the detestable regulations of a commercial enemy; but these proving altogether ineffectual to ward off the effects of the blow, or revenge their cause, the Convention at Annapolis was called for the express purpose of counteracting them on general principles. This Convention found the completion of the business impossible to be effected in their hands; it terminated, as is well known, in calling the Convention who framed the present Constitution, which has perfected a happy revolution in politics and commerce. The general expectation of the country is, that there shall be a discrimination; that those nations, who have not yet explained the terms on which an intercourse shall be carried on, or who have, by establishing regulations bearing hard upon such intercourse, may know our ability and disposition to withhold or bestow advantages, according as we find a principle of reciprocity prevail. A discrimination is necessary; the voice of the people calls for it, and we shall not answer the end for which we came here, by neglecting or refusing to make it."

Nor was the Executive government less explicit in its acknowledgments of its obligations to protect agriculture by discriminating duties. Washington recommended that policy to Congress, in a special message, and, when Congress called upon the Secretary of State to report upon the condition of foreign commerce, and the proper remedies for its amelioration, Mr. Jefferson responded in an elaborate report, from which the following extract is taken:

"But should any nation, contrary to our wishes, suppose it may better find its advantage by continuing its systems of prohibitions, duties and regulations, it behooves us to protect our citizens, their commerce and navigation, by counter prohibitions, duties and regulations also. Free commerce and navigation are not to be given in exchange for restrictions and vexations; nor are they likely to produce a relaxation of them."—(*American State Papers*, vol. i. pp. 350, 351.)

It is not necessary to examine farther the action of the legislature on this interesting, nay vital, question to Virginia. We know the result, and we know that that result has brought disaster and ruin upon the industry of the State.

The proceedings of Congress at its first session, its high-handed measures, its arbitrary assumption of power, and its neglect of the commercial interests of Virginia, greatly soured, as we are informed by the correspondents of Washington, the people of Virginia towards the new government. One of them writes: "*If Mr. Henry has sufficient boldness to aim the blow at its existence, which he has threatened, I think he cannot meet with a more favorable opportunity.* But I doubt whether he possesses so adventurous a spirit."

Henry Lee, of Revolutionary fame, and so staunch a friend of ratification, is represented as having returned from Congress disgusted with the new government.

My authority for this statement is a letter to Washington, under date March 15th, 1790. It was written from Abingdon, Virginia, by his friend Stuart. "A spirit of jealousy, which may become dangerous to the Union, towards the Eastern States, seems to be fast growing amongst us. It is represented, that the Northern phalanx is so firmly united, as to bear down all opposition, while Virginia is unsupported, even by those whose interests are similar to hers. It is the language of all I have seen on their return from New York. Col. Lee tells me, that many, who were warm supporters of the government, are changing their sentiments, from a conviction of the impracticability of union with States whose interests are so dissimilar to those of Virginia. *I fear the colonel is one of the number.* The late applications to Congress, respecting the slaves, will certainly tend to promote this spirit. It gives particular umbrage that the Quakers should be so busy in this business."

To this insolent disregard of the interests upon which the prosperity of Virginia depended, there was soon added, by the sectional legislation of Congress, another evil of great magnitude. The trade, as was predicted by Grayson, was taken from her and given to the North, thus laying her agriculture under the additional burden of a commercial tribute. A total disruption then took place. Lands rapidly sank in value; slave property became a burden, and those towns, once the seat of a growing commerce, fell into ruins. * But the most melancholy and heart-rending consequence of this federal treachery, was the depopulation of the Commonwealth, and

---

* "Of what does the wealth of Virginia consist? Chiefly of lands and slaves. The lands of the Commonwealth were valued, in 1817, at $206,000,-000; what are they now worth? Half that sum? * * * Next, as to slaves. A gentleman sitting near him had, at the period to which he had just referred, sold eighty-five slaves, in families, at $300 round. He had been assured by him, and by other gentlemen, equally well informed, from other portions of the Commonwealth, that $150 for each slave, taking them in families, would be a fair price at the present time. This description of labor, then, *had fallen one half, and lands more than one half*, in very little more than ten years. In the estimate of the last, the tables supplied by the auditor, comprehended $26,500,000 for city and town lots; chiefly for the value of those of Richmond, Petersburg, Norfolk and Fredericksburg; *a value dependent on the fluctuations of foreign and domestic trade. What it is now, I know not; since commerce, that inconstant handmaid of fortune, has turned her helm from our ports to the favored harbor of New York.*"—Mr. MERCER—Debates Va. Convention 1829, p. 173.

"In my poor opinion, every commercial operation of the federal government, since I attained manhood, has been detrimental to the Southern Atlantic slaveholding planting States. In 1800, we had a great West India and a flourishing European trade. We imported for ourselves, and for a good part of North Carolina, perhaps of Tennessee. Where is all that trade now? Annihilated. Where is the capital which carried it on? Gone. Sir we have not an adequate representation in the federal government."—WATKINS LEIGH—*Ibid*, p. 164.

the destruction of that landed system which, from the first settlement of the country, had been growing up in Virginia. Those regions adapted to the growth of the grasses, were converted into pasture lands. The consolidation of farms took place in order to make cattle-ranges and sheep-walks; and the dwellings of the people were abandoned to silent and inevitable decay. Their vestiges alone remain: a ruined and dismantled dwelling, a falling chimney, a neglected graveyard, a decayed orchard; or, perhaps, a rose,

"To tell where a garden has been."

I cannot describe the calamity which had fallen upon them better than by using the language of the historian, which depicts a similar catastrophe which befell their English ancestors: "*Pasturage was found more profitable than tillage; whole estates were laid waste by enclosures; the tenants, regarded as a useless burden, were expelled their habitations; even cottagers, deprived of the commons on which they formerly fed their cattle, were reduced to misery; and a decay of people, as well as a diminution of the former plenty, was remarked in the kingdom.*"

Those sections of the State adapted only to husbandry, were completely destroyed; an utter desolation reigned on every side. It was as though the Angel of Death had passed over the land, blighting whatever he looked upon. Here is a picture drawn by Charles Fenton Mercer, in 1829. It represents that portion of Virginia of which I now speak:

"As I descended the Chesapeake the other day, on my way to this city, impelled by a favoring west wind which, co-operating with the new element applied by the genius of Fulton to navigation, made the vessel on which I stood literally fly through the wave before me, I thought of the early description of Virginia, by the followers of Raleigh and the companions of Smith. I endeavored to scent the fragrance of the gale which reached me from the shore of the capacious bay along which we steered; and I should have thought the pictures of Virginia, which rose in my fancy, not too highly colored, had I not often traversed our lowland country, the land not only of my nativity, but of my fathers, and I said to myself, how much has it lost of its primitive loveliness! Does the eye dwell with most pain on its wasted fields, or its stunted forests of secondary growth of pine and cedar? Can we dwell, but with mournful regret, on the temples of religion sinking in ruin; and those spacious dwellings whose doors, once opened by the liberal hand of hospitality, are now fallen upon their portals, or closed in tenantless silence? Except on the banks of its rivers, the march of desolation saddens this once beautiful country. The cheerful notes of population have ceased, and the wolf and wild deer, no longer scared from their ancient haunts, have descended from the mountains to the plains. They look on the graves of our ancestors, and traverse their former paths. There was a time when the sun, in his course, shone on no land so fair."

So rapid was the work of depopulation that, in 1829, during a space of nine years, according to the auditor's report, the counties of Fairfax and Loudoun had diminished in numbers 5,000. Riots and popular risings were not here, as they had been in England, the result of a ruined agriculture; for the means of a peaceful solution of the social problem were within reach. A fertile and unpeopled country lay on the borders of east Virginia, where this calamity was particularly felt. Strong tides of population began to flow into Kentucky, Georgia, Tennessee and Missouri. The emigrants took with them their slaves, and planted the social institutions of Virginia in their new homes. Others went to Indiana and Illinois, where they vainly attempted to introduce their favorite labor system.

I must here revert to the causes which disconcerted the just expectations of Virginia, that, through the agency of Congress, the exclusive system of Europe would be counteracted.

At one time there existed a perfect unity of commercial interest in all the States, which is proved by the fact that every

State, save one, had agreed to lodge with the federal head, the necessary power over foreign trade. Rhode Island alone objected to that addition to the Federal Articles; * and Rhode Island, it was known, deeply corrupted by paper money, was swayed by dishonest motives. At the period indicated, Massachusetts was as clamorous as the merchants and farmers of Virginia, for commercial retaliation. Not only did her legislature breathe a hostile spirit, but popular outbreaks against the commerce of England, a second time, disturbed the peace of Boston.

Though separate State action had failed to procure commercial freedom, it had, nevertheless, produced to the northward an important change in the public interests. That retaliatory legislation had operated as a protection to domestic manufactures. Establishments of that nature had sprung into existence, and had already become important public interests. So soon as the new Congress had assembled, the fact was at once developed, that the North had become interested in that new branch of industry theretofore almost unknown in America. Mr. Hartley, of Pennsylvania, openly proclaimed, that he wished the government to establish, as a fixed policy, that of protecting the manufactures of the North; and that sentiment was approved and sustained by his co-delegates from that section. Massachusetts, whilst she was unwilling to be taxed on the importation of molasses, from which her people made rum, yet contended that her rum ought to be fenced in by high duties from a competition with the rum of Jamaica, which, whilst it was of a superior quality to her own, could be sold cheaper in the domestic market. Even before the Revolution, the manufacture of rum had, to a considerable extent, engaged the attention of the people of that State. It connected itself with the two most profitable trades which they carried on—the trade in fish to the West India islands, and

* See also Monroe's Report in 1785, already quoted in the text; also, extract from Federalist, quoted in note, pp. 176–7.

the trade in slaves, which were purchased on the coast of Africa, and vended to the Southern planters.

Fisher Ames explains the whole business. Their summer fish they sold to the planters of the West Indies, as food for their slaves, and took molasses in exchange. That molasses they converted into rum, with which they purchased slaves on the barbaric shores of Africa. Pennsylvania sought protection for those manufactures of steel which, she said, could not stand alone, without the crutch of protection; nor could her paper mills, which turned out annually seventy thousand reams of paper. Connecticut had manufactures of woollen and manufactures of cordage, which she humbly petitioned to have protected; for, with great truth, she said, that unless the American consumer was compelled to pay for those articles a price above that at which they could be bought in the general market, those infant establishments would perish. New York demanded that every article should be protected that her people were able to manufacture. Those interests were obviously opposed to a system of commercial retaliation, "the dread of which would have been enough to have struck down the tariffs of England, and have initiated an era of free trade. That deplorable event the Northern States greatly dreaded, and, therefore, in the language of David Stuart, "the Northern phalanx" opposed, to the bitter end, all movements looking in that direction.

The whale and cod fisheries, it was true, were still in agonies; but the government soon found means, by bounties, to still their clamorous cries. But the great interest of the North, which sought and found protection from the liberal hand of the new government, was navigation, which was cherished by high differential duties. This, of course, bore with peculiar hardship on the Southern or producing States, whose commodities were now burdened by a new weight, by the hand of that government which had been so profuse in its promises of protection. Against the whole system, South Carolina lifted up her voice, nor did Virginia tamely submit, although Mr. Madison had embraced that new system with all the ardor of a lover. But his colleague, Mr. Bland, who had no motives to conciliate a popularity in the North, thus pointed out the operations of that class legislation: "*You certainly lay a tax upon the whole community, in order to put money in the pockets of a few, when you burden the importation with a heavy impost.*"

Even the interests of Northern agriculture had undergone a total change. It had no longer to contend with onerous duties in the ports of Europe, where they were only too glad to obtain the breadstuffs of America; for the Revolution in France had already affected the supply of corn. The year 1790 had given to the farmers of New York and Pennsylvania a bountiful harvest of wheat, and "the demand," says Washington, in a letter written, on the 9th January of that year, to Mrs. Catharine Macaulay Graham, "for that article from abroad is great." He proceeds to furnish to his correspondent an account of the prosperous condition of the Northern section of the country, through which he had recently made a tour: "The increase of commerce is visible in every part, and the number of her manufactures introduced in one year is astonishing. I have lately made a tour through the Eastern States. I found the country, in a great degree, recovered from the ravages of war; the towns flourishing, and the people delighted with a government instituted by themselves and for their own good."

Virginia and Maryland stood alone—demanding protection for their agriculture; for the delegates from the other Southern States stood aloof,* and opposed that policy, although

* WASHINGTON TO DAVID STUART, *March 28th*, 1790.—"Was it not always believed, that there are some points which peculiarly interest the Eastern States? And did any one, who reads human nature, and more especially the character of the Eastern people, conceive that they would not pursue them steadily by a combination of their force? Are there not other points which equally concern the Southern States? If these States are less tenacious of their interests, or if, whilst the Eastern move in a solid phalanx, to affect their views, the Southern are always divided—which of the two is most to be blamed?"

the condition of agriculture among their constituents was depressed in the same degree, and by the same causes. Such was its condition in South Carolina, and so little profit attended its operations, that rice and indigo, staple productions, had been in a great measure abandoned. Mr. Tucker, from that State, in a speech, protesting against the protective system, said: "The situation of South Carolina was melancholy; while the inhabitants were deeply in debt, the produce of the State was daily falling in price. Rice and indigo were becoming so low, as to be considered, by many, objects not worthy of cultivation."

I suspect that the cause which disunited the Southern delegates was the course pursued by Madison and other members of the Virginia delegation upon the vital subject of the tariff. He had openly sided with the North on that question, and proved himself to be the ablest and most devoted champion of that sectional legislation. Tonnage duties bore with peculiar severity upon the people of South Carolina and Georgia, and their representatives showed no little irritation at those heavy exactions, the sole benefit of which resulted to the shipping interest of the North. Madison first broke rank; he first left his friends, and took part with his enemies. Could it be expected of those friends to unite with him, when he brought forward the peculiar interest of his constituents for the protecting favor of the government? It was not enough to say, that those measures which sacrificed Carolina, sacrificed Virginia likewise. If he might claim the right to immolate the latter, he certainly had no claim whatever to sacrifice the former to the cupidity of Massachusetts, Connecticut and Pennsylvania.

To the silent operation of these causes is to be ascribed the destruction of that unity of interest which, at one time, pervaded the States, upon which would have been based that commercial league, into which they were ready at one time to embark.

PART II.

How it was Destroyed.

Riches are mine, Fortune is in my hand;
They whom I favor thrive in wealth amain,
While Virtue, Valor, Wisdom sit in want.—PARADISE REGAINED.

In a despotic state, which is every government whose power is immoderately exerted, a real division is perpetually kindled.—GRANDEUR AND DECLENSION OF THE ROMAN EMPIRE.

Every Government has its nature and principle, and its decay begins with the destruction of its principle.—SPIRIT OF LAWS.

A vice in representation, like an error in the first concoction, must be followed by disease, convulsions and finally death itself.—WILSON.

When two nations, of opposite civilizations and differing interests, confederate in the same government, the principle of that government is an Equilibrium. If it be otherwise, the government is a capitulation, by which one party surrenders its independence and, notwithstanding the forms of self-government, is degraded to the condition of a province.

By the Constitution, representatives in the popular branch of Congress, were distributed between the sections, as follows:

NORTH.

New Hampshire,	3 votes.
Massachusetts,	8
Rhode Island,	1
Connecticut,	5
New York,	6
New Jersey,	4
Pennsylvania,	8
Delaware,	1
8 States,	36

SOUTH.

Maryland,	6	votes.
Virginia,	10	
North Carolina,	5	
South Carolina,	5	
Georgia,	3	
5 States,	29	

This division of representatives between the North and South, was based upon the following estimate of population:

New Hampshire,	102,000
Massachusetts,	360,000
Rhode Island,	58,000
Connecticut,	202,000
New York,	238,000
New Jersey,	138,000
Pennsylvania,	360,000
Delaware,	37,000
Maryland (including three-fifths of 80,000 negroes),	218,000
Virginia (including three-fifths of 280,000 negroes),	420,000
North Carolina (including three-fifths of 60,000 negroes),	200,000
South Carolina (including three-fifths of 80,000 negroes),	100,000
Georgia (including three-fifths of 20,000 negroes,)	90,000

The ratio of three-fifths of the slaves gave, according to that estimated census, a majority of seven votes to the North. Gov. Randolph, in the Virginia Convention, when addressing himself to that branch of his subject, says: "The present number, sixty-five, is to be increased according to the progressive augmentation of the number of the people. From the present number of inhabitants, which is estimated at

352,000 whites, and 236,000 blacks,* we shall be entitled to fifteen representatives." This would have reduced the northern majority to two. But upon an examination of Gov. Randolph's calculation, I find that, according to the federal ratio, Virginia would have been entitled to sixteen † representatives, and that would have reduced the Northern majority to one, almost an equilibrium.

When the Northern members in the Federal Convention were accused of exaggerating the population of their respective States, in order to give to the North a larger representation in the outset than it would be entitled to under the compromise, it will be remembered that Col. Mason made light of that fact, because he asserted that the census, to be taken at the end of three years, would set all right—a signal want of foresight in one so wise, as the event soon proved. The point which the Northern members strained every nerve to gain, was to have control of the government in the outset, and in this they succeeded. The government has never passed from under their sway, and the expectations of its framers, that power would speedily be equalized between the North and South, has been falsified; for the North has been as successful in retaining ascendancy in the government as it was in the beginning in obtaining it. The means employed will presently be the subject of examination.

The grand defect of the Constitution, according to the design of its framers, was to have rested power upon a fluctuating basis like that of population. It at once created

---

* It is estimated by Jefferson that not less than *one fifth* of the slaves of Virginia had been carried off by the British.

† I find a singular confirmation of the accuracy of this allotment of *sixteen* votes to Virginia, under the three-fifths ratio, derived from the speech of Mr. Brearly, who was speaking of the share of that State as judged by her quota. He says: "Judging of the disparity of the States by the quota of Congress, Virginia would have *sixteen votes*, &c."—*Madison Papers*, p. 830.

Might not this under estimate of the population of Virginia have been submitted to in order better to reconcile the North to an arrangement which many thought would ultimately take power out of their hands?

13

struggles for power; for to control a mighty government like that created, was an object which might well stir the ambition of any people. The design was good, but the execution bad, and in the frame of the Constitution itself is to be found the cause of those violent agitations which have convulsed the country. If the intended Equilibrium between the Slave and Freesoil powers had been fixed by an absolute provision of the Constitution, the slavery controversy would have been stifled in its birth, and tranquility and good will would have taken the place of the war of sections. It is impossible to estimate the extent of the change that would have been produced by that simple act.*

When Gouverneur Morris, after the government had been placed under Northern influence, in the commencement, openly proposed to allow Congress, from time to time, to arrange the representation in the popular branches of the government, the proposition was voted down. It was said that representation, being in its nature a fundamental article, ought to be fixed in the Constitution; that it was the Constitution itself. Nevertheless, as we shall see, Congress has controlled the

---

* It is not to be concealed, however, that the struggles between the North and South have been the most potential agencies in counteracting the consolidating tendencies of the Federal system, and that a sectional balance of power, by putting at rest sectional jealousies and apprehensions, would have tended greatly to strengthen the government, and lead to an absorption of the States. The South, from its position as a minority, has been compelled to insist upon the strictest limitations of power. If these speculations be well founded, it may have been fortunate that an equilibrium was not successfully introduced into a government of such undefined jurisdiction as that which was created in 1787.

Mr. Calhoun, in his masterly "Disquisition," in which he revives the study of the true science of representative government, remarks that nothing imparts power to governments so much as well adjusted balances and checks. This, beyond doubt, is true. By creating confidence, they extinguish faction, and faction is the destroying agent of popular systems. To have made the Constitution of 1787 safe, it should have contained checks and balances between the States and the central power, as well as checks and balances between the North and South. "Wherever there is danger of attack, there should be given power of defence."

whole matter; for it has, by direct and indirect action, assumed jurisdiction to regulate the tides of population.

The whole system of Federal policy has been designed with that end in view; but the principal instruments by which that consequence was brought about are, First, The protective system. Second, The exclusion of slavery from the territories. Third, The refusal to protect the agriculture of the South. Fourth, The interdiction of the slave trade, without laying a similar disability upon emigration, but, instead, high and unusual encouragements held out to it. Fifth, The use of the credits of the federal government. For none of which is there the slightest warrant in the Constitution. The Equilibrium was the ground-work of the new government, and every part of it, as has been before said, was made with reference to it. After refusing to invest Congress with power over representation, the framers of the instrument, were not guilty of the solecism of allowing that end to be obtained by indirection.

If there is anything demonstrably clear, by evidence extrinsic to the Constitution, it is, that its framers intended it to be a free trade Constitution. The people and the statesmen of the United States, after the close of the Revolution, were disappointed that the policy of foreign nations, and particularly of the English nation, was still opposed to unrestricted commercial intercourse with them, but, instead, loaded their trade with heavy import duties. This fact has been established in these pages by the most authoritative evidence, and that failing to attain the desired object by negotiation and separate State legislation, the States agreed to deposite with Congress the power to regulate their commerce, in order that coercive measures might be employed. In addition to the evidences already submitted, I will here add the unequivocal declarations of Mr. Jefferson upon that point, whilst he sustained the character of the diplomatic agent of the government to France: "The system," says he, "into which the

United States wished to go, was that of freeing commerce from every shackle." (Correspondence, vol. i, p. 355.)

"Our people have a decided taste for navigation and commerce. They take this from their mother country; and their servants are in duty bound to calculate all their measures on this datum: *We wish to do it by throwing open all the doors of commerce, and knocking off all its shackles.*" (Ibid, p. 344.)

The following extract from the report of Mr. Jefferson, when Secretary of State, in 1793, shows that he considered the commercial policy of the United States to be unchanged by the adoption of the new Constitution:

"Instead of embarrassing commerce under piles of regulating laws, duties and prohibitions, could it be relieved from all its shackles in all parts of the world, could every country be employed in producing that which nature has best fitted it to produce, and each be free to exchange with others mutual surpluses for mutual wants, the greatest mass possible would then be produced of those things which contribute to human life and human happiness. Would even a single nation begin with the United States this system of free commerce, it would be advisable to begin it with that nation; since it is one by one, only, that it can be extended to all. Where the circumstances of either party render it expedient to levy a REVENUE, by way of impost, on commerce, its freedom might be modified, in that particular, by mutual and equivalent measures, preserving it entire in all others."

It is not pretended that there is any express authority contained in the Constitution, to justify Congress in embarking in a protective system; but, strange to relate, its advocates pretend to derive the power from that clause which empowers Congress to regulate the foreign trade—a power conferred, beyond all doubt, to enable Congress to realize the opposite policy, and free trade from every shackle. It was given for the protection and benefit of commerce; but when it is employed to build up domestic manufactures, it is evident that the power is used, not for the protection, but for the embarrassment and final destruction of commerce. The object of the protective system is the home supply; the object of a commercial system is the foreign supply. If articles are furnished at home, they cannot be procured from abroad; and it may come to pass, in the realization of the protective system, that foreign trade will be annihilated.

Among all the objections urged against the Constitution in the Convention, by Henry and his compeers, there was not one word said, either by opponent or friend, about the power of Congress to protect domestic manufactures, operating, as it would, to enrich the North out of the pockets of the South. Much was said in opposition to the power to lay import duties for revenue, because of the unequal taxation of which it would be productive, but nothing about the employment of those duties for the purpose of enabling the North to engage in manufactures. So strong was the objection, even to collecting the public dues in that way, that Mr. Madison said that Congress would unquestionably resort to a system of taxation to be composed of direct taxes and imposts.

The power to regulate commerce among the States, is given in the same clause that confers the power to regulate commerce with foreign nations. Is it pretended that, under a grant of power to regulate commerce among the States, it would be competent for Congress to build custom-houses, and institute systems of protective duties among the several States of the Union. If not, why not? We know that, under the Articles of Confederation, the States were in the habit of laying impost duties, directed against each other, and that so soon as the new Constitution was adopted, all such duties became unconstitutional, and that a system of free trade between the States was initiated.*

* "After depicting the great advantages to result from allowing Congress to regulate the foreign trade, "The Federalist" adds: "*An unrestrained intercourse between the States themselves*, will advance the trade of each, by an interchange of their respective productions, not only for the supply of reciprocal wants, but for exportation to foreign markets."

When it is borne in mind that the power to regulate commerce with foreign

It is known that the first tariff, under the present Constitution, was introduced by Mr. Madison, and that it was purely a revenue tariff—a fact in itself significant. It imposed a five per cent. ad valorem upon all imposts, a scale of duties that had been agreed to by the Congress of the Confederation of 1783. But the remarks made by that gentleman on that occasion are important, and prove conclusively that he considered that impost duties could be laid only for the double object, a free commerce and revenue. He said:

"In pursuing this measure, I know that two points occur for our consideration. The first respects the general regulation of commerce; *which, in my opinion, ought to be as free as the policy of nations will admit.* The second relates to revenue alone."

In 1785, as already stated, when the commerce of the United States, to use the language of Jefferson, "was in agonies," the State of Rhode Island excepted, all agreed to invest Congress with the power to regulate their foreign trade. Is it pretended that the transfer of that power to the federal government, would have authorized it to embark in a protective system? On the contrary, do we not, everywhere, find in the memorials of that period that retaliatory, not protective, duties were in contemplation? It was believed that the mere dread of retaliation would have been sufficient to emancipate the trade of America.

Mr. Jefferson says, in speaking of the general action in 1785: "I am well informed that the late proceedings in America have produced a wonderful sensation in England in our favor. I mean the disposition, which seems to be coming general, to invest Congress with the regulation of our commerce."

---

nations, and among the several States, is conferred on Congress, in the same language, nay, in the same breath, we cannot but conclude, that a common object was contemplated by each grant of power, and that if that object was an unrestricted intercourse in one case, it must have been an unrestricted intercourse in the other, excepting such revenue duties as it might be the policy of the government to impose.

If we turn to the speeches of George Mason, in the Virginia Convention of Ratification, we will discover that he spoke on the subject of manufactures, not in connection with the Federal Constitution, but as being a department of industry belonging to nations in an older stage of existence than the United States then were. In the order of nature, they follow after agriculture and commerce, it being from the surpluses of those two branches of industry that manufactures naturally spring, more particularly from the accumulations of trade; for it is the alluvion of commerce that fructifies a land, and prepares it for the growth of manufactures. So far was it from the mind of any man in that assemblage to suspect that there lay hid, under the folds of the new Constitution, a power of that nature.

By a system of protective duties, it is evident that a steady stream of revenue would be produced, which would render nugatory a separate power to lay and collect duties for that object. But, if the power to regulate commerce be confined strictly to commercial objects, and be regarded as a mere mode of reaching free trade, no such result would ensue. Thus the different parts of the Constitution would be brought into symmetry and harmony. Why could not the power to establish a protective system be construed to contain a revenue power, if its constant and necessary result would be productive of revenue? It would not be a greater stretch of the constructive power than to infer the power to impose protective duties from a simple grant to regulate commerce. Not so much; for we have seen that, in their nature, the one is diametrically opposed to the other.

But the strong and, with some, conclusive argument is, that Mr. Madison systematically supported and voted for protective tariffs; but, surely, the very opposite and contradictory modes of construing the Constitution, at different times, adopted by that statesman, greatly impairs the weight of his authority. I believe it may be safely stated that he never committed himself to any important question of constitutional construction, that he did not afterwards take ground inconsistent with it. His chief claim to the public gratitude rests upon the Resolutions and Report of '98 and '99—it is the main pillar of his fame; yet the world knows that, after they had served their turn, and the convenience of the hour had passed, that he employed the evening of his life in undermining the work of his maturity. In his letter to Joseph C. Cabell, in which Mr. Madison labors to prove the constitutionality of a protective tariff, after stating that one member in the Massachusetts Convention of Ratification alluded to it as the probable object of congressional legislation, he adds that "there was nothing said against the existence of that power in any of the Southern conventions." This was strictly true, for, as heretofore stated, there was no allusion whatever made to the subject, any more than to the authority of Congress to create a monarch or an hereditary aristocracy. But their silence on these points would be regarded by every man, except Mr. Madison, as a poor argument in favor of the existence of such a power.

But much was said in the Virginia Convention against the unequal operation of import duties, even for revenue. Here is what Mr. Madison himself said on that subject: "The general government, to avoid these disappointments, which I first described, and to avoid the contentions and embarrassments which I last described, will, in all probability, throw the public burdens on those branches of revenue which will be most in their power. They will be continually necessitated to augment the imposts. If we throw a disproportion of the burdens on that side, *shall we not discourage commerce, and suffer many political evils? Shall we not increase that disproportion of the Southern States, which, for some time, will operate against us? The Southern States, from having fewer manufactures, will import and consume more. They will, therefore, pay more of the imposts. The more commerce is burdened, the more the disproportion will operate against them. If direct taxation be mixed with other taxes, it will* *be in the power of the general government to lessen that inequality. But this inequality will be increased to the utmost extent, if the general government have not this power.*"*—(*Elliot's Deb.*, vol. iii. p. 248.

The reply of Grayson to this part of Madison's speech strengthens the inference against the belief, then, in the existence of the power to use import duties for the protection of Northern manufactures. "But, sir, we are told, that if we do not give up this power to Congress, the impost will be stretched to the utmost extent. I do suppose this might follow, if the thing did not correct itself. But we know that it is in the nature of this kind of taxation, that a small duty will bring more than a large one, &c."—(*Ibid.* pp. 277, 278.

Grayson evidently did not dream of protective duties, else he would not have talked of Congress being confined, by the nature of that kind of taxation, to the revenue standard. Did

---

* This argument was addressed to a *Southern* audience; but refer to the twelfth number of the Federalist, written by Hamilton, where he tells the farmers of New York, that direct taxation, for federal purposes, will cease, and the revenue will be collected wholly from taxes on *commerce.* But he makes no allusion to protective duties; on the contrary, both that and the preceding number are based on the contrary assumption. Here is other evidence looking in the same direction—it is from the pen of Madison—"Federalist, No. 54:"

"In one respect, the establishment of a common measure for representation and taxation will have a very salutary effect. As the accuracy of the census to be obtained by Congress will necessarily depend, in a considerable degree, on the disposition, if not on the co-operation, of the States; it is of great importance that the States feel as little bias as possible, to swell or to reduce the amount of their numbers. Were this share of representation alone to be governed by this rule, they would have an interest in exaggerating their inhabitants. Were the rule to decide the share of taxation alone, a contrary temptation would prevail. By extending the rule to both objects, the States will have opposite interests, which will control and balance each other, and produce the requisite impartiality."

This salutary check against fraud in taking the census was destroyed, when Congress elected to collect all federal taxes through the custom-house. However it may have been with others, it could have occasioned no surprise to Mr. Madison that the North continued to hold the federal reins.

Mr. Madison? It is incontestibly true, that the members of the Virginia Convention were impressed with the belief that the revenue would be principally derived from direct taxes, and with the drawback of a slight revenue tariff, that commerce would be free. Hence the great importance attached to the third of the amendments, which provided that direct taxes should be collected in the first instance through the instrumentality of the State governments.

It has been stated that free trade was, from an ancient date, a darling object with Virginia, and one which she had kept steadily in view through all political changes. I will add another proof. When the Assembly had consented to invest the Congress of the Confederation with the five per cent. impost, and the power to regulate trade, so apprehensive were they of abuse in the exercise of the latter, and that it might be perverted to the purposes of revenue, and thereby made an embarrassment to commerce, that they expressly stipulated the duties, resulting from the regulations of trade, should go into the State treasury.

The reader has not forgotten, when, in the Virginia Convention of Ratification, he (Mr. Madison) was pressed by his able antagonist, as to the wide extent of federal jurisdiction under the Constitution, that he said: "*That the powers of the general government relate to external objects, and are but few; but the power of the States relate to those great objects which immediately concern the prosperity of the people. Let us observe also that the powers of the general government are those which will be exercised mostly in time of war, while those of the State governments will be exercised in time of peace. But I hope the time of war will be little compared to that of peace.*"

By the protective system, the federal legislature boldly exercised the power of controlling the business of the country, of dictating the pursuits of individuals, of regulating prices, and of determining where the people should buy and sell. No power could be, in its nature, more supreme—it is greater than the power of life and death. It is the power of fate, since it fixes the destiny of nations.

After watching the operations of the protective system for half a century, this is the judgment pronounced upon it by the great political luminary of his own day and one of the wisest men who ever lived: "Delays are said to be dangerous, and never was the maxim more true than in the present case, a case of monopoly. *It is the very nature of monopolies to grow. If we take from one side a large portion of the proceeds of its labor, and give it to the other, the side from which we take must constantly decay, and that to which we give must prosper and increase. Such is the action of the protective system. It exacts from the South a large portion of the proceeds of its industry, which it bestows upon the other sections, in the shape of bounties to manufactures and appropriations in a thousand forms; pensions, improvement of rivers and harbors, roads and canals, and in every shape that wit or ingenuity can devise.*" *

William Grayson predicted that the action of the government would be directed by a faction of the Northern against the Southern States. The vote by which the protective tariff of 1828 was passed, realized that prophecy. Watkins Leigh said of it: "A gigantic system of protecting duties is proposed—the Southern States in vain exclaim against its partial and oppressive operation—in vain deprecate, remonstrate, struggle—a bare majority hesitates not to impose the tariff." But it is from Mr. Giles that we have the fullest history and strongest denunciation of that measure. "An excessive tax," said that great man, "has been imposed by that government, as he conceived, in direct violation of morals, principles and the plainest provisions of our written Constitution. It originated in combinations of particular sections of country to tax other sections. These combinations were effected by invitations given by certain political fanatics to other fanatics to meet in convention at Harrisburg, during the recess of Congress; exclud-

* Calhoun.

ing all the sections of country intended to be made tributary from these invitations. Virginia was not honored with an invitation, nor any State south or south-west of Virginia. This convention, thus composed, unblushingly met at Harrisburg in open day, organized themselves into a convention, with all the assumed names and formalities awarded to this convention; and there laid the foundation of the tariff act which was subsequently sanctioned by an act of Congress. This act was passed in direct violation of every principle of taxation heretofore held sacred, and was addressed to the worst passions of the human heart. It was dictated by a spirit of electioneering and of avarice, which, reckless of all principle, invited the manufacturer to rely upon the labor of others, instead of his own labor, not only for suppport, but even for the accumulation of wealth; and actually furnished him with the means of taking the proceeds of the labor of another, which, if done without the sanction of this iniquitous act, would amount to a criminal offence. The effect of this act has been to demoralize the whole country, and to impoverish the whole of the tributary parts of it."

It was by the exercise of that unconstitutional power that remunerative employment was afforded to the idle hands in the North. Emigration to the South* was stopped, and the intention of the framers of the Constitution defeated, who had expected that in this way representative power would be equalized between the sections. The protective system, then, was the first blow aimed at the Equilibrium.

The next blow aimed at the Equilibrium was, by excluding slavery, the characteristic of the South, and the principal source of her political power, from the public territories. By this assumption of power, Congress devoted to the free-soil element the northwest territory, and the large and populous

* Notwithstanding the depressed condition of business in Virginia, there was, according to Gov. Randolph, a steady addition to her population from the North, about the time that the Constitution was ratified.—*Elliot's Debates*, vol. iii. p. 100.

States which have been carved out of it. But for that act of exclusion, slavery would have spread over the whole of it, notwithstanding the fanciful notion of a climate line. * At that time, the slave trade was open, and negroes consequently abundant and cheap. That authority has been pronounced a usurpation on the part of Congress, but it was not on that account less efficacious in making a large addition to the power of the North. It was against the constitutional right of the South, but that disembodied spirit was powerless to restrain aggression until armed with the absolute negative of the judiciary.

It will gratify an enlightened curiosity to know what passed between the leaders of the Opposition and the advocates of the Constitution, upon this subject in the Convention of Virginia. Strictly upon this point, nothing; for it did not occur, even to the most morbid apprehension, that the proposed Constitution clothed Congress with any power whatever to dictate the domestic institutions of any territorial population. That required a flight of imagination of which the men of those days were not capable.

But Mr. Grayson, observing that, by the new Constitution, Congress was invested with something like a discretion in the admission of new States, and, knowing well the instincts of the Northern mind, from the developments of sectional policy which had already been made, expressed his apprehensions that slavery might be construed into a disqualification for admission into the American Union. He said: "It appears to me, sir, under this section, there can never be *a Southern State admitted* † *into the Union.* There are seven States, who

* The western people are already calling out for slaves for their new lands; and will fill that country with slaves, if they can be got through South Carolina and Georgia.—George Mason—Mad. Papers, p. 1391.

† Mr. Webster has declared, that when the Constitution was framed, it was not the expectation that there would ever be an addition to the slave territory of the Union. In this, he is assuredly not supported, but plainly contradicted by historical evidence. Mr. Jefferson, in his correspondence, in-

are a majority, and whose interest it is to prevent it; the balance being actually in their possession. It is not to be supposed, then, that they will admit any Southern State into the Union, so as to lose that majority." Mr. Madison replied, that he thought "this part of the plan *more favorable to the Southern States* than the present Confederation, as there was a greater chance of *new States* being admitted." The subject was here dropped, and was not taken up again.

If the federal government had kept its plighted faith, given under the old system, and extended its protecting power to the agriculture of the slaveholding States, not even the profits of the manufacturing employments in the North could have prevented the migration of population from that region Southward. In order, then, for the Northern majority to keep power in their hands, it was necessary to allow the existing discouragements to Southern enterprise to remain; for these two, in truth, constituted parts of the same system. It had another effect: it discouraged the slave trade, which would have added political elements to Southern society. If the rice of the Carolinas and Georgia had gained admission into the general market, upon advantageous terms, there would speedily have resulted a great development of that interest. The industry of those States would not have sickened, until the cultivation of the cotton plant brought with it riches and power.

---

forms us, that the public men, anterior to the period indicated by Mr. Webster, confidently expected either to conquer or purchase from the Spaniards, the peninsular of Florida. Here is what he speculates about the domain embraced by Louisiana. It would appear that he did not confine his views even to the two acquisitions mentioned: "Our confederacy must be viewed as the nest from which *all* America, North and South, is to be peopled. We should take care, too, not to think it for the interest of that great continent to press too soon on the Spaniards. Those countries cannot be in better hands. My fear is that they are too feeble to hold them till our population can be sufficiently advanced to gain it from them piece by piece. The navigation of the Mississippi, we must have. This is all we are, as yet, ready to receive."—*To Stewart*, Paris, January 25, 1786.

But the profitable cultivation of the tobacco plant would have produced the largest accession to the representative power of the slave section. The tobacco zone stretches over an immense area, and wherever tobacco was cultivated, there slave labor would have been employed. With the markets of Europe thrown open to it, it is not extravagant to say, that tobacco would have been then what cotton is now; for, about that time, plaster of Paris was introduced as a manure into Virginia, so powerful an agency in restoring fertility to lands exhausted by the growth of tobacco. The co-operation, then, of the treacherous federal agent with the vindictive tariffs of Europe, was another blow struck at the Equilibrium.

The interdiction of the African slave trade, under high, unusual and unconstitutional penalties, accompanied by the free admission of European emigration, under high, unusual and unconstitutional encouragements, was still another blow to the Equilibrium. When federal power was derived from population, it is a necessary inference that the sectional compromise must have embraced both the slave trade and the immigration from Europe—then large enough to excite the apprehensions of sober men. To say that the North and South would struggle over the question of population, "even to the twentieth part of one poor scruple," and consume days and weeks in establishing what they believed would be a balance of federal numbers between the two sections, and, at the same time, utterly ignore the copious supplies that were daily arriving from the old world, is to accuse them of a want of foresight that would be discreditable even to a plowman. There was every thing to put the South upon its guard. The American continent, so far as they were peopled with the white race, had been peopled from Europe; and the tide of emigration was growing stronger every day. Then, as now, the great mass of voluntary immigrants preferred to live in the North, being then, as now, repelled from the South by our black peasantry. It is true, then, as now, an element of the foreign influx went Southward, characterised by higher intelligence and greater refinement, being drawn thither by the higher civilization which there prevailed; but the great bulk of the laboring classes went Northward, and planted free-soil society where ever they went. Then, as now, the foreign laborer hated slavery; for how could it be in his nature to feel kindly disposed to him who was a rival in the fields of industry? The foreign laborer occupied not towards the negro slave the same relation which a poor man native to the South occupied; for the latter, looking upon him in the natural light of property, was ever ready to avail himself of his agency in the creation of wealth. But that was not the case with the European peasant, who recognised no difference between the negro and himself, other than that which grew out of the color of the skin and the growth of the hair.

Mr. Wilson, of Pennsylvania, said, that he would not heartily agree to the compromise, in virtue of which three-fifths of the slaves were to be taken into the representative basis, unless some compromise were likewise agreed to with reference to the slave trade. This, however, was not done, until later, and in another connexion—the basis having been agreed to without any restriction being laid on the migration of whites, or the importation of blacks.

Congress was clothed with power, after the year 1808, to prohibit the slave trade under the terms of the importation of persons. Let us see whether the Southern members of the Convention were as attentive to the political interests of their constituents, as Mr. Wilson had proved to his; let us see whether they insisted that Congress should be invested with a similar power of prohibition over the migration of numbers from Europe; and let us see whether the exercise of power over the one was not to be a condition of the exercise of power over the other. If Congress were empowered to interdict the one, and at the same time encourage the other, it is manifest that the work of the Convention would go for nothing, and that to the legislature, after all, would be confided the imperial power to declare which of the two sections should hold the sceptre—whether the North should be the appendage of the South, or the South should be the appendage of the North. The Constitution, if I mistake not, will, upon scrutiny, be discovered to be in accordance with itself, and the principles contained in one part of that instrument will not contradict and nullify the grand idea upon which the whole system is framed.

By the 9th section of the 1st article of the Constitution, it is provided, that "The migration or importation of such persons as any of the States, now existing, shall think proper to admit, shall not be prohibited by the Congress prior to the year one thousand eight hundred and eight, but a tax or duty may be imposed on such importation, not exceeding ten dollars for each person.

It is obvious that this language describes two distinct classes of persons, the one characterized by a voluntary, the other by an involuntary arrival in the country. The terms employed in their natural and customary significance draw distinctly a line of demarcation between the two. To *migrate*, implies a voluntary action, while to be imported, implies an absence of all volition. The word migrate was employed in 1787, in the same sense in which it is now employed. The writings and speeches of that period prove this. In the Declaration of Independence the word 'migration' is used in reference to voluntary arrivals from Europe, and in the speeches of Grayson and others in the Virginia Convention, the word is employed in the same sense. No one in those days spoke, as no one now could with any propriety speak, of the migration of slaves, and no one ever thought of describing the ingress of freemen by the term importation. Migrate is the primitive and uncompounded word, derived from the Latin, from which we have *e*migrate, *com*migrate, *trans*migrate, but they all imply an exercise of the will.

But the Constitution itself has allowed no doubt to rest upon this point, for it has expressly discriminated between the two descriptions of persons mentioned, by imposing upon the admission of the one a tax or duty of ten dollars, but allowing the other to come in without charge.

But with some the authority of a judicial interpretation is stronger than the authority of the Constitution, or even the authority of reason. To reach the closed understandings of such, I beg leave to introduce the well considered opinion of Chief Justice Marshall in the leading case of Gibbons and Ogden, 9th Wheaton, p. 216.

The Chief Justice says: "*The section which restrains Congress from prohibiting the migration or importation of such persons as any of the States may think proper to admit, until the year* 1808, *has always been considered as an exception from the power to regulate commerce, and certainly seems to class migration with importation. Migration applies as appropriately to voluntary, as importation to involuntary, arrivals; and so far as an exception from a power proves its existence, this section proves that the power to regulate commerce applies equally to the regulations of vessels employed in transporting men, who pass from place to place voluntarily, and to those who pass involuntarily.*"

Here, by a great oracle of constitutional law, are not only the two descriptions of persons recognised, but they are placed upon the same footing as regards the prohibitory powers of Congress. Congress had, then, if Gibbons and Ogden be considered authority, power to prohibit European emigration at the same time that it prohibited the slave trade in 1807, and to afflict it with the same penalties.

It remains now to be examined whether it was the duty, as well as the right, of Congress, when it prohibited the slave trade, to prohibit, in the same act, emigration. It would be enough to say, that the preservation of the Equilibrium between the North and South, required this even-handed justice; for the federal legislature was as imperatively bound to observe that fundamental compromise as to respect any part of the instrument whatever.

But the language of the 9th section, if properly understood, gives countenance to this idea. It is wholly negative in its character, and gives no sort of power to Congress to discriminate between the two classes of persons described, no authority to treat them after different modes. It simply declares that previous to 1808 neither the migration nor importation of persons shall be prohibited, but that a tax or duty may be collected upon the admission of one of them. In the case of Smith *v.* Turner, Chief Justice Taney determines that the migration or importation of persons was used to describe the subjects of the slave trade. He confounds, as will be seen, the distinct classes of persons indicated in the 9th section, and for no better reason than that he may by that means avoid the conclusion here sought to be established—that they are equivalent political forces, and were to be dealt with alike: "If the word can be applied to voluntary immigrants, the construction put upon it by those who opposed the Constitution, is certainly the just one, for it is difficult to imagine why a power should be so explicitly and carefully conferred on Congress to prohibit immigration, unless a majority of the States desired to put an end to it, and to prevent any particular State from contravening this policy. But it is admitted, on all hands, that it was then the policy of all the States to encourage immigration, as it was then the policy of the far greater number of them to discourage the African slave trade. With these opposite views upon these two subjects, the *framers of the Constitution would never have bound them both together in the same clause, and spoken of them as kindred subjects which ought to be treated alike, and which it would be the probable policy of Congress to prohibit at the same time.*"

If Chief Justice Taney had adhered to the interpretation of the 9th section, unanimously made by the Court in Gibbons *v.* Ogden, that two classes of people were described, he would have come to the very result, and placed upon its language the very construction contended for here. It may well excite the amazement of the reader, that his Honor should assume the power to expunge from the Constitution a word of significant import, and apply that to slaves, which, by the common proprieties of speech, was applicable only to freemen, as it may well excite surprise that he should go outside of the Constitution, and upon what he chooses to assume was the state of public opinion in the South, erase from that solemn instrument an important and, as I think, vital part. Mr. Webster says, that the Constitution must be read by its own lights, but Judge Taney appeals to the authority of loose tradition. What evidence is there that the Southern States were willing, after population had been made political power, that the North should receive accessions from Europe, and themselves be cut off from accessions from Africa? This is the point to which the Chief Justice must address his historical inquiries. The history of the 9th section in the Constitutional Convention will throw some light on the question.

The sectional compromise was in the first place agreed to without any reference whatever to emigration or the slave trade. The question was laid by as one of the conclusions to which the Convention had come. It appears rather to have been the understanding, that no limitation whatever should be put to supplies of population derived from either of those sources; for when, towards the close of the Convention, a committee of detail was appointed to embody the conclusions to which the Convention had come, there was a positive provision in their report that "no tax or duty shall be laid by the federal legislature on articles exported from any State; *nor on the migration nor importation of such persons as the several States shall think proper to admit, nor shall such migration or importation be prohibited.*"

But the report omitted the sectional compromise which had been agreed to, touching representation, which Mr. Williamson of North Carolina remarked upon. He moved to insert it. It was inserted, New Jersey and Delaware alone voting against it. The report then stood, so far as this question is concerned, that three-fifths of the slaves were to be admitted into the representation, with no restriction whatever upon the slave trade or its equivalent European emigration.

But Mr. King, of Massachusetts, took exceptions to it, and said that he *could never agree to leave the slave trade open unless Congress were allowed to tax exports*, and that South Carolina would not consent to it. A warm debate sprung up upon the merits of the slave trade and slavery, in which South Carolina and Georgia declared that they would not confederate if their right to import slaves was restrained. A committee of compromise was appointed, of which Mr. Livingston of New York was chairman.

On the 24th August, Livingston reported: "Strike out so much of the 4th section as was referred to the committee, and insert, 'The migration and importation of such persons as the several States, now existing, shall think proper to admit, shall not be prohibited by the legislature prior to the year 1800; but a tax or duty may be imposed on such migration or importation, at a rate not exceeding the average of duties laid on imports.' "*

* It must not be inferred from the language here employed, that it was the intention of Livingston's committee to consider slaves as property. In the first Congress, Mr. Madison said, "The collector may mistake, for he would not presume to apply the term goods, wares, merchandise, to any person whatever. But if that general definition of goods, wares, and merchandise is supposed to include African slaves, why may we not particularly enumerate them, and lay the duty pointed out by the Constitution, which, as gentlemen tell us, is no more than five per cent. upon their value." Mr. Sherman said, "The Constitution does not consider these persons as a species of property; it speaks of them as persons, and says, that a tax or duty may be imposed on the importation of them." (Annals of Congress, vol. i, pp. 341, 342.)

But what Mr. Madison said is important in another point of view. If ten dollars, upon the importation of each person, was in truth but five per cent. on the average value of imported negroes, and it was the intention of the Constitution to "tax them at a rate not exceeding the average of duties laid on imports," the inference is very strong that it was the expectation of the framers of the Constitution, that an impost of five per cent. was to be exacted on all merchandise, and this is strengthened by the revenue tariff which Mr. Madison first introduced. It would seem to follow, that the framers of the Constitution did not contemplate the establishment of protective duties.

Mr. Davie, who had been a member of the Federal Convention, thus spoke

"It was finally agreed," says Mr. Madison, "without dissent, to make the clause read 'but a tax or duty may be imposed on such *importation*, not exceeding ten dollars for each person.'"

The determination of the Convention to discriminate between the two classes of persons, embraced in the ninth section, is certain; and it is equally certain, from their being constantly classed together by the committee of detail, as well as by Livingston's committee, that it was intended they should be dealt with alike by the prohibitory legislation of Congress. This is the impartial conclusion to be drawn from the history of the ninth section and the alterations which it underwent in the Convention, as well as from its immediate connection with the Equilibrium in federal numbers, which it was the avowed intention of the Convention to establish between the North and South. Population in a country, with an unoccupied and fertile domain, is national wealth, and national wealth is, in turn, the parent of population. This

---

to this subject in the North Carolina Convention, 23d July, 1788: "The Eastern States had great jealousies on this subject. They insisted that their cows and horses were equally entitled to representation; that the one was property as well as the other. It became our duty on the other hand, to acquire as much weight as possible in the legislation of the Union; and as the Northern States were the more populous in whites, this only could be done by insisting that a certain proportion of our slaves should make a part of *the computed* population. It was attempted to form a rule of representation from a compound ratio of wealth and population; but, on consideration, it was found to be impracticable to determine the comparative value of lands and other property, in so extensive a territory, with any degree of accuracy; *and population alone* was adopted as the only practicable rule or criterion of representation. It was urged by the deputies of the Eastern States, that a representation of two-fifths would be of little utility, and that this representation would be unequal and burdensome; and furthermore, that in time of war, slaves rendered a country more vulnerable, whilst its defence devolved on its free inhabitants. On the other hand, we insisted that, in time of peace, they contributed, by their labor, to the general wealth, as well as other members of the community; *that, as rational beings*, they had a right to representation, and, in some instances, *might be highly useful in war. On these principles, the Eastern States gave the matter up, and consented to the regulation as it has been read.* It is the same rule or principle which was proposed some years ago by Congress, and assented to by twelve States."

great productive power Congress threw into the Northern scale, and confirmed, in the Northern majority, the means of a sectional domination.

Calhoun says, that "it is the negative power—the power of preventing or arresting the action of the government—be it called by what name it may—veto, interposition, nullification, check or balance of power—which, in fact, forms the Constitution. It is the negative power which makes the Constitution, and the positive which makes the government." Then, the positive powers of our system have destroyed its negative powers, and Congress has destroyed the Constitution.

The far-sighted Democrats in Virginia were well persuaded that, through the agency of the new government, the North would manage to monopolize the commerce of Virginia and the rest of the South, and subject that devoted region to a commercial tribute. In this, as in their other gloomy apprehensions, the event has justified the prophecy. The United States Bank, banking on federal capital, was one of the early agencies employed. The funding of the public debt was a great stride in that direction. The great mass of the Revolutionary debt had been bought up by Northern speculators at a heavy discount, who had it, according to the statement of Patrick Henry, "barreled up."* One of the first acts of the new government was to touch, with the wand of the public credit, that lifeless mass. A mighty value was created in the North, which was applied, under its patronage, to manufactures, commerce, agriculture and the mechanic arts. These acts were but links in the long chain of Federal policy, the object of which was to despoil the South, and, with that ill-gotten wealth, enrich the North.

The Romans conquered the world. With the spoils of conquest, they built and adorned their Imperial city, the ruins of which only remain. But not the Romans in so short a time aggregated such wealth in the garden of Italy, as the central

---

* See Mr. Jackson's speech, Annals of Congress, vol. i. pp. 1137, 1138.

power has lavished on the favorite North. Compare Massachusetts now with what she was in 1787. Compare New England, compare the whole North, with what it was in 1787. Then compare Virginia—dilapidated and broken down, her population scattered, her statesmen converted into politicians, engaged in the wild hunt after federal office—with what she then was; and we have before us the fruits of the Constitution, ratified in Richmond, in June, 1788.

When it was proposed to proportion representation according to contribution, the suggestion was discarded. No mode of representation could have been more unjust, or more unequal, whether the standard be regulated by indirect or direct contribution. Wealth arises, in either case, from causes extrinsic to the community, and is often derived from and properly belongs to the very States and communities over which it gives the advantage. The unrestricted trade, which exists among the several States, makes them but members of the same body. New York city reaps the harvest of wealth from the export and import commerce of every State in the Union, and her contribution, and, in consequence, her representation, would have been derived from and founded upon that wealth. "Of all things, this representation, to be measured by contribution, is the most difficult to settle upon principles of equity, in a country which renders its districts members of a whole." It affords, then, no matter of surprise that such a measure of power should have been repudiated.

Whilst the States subsisted under the former Constitution, it might have been a just standard of political power; for the possession of the custom-house enabled each of them to maintain a separate and independent system, and placed them, in this respect, in an independent attitude towards each other—for the custom-house is the great means of restraining commerce, and dictating the channels in which it shall flow.

But after rejecting the proposition to apportion political influence according to contribution, the Convention determined to measure it out according to *population*, but which all agreed was an invariable measure of wealth. In this way they did, by indirection, the very thing which, by a great vote, they had already determined not to do.

The result of the arrangement has been to swell the representative power of the commercial classes of the North, and to increase the preponderance over the South, by the wealth derived from the export and import trade of the South. And the same may be said with respect to the non-commercial States of the West. It has been estimated that not less than *three millions of people* at the North are in this way sustained. This has been the result of the theoretical experiments on the representative basis.

It is not going too far to say, that never was there a more splendid failure in government, never a more wretched conclusion of a grand and ostentatious experiment. Judging the Constitution by its blasting effects, it was the great delusion of the century that gave it birth—it has well nigh ruined the oldest and richest part of the Confederacy—it has pampered with ill-gotten riches the frozen hills and bleak valleys of New England—it has corrupted by the extravagant and lawless expenditures to which it has given birth, the morality of a portion, and will, unless amended or destroyed, gradually undermine that of the whole of the people—it has embittered into deadly hate the animosities between the North and South, a feeling which found its natural expression in the insurrectionary movement of John Brown—it has done all this, because of the vice which its makers introduced in the representation, which, like an error in the first concoction, must be followed by disease, convulsions and finally death itself.

Before I close this part of the subject, I wish to bring prominently before the reader a prophecy of Patrick Henry. He said that the Federal Government, under the inspirations of the North, would tend to assimilate the social institutions of the South to the Northern model, and that it would abolish African slavery in Virginia. George Mason thought that abolition would be brought about through the instrumentality of the taxing power, but Henry said, that, whilst he could not designate the means that would be employed, he was very sure the government would find means to attain that result. We are at no loss at this day to know by what instrumentalities that anticipated result is to be achieved. The first act was to interdict the slave trade, the next by annexation and purchase to extend the Southern frontier over regions where slave labor would be greatly more valuable than in the neglected and impoverished tobacco fields of Virginia. The mercantile principle of supply and demand would very soon draw off the slaves of Maryland and Virginia, at the same time the tide of European emigration would be pressing upon those States from the Northward.

This policy was avowed by a Senator from Pennsylvania, as the one which persuaded him to vote for the annexation of the great cotton and sugar regions of Texas. Here, then, was an avowed conspiracy of the central agent against the domestic institutions of those States, and was a complete realization of the marvellous foresight of Patrick Henry.

PART III.

How it may be Restored.

Union in a body politic is a very equivocal term; true union is such a harmony as makes all the particular parts, as opposite as they may seem to us, concur in the general welfare of society, in the same manner as discords in music contribute to the general melody of sound. Union may prevail in a State full of seeming commotion; or, in other words, there may be an harmony whence results prosperity, which alone is true peace, and may be considered in the same view as different parts of this universe, which are eternally connected by the action of some, and the re-action of others.—GRANDEUR AND DECLENSION OF THE ROMAN EMPIRE.

To propose alterations, belongs only to those who are so happy as to be born with a genius capable of penetrating into the entire Constitution of a State.—SPIRIT OF LAWS.

With this admonition before my eyes, I am not disposed rashly to plunge into the work of reform; since it is as difficult to mend as to make a Constitution. To restore a principle which has been lost from the political frame, would not be a task of such magnitude, and would imply no other reform than in the mere means of attaining an immediate object, and that, experience of defects will enable us to do. So to alter the Constitution, as to give to each of the sections a fixed and absolute negative on the action of the government in all its departments, would be only to do that which the framers of the Constitution thought they had done by their unique construction of the popular basis. Why they did not proceed directly to the attainment of that end, and positively establish an Equilibrium, may excite surprise; but the framers of the Constitution, as we are told by Madison in the Federalist, had adopted, as a fixed and pre-determined point, that federal representation was to be the offspring and result of population.

We are at no loss, after an examination of the Debates in 1787, to ascertain their motive for this ; it was to accommodate the populous States with a proportionate power. It was that departure from the principles of the Articles of Confederation, that so infinitely complicated the work. Had they adopted the idea of a fixed negative between the North and South, they must have abandoned the idea of a proportion between power and population, and that neither the large States of the North, nor the large States of the South, were willing to do. It was impossible, then, with that foregone conclusion, for the Federal Convention to have made a good Constitution for the North and South. But it is manifest, at this day, as it was then manifest to Mr. Madison, that the dividing line of interest was not on the question of magnitude between the States, but upon the question of slavery. It may well excite the surprise of his posterity, being so fully possessed of that truth as he appears to have been, that that great man had not acted on his conviction, and have insisted upon an equal representation of all the States, together with a sectional Equilibrium.

To restore, then, the Lost Principle to the government, it is only necessary for us to profit by the errors of the past, and, avoiding those breakers upon which our ship of State has been wrecked, to rest upon an immutable basis, a balance of power between the North and South.

But a grave question interposes: Would that which was expedient in 1787, be expedient in 1860? The Equilibrium or negative power is, in its nature, a conservative principle; its object and tendency being to preserve the relative condition of parties to the compact of government. Would the South be content with this? In 1787, each section stood upon its natural resources, but that is not the case now. Power, under the present Constitution, has been employed to dignify and enrich the free-soil section, but to degrade and despoil the slave section. It has given to the inhabitants of the sterile and inhospitable North all the advantages of right belonging to the fruitful and pleasant South, and to the South, the disabilities and the embarrassments naturally belonging to the North. To embark anew on an experiment of government with the Northern States, under these altered and disadvantageous circumstances, would be, in the South, the extremest folly.

The experience of the United States, under the present Constitution, and the experience under the former Constitution, places the people of this country in possession of ample stores of political knowledge. It will be necessary in reforming the federal compact to go beyond the mere restoration of the Equilibrium, and place in the power of the States, larger powers of self-development than, under the new Constitution, they have. But, in order to make that a valuable acquisition, the wealth of the federal government must be diminished so as not to operate as an attraction to draw intellectual power from the service of the several States; and this will operate as a purification of, and will impart a greater stability to the general government.

A great and irresponsible money power leads necessarily to despotism, but to despotism by the vile paths of corruption; that it does lead to despotism we have the authority of Madison, who with open eyes, as his history proves, conferred upon Congress the power of a revenue, for the collection and expenditure of which they are not and never have been responsible to those from whom the money is extracted.

"*At one period of the Congressional history they had power to trample on the States.* When they had that fund of paper money in their hands, and could carry on all their measures without any dependence on the States, was there any disposition to debase the State governments?"

The necessary reforms would lead to a simple reiteration of the Articles of Confederation, amended in those particulars in which Henry, and Grayson, and Jefferson admitted they needed reform, with the addition, I conceive, of a sectional

Equilibrium, which none of them, so far as I can discover, appear to have contemplated.

Of the Articles of Confederation, Jefferson thus expressed himself: "With all the imperfections of our present government, it is, without comparison, the best existing or the best that ever did exist." The sentiment of Jefferson was the almost unanimous opinion in the United States at the time when that sentiment was uttered. It was not until a later period that the faults of that system were exaggerated, or its admirable perfections denied. At the time of the meeting of the Convention at Annapolis, all parties agreed that the commercial jurisdiction of the federal government ought to be enlarged, but that that power, as we have seen from the letter of Washington, must be placed under safeguards against abuse. The re-organization of the departments of the government was necessary for the dispatch of business, but those defects the Congress had in part supplied, by the establishment of executive bureaus. The condition of the taxing power, under the Articles of Confederation, was one of the most important particulars in which that Constitution differed from the present Constitution. By the former arrangement the custom house was left in the possession of the States, and consequently the revenue from customs went into the State treasury, out of which, for the most part, the federal quota was paid. As we have seen, the proposition to endow Congress with an enlarged commercial jurisdiction, did not imply a surrender of the custom house to federal authority, the Congress being used as a mere organ for negotiating a commercial league among the States. No inconvenience had ever resulted from the possession of the custom house by the States, so long as the States employed it only as a means of collecting revenue from imports. The revenue standard, as Grayson tells us, had been ascertained. None could afford to fall below that standard, nor were any inclined to rise above it, until the State legislatures embarked on the fatal policy of retaliating on European commerce the burden imposed on their own, without first having negotiated among themselves, and settled a rate of discriminination to be observed by all.

The possession of the custom house by the State government necessitates a free trade policy, and that would be one of its most precious fruits. It would compel the States to be just in their domestic policy, and not by plundering one class to enrich another. The failure of the States to comply with their federal obligations, was referable wholly to inability; the country having emerged from a long and exhausting war, in a condition of feebleness and poverty, accompanied by the pressure of public and private debt. It was under those disabling circumstances that the old Constitution was tried, circumstances which would never recur. And yet, notwithstanding those adverse events, it was pronounced by the sages of the land the best Constitution for a republican community that the world had ever seen.

Never were a people so devotedly attached to a political system as were the people of Virginia to the Articles of Confederation. It was a commodious and elegant structure which they sought to repair, but which rash innovators destroyed instead, and erected this mighty despotism in its place. I have quoted Jefferson's opinion of the old Constitution, I will now quote his opinion of the new: "I confess there are things in it which stagger all my dispositions to subscribe to what such an assembly has proposed. Their President seems a bad edition of a Polish king. * * Indeed, I think, all the good of this new Constitution might have been couched in three or four articles to be added to the old and venerable fabric." On another occasion he says: "Our Convention has been too much impressed by the insurrection in Massachusetts, and on the spur of the moment they are setting up a kite to keep the hen yard in order." And he strenuously demanded a new Convention.

It was very evident, from the sectional tendencies in the Congress of the Confederation, and the sectional struggles which already had thence ensued, that the North and South would not have been able to have lived long under any government which did not, in the first place, equalize power between them, and rest it upon an immovable basis.

A proposition from a highly intelligent and influential source, has been recently made, that the federal Constitution should be so amended as to arm the South with a negative power in the Senate, leaving the other department of the legislature and the Executive department to remain subject to the dominion of the Northern majority. The error, as I esteem it, of the proposed amendment is, that it stops short of the full object of a negative power; for the South is as well, or better, entitled to claim an Equilibrium in the remaining branch of the Legislature and in the College of Electors, than in the Senate alone. If the principle be good, why not apply it to every object that falls within the scope of that principle?

The history of the Roman Republic is instructive in this regard. The plebeian class abandoned Rome, until the aristocratic order consented to arm them with the Tribunitian power, which, being a check upon the action of the Senate, it was hoped would quiet the agitations which convulsed the city and heal those discords which threatened its destruction. But that hope was disappointed, for the reign of faction continued. The healing principle of the veto had been but partially developed, and it was only in its full development that Rome could recover tranquility, and her political institutions be accomodated to the necessities of her condition. The plebeian order claimed a full participation in government. They claimed an equal share of the consular and priestly powers, and ultimately the right of intermarriage with their insolent patrician neighbors. Civil dissensions continued to distract the State until those concessions were made. The reign of order was the immediate offspring of those changes in the Roman constitution, and Roman power soon began to threaten the world. So it happened most naturally that external war was the product of internal peace.

The North and South are two nations forming a government, and it is the dictate of policy as well as of natural justice, irrespective of wealth and populousness, that each should be armed with the protecting power of the Equilibrium.

But if the North, drunk with insolence, will not consent to a restoration of the Equilibrium, and to such other amendments as experience has proved to be necessary, the South has only to withdraw from the violated league and destroy the government growing out of it. "A breach of the fundamental principles of the compact," said Mr. Madison, whilst this very Constitution was on the anvil, "by a part of the society, would certainly absolve the other part from their obligations to it,"—and much more so, if the history of that compact is an unbroken chain of usurpations.

Not because the slave section, constituting a large and powerful empire, would not be able to maintain a separate existence and become renowned among the nations of the earth, but because there would be too much homogeneousness pervading its social and political elements, that it would be well to offer to the free-soil States of the west to form a new federal union. Everything would invite those parties to such a compact. The west is a great region lying contiguous to the slave section, but without a sea front or an independent outlet to the sea. The slave section then might become the merchant for conducting the foreign exchanges of the west. As already intimated, the very antagonism between, and contrary tendency of the institutions of the two countries, under a well made government, would impart to it a greater stability. Each of these parties is in about the same stage of development—neither are manufacturing, both agricultural, and one is eminently qualified from geographical position for an extended foreign trade. Deep and navigable streams which almost deserve, as they have received, the name of inland seas, bind them closely together, and numerous artificial channels of communication multiply the means of internal trade. But if the North be hopelessly corrupted by abolitionism, in the west a strong conserva-

15

tive feeling survives, which, with encouragement, would rise to the ascendant. Under the benign influence of a government established on the principle of equality, a brotherhood would soon be re-established, and the embers of the old feud would grow cold.

By the Constitution of the Helvetic Confederacy, religious subjects are not allowed to be acted on, or even discussed by the Diet, and notwithstanding that some of the Cantons which compose it were Catholic and others Protestant, that association retained its integrity unimpaired throughout the religious wars which, for so long a period desolated Europe. Kingdoms were plunged in civil strife; empires were torn asunder, and old monarchies uprooted; but amid all vicissitudes, the Republic of the Alps, cemented by that harmonizing negative, stood firm, and exists at this day in pristine vigor to protect the independence and defend the liberty of those brave and politic mountaineers.*

If a similar principle, under some modification, had been introduced into our federative system, there cannot be a doubt that it would have expelled from the federal theatre, every question calculated to disturb the relations of the sections which compose the Union.

If it be true that feebleness in the federal agent was about to destroy, in 1787, the confederacy of the States, there can be no sort of doubt that the excessive power conferred upon it by the present Constitution, is about to destroy the union between the North and South. The manifestations of the present day establish the truth of this proposition. A speedy and radical reform of that Constitution, which by fraudulent devices, in 1788, was forced on the people of Virginia, can alone save the government from destruction. Reform is the parent of conservatism; but the neglect of it, of revolution.

* It is a remarkable fact that in the discussions which the Confederacy of Switzerland underwent, in the Federal as well as in the Virginia Convention, that this cardinal point of the Constitution was not commented on. Mr. Ranke, in his History of the Popes, takes notice of it as a fundamental provision.

This is the lesson of history, and if the people of the United States would, indeed, preserve and extend the political union among their republican communites, they must, by prompt and energetic action, reform the government which creates it.

In this grand movement, Virginia, as well from the deep wrongs which she has sustained, as from other circumstances, is entitled to lead. With a powerful military organization, and fortified by Southern unity, she may yet play a great and useful part on the theatre of American affairs.

"Methinks I see in my mind a noble and puissant Nation arousing herself like a strong man after sleep, and shaking her invincible locks; methinks I see her as an Eagle mewing her mighty youth, and kindling her undazzled eyes, at the full mid-day beam; purging and unscaling her long-abused sight at the fountain itself of heavenly radiance; while the whole noise of timorous and flocking birds with those also that love the twilight, flutter about, amazed at what she means, and in their envious gabble would prognosticate a year of Sects and Schisms."*

---

* Areopagitica.

APPENDIX I.

Extract from the Journal of the House of Delegates of Virginia, Thursday, October 30, 1788.

"The House, then, according to the order of the day, resolved itself into a committee of the whole House on the state of the Commonwealth; and, after some time spent therein, Mr. Speaker resumed the Chair, and Mr. Briggs reported, that the committee had, according to order, again had the state of the Commonwealth under their consideration, and had come to several resolutions thereupon, which he read in his place, and afterwards delivered in at the clerk's table, where the same were again read, and are as followeth :

"Whereas, the convention of delegates of the people of this Commonwealth, did ratify a Constitution or form of government for the United States, referred to them for their consideration, and did also declare that sundry amendments to exceptionable parts of the same ought to be adopted; and whereas, the subject matter of the amendments agreed to by the said Convention involves all the great essential and inalienable rights, liberties and privileges of freemen; many of which, if not cancelled, are rendered insecure under the said Constitution, until the same shall be altered and amended;

"*Resolved, That it is the opinion of this committee*, that for quieting the minds of the good citizens of this Commonwealth, and securing their dearest rights and liberties, and preventing those disorders which must arise under a government *not founded in the confidence of the people*, application be made to the Congress of the United States, so soon as they shall assemble under the said Constitution, *to call a Conven-*

tion for proposing amendments to the same, according to the mode therein directed.

"*Resolved, That it is the opinion of this Committee,* that a committee ought to be appointed to draw up and report to this House, a proper instrument of writing, expressing the sense of the General Assembly, and pointing out the reason which induced them to urge their application thus early for calling the aforesaid Convention of the States.

"*Resolved, That it is the opinion of this Committee,* that the said committee ought to be instructed to prepare the draft of a letter in answer to one received from His Excellency, George Clinton, Esq., President of the Convention of New York, and a circular letter on the aforesaid subject of the other States in the Union, expressive of the wish of the General Assembly of this Commonwealth, that they may join in an application to the new Congress to appoint a Convention of the States so soon as the Congress shall assemble under the new Constitution.

"And the said resolutions being severally again read, a motion was made, and the question being put, to amend the same by striking out from the word "whereas," in the first line, to the end, and inserting, in lieu thereof, the following words:

"Whereas, 'the delegates appointed to represent the good people of this Commonwealth in the late Convention, held in the month of June last, did, by their act of the 25th of the said month, assent to and ratify the Constitution recommended, on the 17th day of September, 1787, by the Federal Convention, for the government of the United States, declaring themselves, with a solemn appeal to the Searcher of Hearts for the purity of their intentions, under the conviction, 'that whatsoever imperfections might exist in the Constitution, ought rather to be examined in the mode prescribed therein, than to bring the Union into danger by a delay, with a hope of obtaining amendments, previous to the ratification;' and whereas, in pursuance of the said declaration, the same Convention did, by their subsequent act of the 27th of June aforesaid, agree to such amendments to the said Constitution of government for the United States, as were by them deemed necessary to be recommended to the consideratien of the Congress which shall first assemble under the said Constitution, to be acted upon according to the mode prescribed in the fifth article thereof; at the same time enjoining it upon their representatives in Congress to exert all their influence, and use all reasonable and legal methods to obtain a ratification of the foregoing alterations and provisions in the manner provided by the fifth article of the said Constitution, and in all Congressional laws to be passed in the meantime, to conform to the spirit of those amendments as far as the Constitution would admit.'

"*Resolved, therefore, That it is the opinion of this Committee*, that an application ought to be made in the name and on the behalf of the legislature of this Commonwealth to the Congress of the United States, so soon as they shall assemble under the said Constitution, to pass an act, recommending to the legislatures of the several States, the ratification of the Bill of Rights, and of certain articles of amendment proposed by the Convention of this State for the adoption of the United States, and that until the said act shall be ratified, in pursuance of the fifth article of the said Constitution of government of the United States, Congress do conform their ordinances to the true spirit of the said Bill of Rights and Articles of Amendment.

"*Resolved, That it is the opinion of this Committee*, that the Executive ought to be instructed to transmit a copy of the foregoing resolution to the Congress of the United States so soon as they shall assemble, and to the legislative and executive authorities of each State in the Union.

"It passed in the negative.

	"Ayes 39	Nays 85
		39
Majority		46

"The ayes and noes being called for by Mr. Bland, seconded by Mr. Turberville—

"The names of those who voted in the affirmative are: Francis Walker, Zachariah Johnson, John Tate, Joseph Swearingen, Martin McFerran, Lawr. Battaile, Roger West, David Stuart, John Shearman Woodcock, Thomas Smith, Geo. Clendennin, Daniel Fisher, Hezekiah Davison, Wm. Heath, Dan'l Brodhead, Larkin Smith, Wm. Thornton, Daniel Fitzhugh, Bernard Moore, Thos. Pinkard, Levin Powell, Richard Bland Lee, Wm. Overton Callis, Richard Morris, James Knox, Sam'l Taylor, Francis Corbin, Ralph Wormley, Thomas Laidley, Willis Wilson, Hardin Burnley, Jonathan Parsons, John Elliott, George Lee Turberville, Francis Kertley, Geo. Baxter, William Stuart, James Wilkinson, and John Allen.

"The names of those who voted in the negative are: Jabez Pitt, Edmund Custis, Davis Booker, Peter Randolph, William Cabell, Samuel Jordan Cabell, John Trigg, Thomas Leftwich, James Barnett, Henry Lee, Notlay Conn, Binns Jones, Andrew Meade, Thomas Anderson, John Clarke, John Hunter, Anthony New, Thomas Bedford, John B. Scott, Henry Southall, Benjamin Harrison, Matthew Cheatham, George Markham, French Strother, John Early, George Pegram, Robert Bolling Jr., George Booker, James Upshaw, John McDowell, James Trotter, Elias Edmonds, John Thompson, William Payne, Joel Early, Joshua Rentfro, John Guerrant, Batt Peterson, Thomas Watkins, Thomas Macon, John Garland, Miles Selden, Nathaniel Wilkinson, Thomas Cooper, Abraham Penn, John Green Clay, Thomas Kennedy, Alexander Robinson, Richard Kennon, Lewis Burwell, Daniel Trigg, John Dandridge, William McClung, Henry Guy, William Nutt, Abraham Beacham, Benjamin Lankford, Patrick Henry, Tarlton Woodson, Theoderick Bland, Cuthbert Bullitt, William Grayson, Thomas Kemp, William McKee, Charles Campbell, Andrew Cowen, Thomas Carter, James Monroe, John Dawson, Lemuel Cocke, John Howell Briggs, Thomas Edmunds, Thomas

West, John S. Lanhorne, Samuel Edmiston, John Lowry, Richard Lee and Robert Shield.

"And then the main question being put, that the House do agree with the committee of the whole House, in the said resolutions;

"It was resolved in the affirmative.

"*Ordered*, That a committee be appointed pursuant to the said resolutions; and that Messrs. Briggs, Henry, Benjamin Harrison, Grayson, Bullitt, William Cabell, Selden, Monroe, Bland, Dawson, Strother, John B. Scott and Roane be of the said committee."

Here is revealed a most singular and instructive fact, in connection with ratification in Virginia, and discloses the true temper of the popular mind in reference to that momentous event. It will be perceived, by an inspection of the foregoing extract of the Journal, that the Federalists and Democrats divided by a distinct line, the latter calling for another Convention to make another Constitution, but the former proposing to preserve it, and yet cure its admitted defects by amendments. The majority in favor of setting aside the new government, before even it was installed, was, notwithstanding the restricted suffrage, and the partial representation which prevailed, as great as *forty-six*.

Jefferson wrote to Short, that the Assembly was possessed "*by a vast majority of anti-Federalists*, and that Henry was supreme." In respect to the party line, he says: "*The friends of the new government will oppose the method of amendment by a federal convention, which would subject the whole instrument to change, and they will support the other method, which admits Congress, by a vote of two-thirds, to submit specific changes to the Assemblies, three-fourths of whom must concur, to establish them.*"

Are we to measure the popularity of the Constitution by this vote? What interpretation shall be put upon it? The members which composed the popular branch of the legislature n '88 had been elected in the previous April, a month after the members of the Convention had been chosen. They must have been selected with reference to their opinions about the new Constitution, for that was the absorbing topic. If we judge, then, the politics of the members of the Convention, as they were supposed to be at the time of the election, by the politics of the popular branch of the legislature, the list of those who changed sides in the Convention, must be greatly enlarged.

But if we adhere to the idea that parties in the Convention were more nearly balanced, and that the defection of Randolph and "the few" who were influenced by him cast the scale in favor of the Federalists, the proceedings in the legislature are nevertheless significant of the disposition of the people.

The legislature held a short session, beginning the 23d of June, two days before the Convention adjourned, and after transacting business of an ordinary character, the members "hurried home," as we are told, "to gather in their harvests." But that short visit to their constituents appears to have instilled into the minds of a great majority of them a most determined opposition to the Constitution, which had just been accepted by the Convention.

The legislature convened again in the month of October, at which time the proceedings above quoted transpired. It will be observed, by comparing the votes given on the two occasions that several members who had voted for ratification, now gave their votes for calling a Convention to make another Constitution, and for undoing the work which they had but just assisted to accomplish. The means which had been adopted to stifle their voice in the Convention created, no doubt, great indignation in the particular constituencies which had been misrepresented, and produced a strong general revulsion against the new government. I have but little doubt, owing to the operation of this cause, that the enemies of the Constitution had been multiplied, and that that which was unpopular in spring had become odious in autumn.

APPENDIX II.

I insert here the counties represented in the Convention, together with the names of the delegates from each county, taken from a printed copy of the Journal of the Convention, to be found in the State library:

DELEGATES

Returned to serve in Convention, March, 1788.

COUNTIES.	DELEGATES.
Accomack,	Edmund Custis,* *George Parker.*
Albemarle,	George Nicholas, Wilson Nicholas.
Amelia,	John Pride,* Edmund Booker.*
Amherst,	William Cabell,* Samuel Jordan Cabell.*
Augusta,	Zachariah Johnston, Archibald Stuart.
Bedford,	John Trigg,* Charles Clay.*
Berkeley,	William Dark, Adam Stephen.
Botetourt,	William Fleming, Martin McFerran.
Bourbon,	Henry Lee,* *Notley Conn.*†
Brunswick,	John Jones,* Binns Jones.*
Buckingham,	Charles Patteson,* David Bell.*
Campbell,	Robert Alexander,* Edmund Winston.*

† Notley Conn, one of the delegates from Bourbon, I do not find to have voted on the Constitution; yet he was a Democrat, judging his politics by those of his colleague. He may have *dodged* in June, but he stood out in October for a new Convention. Nor do I find any trace whatever of Thomas Pierce's vote. If, like Conn, he was a Democrat, who, if present, would have voted against ratification, the majority for ratification, on the test vote, would have been reduced to six votes—to *three* delegates.

COUNTIES.	DELEGATES.
Caroline,	Hon. Edmund Pendleton, James Taylor.
Charlotte,	Thomas Read,* *Hon. Paul Carrington.*
Charles City,	Benjamin Harrison,* John Tyler.*
Chesterfield,	David Patteson,* Stephen Pankey, jun.*
Cumberland,	Joseph Michaux,* Thomas H. Drew.*
Culpeper,	French Strother,* Joel Early.*
Dinwiddie,	Joseph Jones,* William Watkins.*
Elizabeth City,	Miles King, Worlich Westwood.
Essex,	James Upshaw,* Meriwether Smith.*
Fairfax,	David Stuart, Charles Simms.
Fayette,	*Humphrey Marshall,* John Fowler.*
Fauquier,	Martin Pickett, Humphrey Brooke.
Fluvanna,	Samuel Richardson,* Joseph Haden.*
Frederick,	John S. Woodcock, Alexander White.
Franklin,	John Early,* Thomas Arthurs.*
Gloucester,	Warner Lewis, Thomas Smith.
Goochland,	John Guerrant,* William Sampson.*
Greenbrier,	George Clendinen, John Stuart.
Greenesville,	William Mason, Daniel Fisher.
Halifax,	Isaac Coles,* George Carrington.*
Hampshire,	Andrew Woodrow, Ralph Humphreys.
Hanover,	Parke Goodall,* John Carter Littlepage.*
Harrison,	George Jackson, John Prunty.
Hardy,	Isaac Vanmiter, Abel Seymour.
Henrico,	*His Exc'y Gov. Randolph,* John Marshall.
Henry,	Thomas Cooper,* John Marr.*
Isle of Wight,	Thomas Pierce, James Johnson.
James City,	Nathaniel Burwell, Robert Andrews.
Jefferson,	Robert Breckenridge, Rice Bullock.
King and Queen,	*William Fleet,* Thomas Roane.*
King George,	Burdet Ashton, William Thornton.
King William,	Holt Richeson,* Benjamin Temple.*
Lancaster,	James Gordon, Henry Towles.
Loudoun,	Stephens T. Mason,* *Levin Powell.*
Louisa,	*William Overton Callis,* William White.*
Lunenburg,	Jonathan Patteson,* Christopher Robertson.*
Lincoln,	John Logan,* Henry Pawling.*

COUNTIES.	DELEGATES.
Madison,	John Miller,* Green Clay.*
Mecklenburg,	Samuel Hopkins,* Richard Kennon.*
Mercer,	Thomas Allen,* Alexander Robertson.*
Monongalia,	John Evans,* *William McClerry.*
Middlesex,	Ralph Wormley, Jr., Francis Corbin.
Montgomery,	Walter Crocket,* Abraham Trigg.*
Nansemond,	Willis Riddick, Solomon Shepherd.
New Kent,	William Clayton, Burwell Bassett.
Nelson,	Matthew Walton,* John Steele.*
Norfolk,	James Webb, James Taylor.
Northampton,	John Stringer, Littleton Eyre.
Northumberland,	Walter Jones, Thomas Gaskins.
Ohio,	Archibald Woods, Ebenezer Zane.
Orange,	James Madison, Jr., James Gordon.
Pittsylvania,	Robert Williams,* John Wilson.*
Powhatan,	*William Ronald,* Thomas Turpin, Jr.*
Prince Edward,	Patrick Henry,* Robert Lawson.*
Prince George,	Theodrick Bland,* Edmund Ruffin.*
Prince William,	William Grayson,* Cuthbert Bullitt.*
Princess Ann,	Anthony Walke, Thomas Walke.
Randolph,	Benjamin Wilson, John Wilson.
Richmond,	Walker Tomlin, William Peachy.
Rockbridge,	William McKee, Andrew Moore.
Rockingham,	Thomas Lewis, Gabriel Jones.
Russell,	Thomas Carter,* Henry Dickenson.*
Shenandoah,	Jacob Rinker, John Williams.
Southampton,	Benjamin Blount, Samuel Kello.
Spottsylvania,	James Monroe,* John Dawson.*
Stafford,	George Mason,* Andrew Buchanan.*
Surry,	John Hartwell Cocke, John Allen.
Sussex,	John Howell Briggs,* Thomas Edmunds.*
Warwick,	*Cole Diggs,* Richard Cary.*
Washington,	Samuel Edmison,* James Montgomery.*
Westmoreland,	Henry Lee, Bushrod Washington.
York,	Hon. John Blair, Hon. George Wythe.
Williamsburg,	James Innes.
Norfolk Borough,	Thomas Mathews.

In the above list, the Democrats who stood firm are designated by an asterisk (*), and those Democrats who are believed to have voted with the Federalists are in *italics*. I have ascertained them, I think, with tolerable certainty, by the following process: It is not pretended, I repeat, that any one of the Federalists voted with the Democrats; but it is positively stated by Bushrod Washington, who appears to have been very active on the occasion, that the hope of ratification rested upon conversions to be made from the Democrats. It results, from this test, where a delegate from any county voted with the Opposition, that the politics of that county partook of that complexion, and that where his co-delegate sided with the Federalists on the test vote, that he did so contrary to the declared wishes of his constituents. This test, it is true, may not tell the whole truth, for it may have chanced that the entire delegation from a county may have gone over to the Federalists.

APPENDIX III.

RATIFICATION OF THE CONSTITUTION.

From the Journal of the Convention of Virginia, held in Richmond, on the first Monday in June, 1788.

WEDNESDAY, JUNE 25, 1788.—The Convention, according to the order of the day, resolved itself into a committee of the whole Convention, to take into farther consideration the proposed Constitution of Government for the United States; and after some time spent therein, Mr. President resumed the chair, and Mr. Mathews reported, that the committee had, according to order, again had the said proposed Constitution under their consideration, and had gone through the same, and come to several resolutions thereupon, which he read in his place, and afterwards delivered in at the clerk's table, where the same were again read, and are as followeth:

Whereas, the powers granted under the proposed Constitution are the gift of the people, and every power, not granted thereby, remains with them, and at their will: No right, therefore, of any denomination can be cancelled, abridged, restrained or modified by the Congress, by the Senate, or House of Representatives, acting in any capacity; by the President, or any department, or officer of the United States, except in those instances in which power is given by the Constitution for those purposes: and among other essential rights, liberty of conscience and of the press cannot be cancelled, abridged, restrained or modified by any authority of the United States.

And whereas, any imperfections which may exist in the said Constitution ought rather to be examined in the mode prescribed therein for obtaining amendments, than by a delay, with a hope of obtaining previous amendments, to bring the Union into danger:

Resolved, that it is the opinion of this committee, That the said Constitution be ratified.

But in order to relieve the apprehension of those who may be solicitous for amendments,

Resolved, that it is the opinion of this committee, That whatsoever amendments may be deemed necessary, be recommended to the consideration of the Congress, which shall first assemble under the said Constitution, to be acted upon according to the mode prescribed in the fifth article thereof.

The first resolution being read a second time, a motion was made, and the question being put to amend the same, by substituting, in lieu of the said resolution and its preamble, the following resolution:

"*Resolved,* That previous to the ratification of the new Constitution of Government, recommended by the late Federal Convention, a Declaration of Rights, asserting and securing from encroachment the great privileges of Civil and Religious Liberty, and the inalienable rights of the PEOPLE, together with amendments to the most exceptionable parts of the said Constitution of Government, ought to be referred by this Convention to the other States in the American Confederacy for their consideration."

It passed in the negative—ayes, 80; noes, 88.

On motion of Mr. Patrick Henry, seconded by Mr. Theoderick Bland, the ayes and noes on the said question were taken, as followeth:

Ayes—Messrs. Edmund Custis, Jno. Pride, Edmund Booker, William Cabell, Samuel Jordan Cabell, John Trigg, Charles Clay, Henry Lee (of Bourbon), The Honorable John Jones,

Binn Jones, Charles Patteson, David Bell, Robert Alexander, Edmund Winston, Thomas Read, Benjamin Harrison, The Honorable John Tyler, David Patteson, Stephen Pankey, Jr., Joseph Michaux, Thomas H. Drew, French Strother, Joel Early, Joseph Jones, William Watkins, Meriwether Smith, James Upshaw, John Fowler, Samuel Richardson, Joseph Haden, John Early, Thomas Arthurs, John Guerrant, William Sampson, Isaac Coles, George Carrington, Parke Goodall, John Carter Littlepage, Thomas Cooper, John Marr, Thomas Roane, Holt Richeson, Benjamin Temple, Stephens Thompson Mason, William White, Jonathan Patterson, Christopher Robertson, John Logan, Henry Pawling, John Miller, Green Clay, Samuel Hopkins, Richard Kennon, Thomas Allen, Alexander Robertson, John Evans, Walter Crocket, Abraham Trigg, Matthew Walton, John Steele, Robert Williams, John Wilson (of Pittsylvania), Thomas Turpin, Patrick Henry, Robert Lawson, Edmund Ruffin, Theoderick Bland, William Grayson, Cuthbert Bullitt, Thomas Carter, Henry Dickenson, James Monroe, John Dawson, George Mason, Andrew Buchanan, John Howell Briggs, Thos. Edmunds, The Honorable Richard Cary, Samuel Edmison and James Montgomery—80.

Noes—The Honorable Edmund Pendleton, Esq., President, Messrs. George Parker, George Nicholas, Wilson Nicholas, Zachariah Johnson, Archibald Stuart, William Dark, Adam Stephen, Martin McFerran, William Fleming, James Taylor (of Caroline), The Honorable Paul Carrington, Miles King, Worlich Westwood, David Stuart, Charles Simms, Humphrey Marshall, Martin Pickett, Humphrey Brooke, John S. Woodcock, Alexander White, Warner Lewis, Thomas Smith, George Clendinen, John Stuart, William Mason, Daniel Fisher, Andrew Woodrow, Ralph Humphreys, George Jackson, John Prunty, Isaac Vanmiter, Abel Seymour, His Excellency Governor Randolph, John Marshall, Nathaniel Burwell, Robert Andrews, James Johnson, Robert Breckenridge, Rice Bullock, William Fleet, Burdet Ashton, William Thornton, James Gordon (of Lancaster), Henry Towles, Levin Powell, Wm. Overton Callis,

Ralph Wormeley, Jr., Francis Corbin, William McClerry, Willis Riddick, Solomon Sheppard, William Clayton, Burwell Bassett, Jas. Webb, Jas. Taylor (of Norfolk), John Stringer, Littleton Eyre, Walter Jones, Thomas Gaskins, Archibald Woods, Ebenezer Zane, The Honorable James Madison, James Gordon (of Orange), William Ronald, Anthony Walke, Thomas Walke, Benjamin Wilson, John Wilson (of Randolph), Walker Tomlin, William Peachey, William McKee, Andrew Moore, Thomas Lewis, Gabriel Jones, Jacob Rinker, John Williams, Benjamin Blunt, Samuel Kello, John Hartwell Cocke, John Allen, Cole Digges, Henry Lee (of Westmoreland), Bushrod Washington, The Honorable John Blair, The Honorable George Wythe, James Innes and Thomas Mathews—88.

And then the main question being put, that the Convention do agree with the committee in the said first resolution,

It was resolved in the affirmative—ayes, 89; noes, 79.

On motion of Mr. George Mason, seconded by Mr. Patrick Henry, the ayes and noes on the said main question were taken as followeth:

Ayes—The Honorable Edmund Pendleton, Esq., President, Messrs. George Parker, George Nicholas, Wilson Nicholas, Zachariah Johnson, Archibald Stuart, William Dark, Adam Stephen, Martin McFerran, William Fleming, James Taylor (of Caroline), The Honorable Paul Carrington, David Patteson, Miles King, Worlich Westwood, David Stuart, Charles Simms, Humphrey Marshall, Humphrey Brooke, Martin Pickett, John Shearman Woodcock, Alexander White, Warner Lewis, Thomas Smith, George Clendinen, Jno. Stuart, William Mason, Daniel Fisher, Andrew Woodrow, Ralph Humphreys, George Jackson, John Prunty, Isaac Vanmiter, Abel Seymour, His Excellency Governor Randolph, John Marshall, Nathaniel Burwell, Robert Andrews, James Johnson, Robert Breckenridge, Rice Bullock, William Fleet, Burdet Ashton, William Thornton, James Gordon (of Lancaster), Henry Towles, Levin Powell, William Overton Callis, Ralph Wormeley, Jr., Francis Corbin, William McClerry, Willis Riddick, Solomon Sheppard,

William Clayton, Burwell Bassett, James Webb, James Taylor (of Norfolk), John Stringer, Littleton Eyre, Walter Jones, Thomas Gaskins, Archibald Woods, Ebenezer Zane, The Honorable James Madison, James Gordon (of Orange), William Ronald, Anthony Walke, Thomas Walke, Benjamin Wilson, John Wilson (of Randolph), Walker Tomlin, William Peachey, William McKee, Andrew Moore, Thos. Lewis, Gabriel Jones, Jacob Rinker, John Williams, Benjamin Blunt, Samuel Kello, John Hartwell Cocke, John Allen, Cole Digges, Henry Lee (of Westmoreland), Bushrod Washington, The Honorable John Blair, The Honorable George Wythe, James Innes and Thomas Mathews—89.

Noes—Messrs. Edmund Custis, Jno. Pride, Edmund Booker, William Cabell, Samuel Jordan Cabell, John Trigg, Charles Clay, Henry Lee (of Bourbon), The Honorable John Jones, Binns Jones, Charles Patteson, David Bell, Robert Alexander, Edmund Winston, Thomas Read, Benjamin Harrison, The Honorable John Tyler, Stephen Pankey, Jr., Joseph Michaux, Thomas H. Drew, French Strother, Joel Early, Joseph Jones, William Watkins, Meriwether Smith, James Upshaw, John Fowler, Sam'l Richardson, Joseph Haden, Jno. Early, Thomas Arthurs, Jno. Guerrant, William Sampson, Isaac Coles, George Carrington, Parke Goodall, John Carter Littlepage, Thomas Cooper, John Marr, Thomas Roane, Holt Richeson, Benjamin Temple, Stephens Thompson Mason, William White, Jonathan Patteson, Christopher Robertson, John Logan, Henry Pawling, John Miller, Green Clay, Samuel Hopkins, Richard Kennon, Thomas Allen, Alexander Robertson, John Evans, Walter Crockett, Abraham Trigg, Matthew Walton, John Steele, Robert Williams, John Wilson (of Pittsylvania), Thomas Turpin, Patrick Henry, Robert Lawson, Edmund Ruffin, Theoderick Bland, William Grayson, Cuthbert Bullitt, Thomas Carter, Henry Dickenson, Jas. Monroe, John Dawson, George Mason, Andrew Buchanan, John Howell Briggs, Thomas Edmunds, The Honorable Richard Cary, Samuel Edmison and James Montgomery—79.

The second resolution being then read a second time, a motion was made, and the question being put to amend the same by striking out the preamble thereto,

It was resolved in the affirmative.

And then the main question being put, that the Convention do agree with the committee in the second resolution so amended,

It was resolved in the affirmative.

On motion,

Ordered, That a committee be appointed to prepare and report a form of ratification, pursuant to the first resolution; and that his Excellency Governor Randolph, Messrs. Nicholas, Madison, Marshall and Corbin compose the said committee.

On motion,

Ordered, That a committee be appointed to prepare and report such amendments as shall by them be deemed necessary to be recommended, pursuant to the second resolution; and that the Honorable Geo. Wythe, Messrs. Harrison, Mathews, Henry, His Excellency Governor Randolph, George Mason, Nicholas, Grayson, Madison, Tyler, John Marshall, Monroe, Ronald, Bland, Meriwether Smith, The Honorable Paul Carrington, Innes, Hopkins, The Honorable John Blair and Simms compose the said committee.

His Excellency Governor Randolph reported, from the committee appointed, according to order, a form of ratification, which was read and agreed to by the Convention, in the words following:

Virginia, to wit:

WE, the DELEGATES of the PEOPLE of VIRGINIA, duly elected in pursuance of a recommendation from the General Assembly, and now met in Convention, having fully and freely investigated and discussed the proceedings of the Federal Convention, and being prepared, as well as the most mature deliberation hath enabled us, to decide thereon, DO, in the name and in behalf of the PEOPLE of VIRGINIA, declare and make known, that the powers granted under the Constitution, being derived from the PEOPLE of the UNITED STATES, may be resumed by them whensoever the same shall be perverted to their injury or oppression, and that every power, not granted thereby, remains with them, and at their will: that, therefore, no right, of any denomination, can be cancelled, abridged, restrained, or modified, by the Congress, by the Senate or House of Representatives, acting in any capacity; by the President, or any department, or officer of the UNITED STATES, except in those instances in which power is given by the CONSTITUTION, for those purposes; and that, among other essential rights, the liberty of conscience, and of the press, cannot be cancelled, abridged, restrained, or modified, by any authority of the UNITED STATES.

With these impressions, with a solemn appeal to the Searcher of Hearts for the purity of our intentions, and under the conviction, that whatsoever imperfections may exist in the Constitution, ought rather to be examined in the mode prescribed therein, than to bring the Union into danger by a delay, with a hope of obtaining amendments, previous to the ratification:

WE, the said DELEGATES, in the name and in behalf of the PEOPLE of VIRGINIA, DO, by these presents, ASSENT TO and RATIFY the CONSTITUTION, recommended on the seventeenth day of September, one thousand seven hundred and eighty-seven, by the FEDERAL CONVENTION for the Government of the UNITED STATES, hereby announcing to all those whom it may concern, that the said Constitution is binding upon the said People, according to an authenticated copy hereto annexed, in the words following, &c.

THE VIRGINIA AMENDMENTS.

FRIDAY, JUNE 27, 1788.—Another engrossed form of the ratification agreed to on Wednesday last, containing the proposed Constitution of Government, as recommended by the Federal Convention, on the seventeenth day of September, one thousand seven hundred and eighty-seven, being prepared by the Secretary, was read, and signed by the President, in behalf of the Convention.

On motion,

Ordered, That the said ratification be deposited, by the Secretary of this Convention, in the archives of the General Assembly of this State.

Mr. Wythe reported, from the committee appointed, such amendments to the proposed Constitution of Government for the United States, as were by them deemed necessary to be recommended to the consideration of the Congress which shall first assemble under the said Constitution, to be acted upon according to the mode prescribed in the fifth article thereof; and he read the same in his place, and afterwards delivered them in at the clerk's table, where the same were again read, and are as followeth:

That there be a Declaration or Bill of Rights, asserting and securing from encroachment the essential and unalienable rights of the people in some such manner as the following:

1. That there are certain natural rights, of which men, when they form a social compact, cannot deprive or divest their posterity; among which are the enjoyment of life and liberty, with the means of acquiring, possessing and protecting property, and pursuing and obtaining happiness and safety.

2. That all power is naturally vested in, and consequently

derived from, the people; that magistrates, therefore, are their trustees and agents, and at all times amenable to them.

3. That government ought to be instituted for the common benefit, protection and security of the people; and that the doctrine of non-resistance against arbitrary power and oppression is absurd, slavish and destructive to the good and happiness of mankind.

4. That no man, or set of men, are entitled to exclusive or separate public emoluments or privileges from the community, but in consideration of public services; which not being descendible, neither ought the offices of magistrate, legislator, or any other public office to be hereditary.

5. That the legislative, executive and judiciary powers of government should be separate and distinct; and that the members of the two first may be restrained from oppression, by feeling and participating the public burthens, they should, at fixed periods, be reduced to a private station, return into the mass of the people, and the vacancies be supplied by certain and regular elections; in which all or any part of the former members to be eligible or ineligible, as the rules of the Constitution of Government and the laws shall direct.

6. That the elections of representatives in the legislature ought to be free and frequent, and all men, having sufficient evidence of permanent common interest with and attachment to the community, ought to have the right of suffrage; and no aid, charge, tax or fee can be set, rated or levied upon the people, without their own consent, or that of their representatives so elected, nor can they be bound by any law, to which they have not, in like manner, assented for the public good.

7. That all power of suspending laws, or the execution of laws, by any authority, without the consent of the representatives of the people in the legislature, is injurious to their rights, and ought not to be exercised.

8. That in all criminal and capital prosecutions, a man hath

a right to demand the cause and nature of his accusation, to be confronted with the accusers and witnesses, to call for evidence and be allowed counsel in his favor, and to a fair and speedy trial by an impartial jury of his vicinage; without whose unanimous consent he cannot be found guilty, (except in the government of the land and naval forces,) nor can any man be compelled to give evidence against himself.

9. That no freeman ought to be taken, imprisoned or disseized of his freehold, liberties, privileges or franchises, or outlawed or exiled, or in any manner destroyed or deprived of life, liberty or property, but by the law of the land.

10. That every freeman, restrained in his liberty, is entitled to a remedy to inquire into the lawfulness thereof, and to remove the same, if unlawful, and that such remedy ought not to be denied nor delayed.

11. That in controversies respecting property, and in disputes between man and man, the ancient trial by jury is one of the greatest securities to the rights of the people, and ought to remain sacred and inviolable.

12. That every freeman ought to find a certain remedy, by recourse to the laws, for all injuries and wrongs he may receive in his person, property or character. He ought to obtain right and justice freely, without sale; completely, and without denial; promptly, and without delay; and that all establishments or regulations contravening these rights are oppressive and unjust.

13. That excessive bail ought not to be required, nor excessive fines imposed, nor cruel and unusual punishments inflicted.

14. That every freeman has a right to be secure from all unreasonable searches and seizures of his person, his papers and property; all warrants, therefore, to search suspected places, or seize any freeman, his papers or property, without information upon oath (or affirmation of a person religiously scrupulous of taking an oath) of legal and sufficient cause, are

grievous and oppressive; and all general warrants, to search suspected places, or to apprehend any suspected person, without specially naming or describing the place or person, are dangerous, and ought not to be granted.

15. That the people have a right peaceably to assemble together to consult for the common good, or to instruct their representatives; and that every freeman has a right to apply to the legislature for redress of grievances.

16. That the people have a right to freedom of speech, and of writing and publishing their sentiments; that the freedom of the press is one of the greatest bulwarks of liberty, and ought not to be violated.

17. That the people have a right to keep and bear arms; that a well-regulated militia, composed of the body of the people trained to arms, is the proper, natural and safe defence of a free State. That standing armies in time of peace are dangerous to liberty, and, therefore, ought to be avoided, as far as the circumstances and protection of the community will admit; and that, in all cases, the military should be under strict subordination to, and governed by, the civil power.

18. That no soldier in time of peace ought to be quartered in any house without the consent of the owner, and in time of war in such manner only as the laws direct.

19. That any person religiously scrupulous of bearing arms ought to be exempted, upon payment of an equivalent to employ another to bear arms in his stead.

20. That religion, or the duty which we owe to our Creator, and the manner of discharging it, can be directed only by reason and conviction, not by force or violence, and, therefore, all men have an equal, natural and unalienable right to the free exercise of religion, according to the dictates of conscience, and that no particular religious sect or society ought to be favored or established by law in preference to others.

AMENDMENTS TO THE CONSTITUTION.

1. That each State in the Union shall respectively retain every power, jurisdiction and right, which is not by this Constitution delegated to the Congress of the United States, or to the Departments of the Federal Government.

2. That there shall be one Representative for every thirty thousand, according to the enumeration or census mentioned in the Constitution, until the whole number of Representatives amounts to two hundred; after which that number shall be continued or increased, as Congress shall direct, upon the principles fixed in the Constitution, by apportioning the Representatives of each State to some greater number of people, from time to time, as population increases.

3. When the Congress shall lay direct taxes or excises, they shall immediately inform the Executive power of each State, of the quota of such State according to the census herein directed, which is proposed to be thereby raised; and if the Legislature of any State shall pass a law which shall be effectual for raising such quota at the time required by Congress, the taxes and excises laid by Congress shall not be collected in such State.

4. That the members of the Senate and House of Representatives shall be ineligible to, and incapable of holding, any civil office under the authority of the United States, during the time for which they shall respectively be elected.

5. That the Journals of the proceedings of the Senate and House of Representatives shall be published at least once in every year, except such parts thereof relating to treaties, alliances, or military operations, as in their judgment require secrecy.

6. That a regular statement and account of the receipts and expenditures of all public moneys shall be published once in every year.

7. That no commercial treaty shall be ratified without the

concurrence of two-thirds of the whole number of the members of the Senate; and no treaty, ceding, contracting, restraining or suspending the territorial rights or claims of the United States, or any of them, or their, or any of their rights or claims to fishing in the American Seas, or navigating the American Rivers, shall be made but in cases of the most urgent and extreme necessity, nor shall any such treaty be ratified without the concurrence of three-fourths of the whole number of the members of both Houses respectively.

8. That no navigation law, or laws, regulating Commerce, shall be passed without the consent of two-thirds of the members present in both Houses.

9. That no standing army or regular troops shall be raised or kept up in time of peace, without the consent of two-thirds of the members present in both Houses.

10. That no soldier shall be enlisted for any longer term than four years, except in time of war, and then for no longer term than the continuance of the war.

11. That each State respectively shall have the power to provide for organizing, arming and disciplining its own militia, whensoever Congress shall omit or neglect to provide for the same. That the militia shall not be subject to martial law, except when in actual service in time of war, invasion or rebellion; and when not in the actual service of the United States, shall be subject only to such fines, penalties, and punishments, as shall be directed or inflicted by the laws of its own State.

12. That the exclusive power of legislation given to Congress over the Federal Town and its adjacent district, and other places purchased or to be purchased by Congress of any of the States, shall extend only to such regulations as respect the police and good government thereof.

13. That no person shall be capable of being President of the United States for more than eight years in any term of sixteen years.

14. That the Judicial power of the United States shall be

vested in one Supreme Court and in such Courts of Admiralty as Congress may from time to time ordain and establish in any of the different States. The Judicial power shall extend to all cases in law and equity arising under treaties made, or which shall be made, under the authority of the United States; to all cases affecting Ambassadors, other foreign Ministers and Consuls; to all cases of admiralty and maritime jurisdiction; to controversies to which the United States shall be a party; to controversies between two or more States, and between parties claiming lands under the grants of different States. In all cases affecting Ambassadors, other foreign Ministers and Consuls, and those in which a State shall be a party, the Supreme Court shall have original jurisdiction; in all other cases the Supreme Court shall have appellate jurisdiction, as to matters of law only; except in cases of equity and of admiralty and maritime jurisdiction, in which the Supreme Court shall have appellate jurisdiction both as to law and fact, with such exceptions and under such regulations as the Congress shall make: but the judicial power of the United States shall extend to no case where the cause of action shall have originated before the ratification of this Constitution; except in disputes between States about their territory; disputes between persons claiming lands under the grants of different States, and suits for debts due the United States.

15. That in criminal prosecutions, no man shall be retrained in the exercise of the usual and accustomed right of challenging or excepting to the jury.

16. That Congress shall not alter, modify, or interfere in the times, places, or manner of holding elections for Senators and Representatives, or either of them, except when the Legislature of any State shall neglect, refuse, or be disabled by invasion or rebellion to prescribe the same.

17. That those clauses which declare that Congress shall not exercise certain powers be not interpreted in any manner whatsoever, to extend the powers of Congress; but that they be construed either as making exceptions to the specified

powers of Congress where this shall be the case, or otherwise, as inserted merely for greater caution.

18. That the laws ascertaining the compensation of Senators and Representatives for their services be postponed in their operations until after the election of Representatives immediately succeeding the passing thereof, that excepted, which shall first be passed on the subject.

19. That some tribunal other than the Senate be provided for trying impeachments of Senators.

20. That the salary of a Judge shall not be increased or diminished during his continuance in office, otherwise than by general regulations of salary which may take place on a revision of the subject at stated periods of not less than seven years, to commence from the time such salaries shall be first ascertained by Congress.

And the Convention do, in the name and behalf of the people of this Commonwealth, enjoin it upon their Representatives in Congress, to exert all their influence and use all reasonable and legal methods to obtain a ratification of the foregoing alterations and provisions in the manner provided by the fifth article of the said Constitution; and in all Congressional laws be passed in the mean time, to conform to the spirit of these amendments as far as the said Constitution will admit.

And so much of the said amendments as is contained in the first twenty articles, constituting the Bill of Rights, being again read:

Resolved, That this Convention doth concur therein.

The other amendments to the said proposed Constitution, contained in twenty-one articles, being then again read, a motion was made, and the question being put, to amend the same by striking out the third article, containing these words:

"When Congress shall lay direct taxes or excises, they shall immediately inform the Executive power of each State, of the quota of such State according to the census herein directed, which is proposed to be thereby raised; and if the Legislature of any State shall pass a law which shall be effectual for raising such quota at the time required by Congress, the taxes and excises laid by Congress, shall not be collected in such State;"

It passed in the negative—ayes, 65; noes, 85.

On motion of Mr. George Nicholas, seconded by Mr. Benjamin Harrison, the ayes and noes on the said question were taken as followeth:

Ayes—Messrs. George Parker, George Nicholas, Wilson Nicholas, Zachariah Johnston, Archibald Stuart, William Dark, Adam Stephen, Martin McFerran, James Taylor (of Caroline), David Stuart, Charles Simms, Humphrey Marshall, Martin Pickett, Humphrey Brooke, John Shearman Woodcock, Alexander White, Warner Lewis, Thomas Smith, John Stuart, Daniel Fisher, Alexander Woodrow, George Jackson, John Prunty, Abel Seymour, His Excellency Governor Randolph, John Marshall, Nathaniel Burwell, Robert Andrews, James Johnson, Rice Bullock, Burdet Ashton, William Thornton, Henry Towles, Levin Powell, William Overton Callis, Ralph Wormeley, Francis Corbin, William McClerry, James Webb, James Taylor (of Norfolk), John Stringer, Littleton Eyre, Walter Jones, Thomas Gaskins, Archibald Woods, The Honorable James Madison, James Gordon (of Orange), William Ronald, Thomas Walke, Benjamin Walke, John Wilson, William Peachey, Andrew Moore, Thomas Lewis, Gabriel Jones, Jacob Rinker, John Williams, Benjamin Blunt, Samuel Kello, John Allen, Cole Digges, Bushrod Washington, The Honorable George Wythe and Thomas Mathews—65.

Noes—The Honorable Edmund Pendleton, Esquire, President, Messrs. Edmund Custis, John Pride, William Cabell, Samuel Jordan Cabell, John Trigg, Charles Clay, William Fleming, Henry Lee (of Bourbon), John Jones, Binns Jones, Charles Patteson, David Bell, Robert Alexander, Edmund Winston, Thomas Read, The Honorable Paul Currington, Benjamin Harrison, The Honorable John Tyler, David Patteson, Stephen Pankey, Jr., Joseph Michaux, French Strother, Joseph Jones, Miles King, Joseph Haden, John Early, Thomas Arthurs, John Guerrant, William Sampson, Isaac Coles, George Carrington, Parke Goodall, John Carter Littlepage, Thomas Cooper, William Fleet, Thomas Roane, Holt Richeson, Benjamin Temple, James Gordon (of Lancaster), Stephens Thompson Mason, William White, Jonathan Patteson, John Logan, Henry Pawling, John Miller, Green Clay, Samuel Hopkins, Richard Kennon, Thomas Allen, Alexander Robertson, Walter Crockett, Abraham Trigg, Solomon Shepherd, William Clayton, Burwell Bassett, Mathew Walton, John Steele, Robert Williams, John Wilson, Thomas Turpin, Patrick Henry, Edmund Ruffin, Theoderick Bland, William Grayson, Cuthbert Bullitt, Walker Tomlin, William McKee, Thomas Carter, Henry Dickenson, James Monroe, John Dawson, George Mason, Andrew Buchanan, John Hartwell Cocke, John Howell Briggs, Thomas Edmunds, The Honorable Richard Cary, Samuel Edmison and James Montgomery—85.

And then the main question being put, that this Convention doth concur with the committee in the said amendments,

It was resolved in the affirmative.

On motion,

Ordered, That the foregoing amendments be fairly engrossed upon parchment, signed by the President of this Convention, and by him transmitted, together with the ratification of the Federal Constitution, to the United States in Congress assembled.

On motion,

Ordered, That a fair engrossed copy of the ratification of the Federal Constitution, with the subsequent amendments this day agreed to, signed by the President, and attested by the Secretary of this Convention, be transmitted by the President in the name of this Convention to the Executive or Legislature of each State in the Union.

Ordered, That the Secretary do cause the Journal of the proceedings of this Convention to be fairly entered in a well-bound book, and after being signed by the President, and attested by the Secretary, that he deposit the same in the archives of the Privy Council or Council of State.

On motion,

Ordered, That the Printer to this Convention do strike, forthwith, fifty copies of the ratification and subsequent amendments of the Federal Constitution, for the use of each county in the Commonwealth.

APPENDIX IV.

Extracts from Speeches of Governor Randolph and Patrick Henry.

On the 4th June, 1788, the Preamble and Art. I. sect. 1 and 2, being under consideration, Governor RANDOLPH said (*Elliot's Debates*, vol. iii. pp. 48, 49):

"Mr. Chairman, had the most enlightened statesman, whom America has yet seen, foretold but a year ago, the crisis which has now called us together, he would have been confronted by the universal testimony of history; for never was it yet known, that in so short a space, by the peaceable working of events, without a war or even the menace of the smallest force, a nation has been brought to agitate a question, an error in the issue of which, may blast their happiness. It is, therefore, to be feared, lest to this trying exigency, the best wisdom should be unequal, and here, (if it were allowable to lament any ordinance of nature) might it be deplored, that in proportion to the magnitude of a subject, is the mind intemperate. Religion, the dearest of all interests, has too often sought proselytes by fire rather than by reason; and politics, the next in rank, is too often nourished by passion, at the expense of the understanding. Pardon me, however, for expecting one exception to this tendency of mankind—from the dignity of this convention, a mutual toleration, and a persuasion that no man has a right to impose his opinion on others. Pardon me too, Sir, if I am particularly sanguine in my expectations from the chair—it well knows what is order, how to command obedience, and that political opinions may be as honest on one side as on the other. Before I press into the body of the argument, I must take the liberty of mentioning the part I have already borne in this great question: but let me not here be misunderstood. I come not to apologize to any individual within these walls, to the convention as a body, or even to my fellow-citizens at large. Having obeyed the impulse of duty, having satisfied my conscience, and I trust, my God, I shall appeal to no other tribunal; no do I come a candidate for popularity: my manner of life has never yet betrayed such a desire. The highest honors and emoluments of this commonwealth, are a poor compensation for the surrender of personal independence. The history of England, from the revolution, and that of Virginia, for more than twenty years past, shew the vanity of a hope, that general favor should ever follow the man, who without partiality or prejudice, praises or disapproves the opinions of friends or of foes: nay, I might enlarge the field, and declare from the great volume of human nature itself, that to be moderate in politics, forbids an ascent to the summit of political fame. But, I come hither regardless of allurements, to continue as I have begun, to repeat my earnest endeavors for a firm energetic government, to enforce my objections to the constitution, and to concur in any practical scheme of amendments; but I never will assent to any scheme that will operate a dissolution of the union, or any measure which may lead to it. This conduct may possibly be upbraided as injurious to my own views; if it be so, it is, at least, the natural offspring of my judgment. I refused to sign, and if the same were to return, again would I refuse. Wholly to adopt or wholly to reject, as proposed by the convention, seemed too hard an alternative to the citizens of America, whose servants we were, and whose pretensions amply to discuss the means of their happiness were undeniable. Even if adopted under the terror of impending anarchy, the government must have been without that safest bulwark, the hearts of the people—and if rejected because the chance for amendments was cut off, the union would have been irredeemably lost. This seems to have been verified by the event in Massachusetts; but our Assembly have removed these inconveniences, by propounding the constitution to our full and free enquiry. When I withheld my subscription, I had not even the glimpse of the genius of America, relative to the principles of the new constitution. Who, arguing from the preceding history of Virginia, could have divined that she was prepared for the important change? In former times indeed, she transcended every colony in professions and practices of loyalty; but she opened a perilous war, under a democracy almost as pure as representation would admit: she supported it under a constitution which subjects all rule, authority and power, to the legislature: every attempt to alter it had been baffled: the increase of congressional power, had always excited an alarm. I therefore would not bind myself to uphold the new constitution, before I had tried it by the true touchstone; especially too, when I foresaw, that even the members of the General Convention, might be instructed by the comments of those who were without doors. But, I had moreover objections to the constitution, the most material of which, too lengthy in detail, I have as yet barely stated to the public, but shall explain when we arrive at the proper points. Amendments were consequently my wish; these were the grounds of my repugnance to subscribe, and were perfectly reconcileable with my unalterable resolution, to be regulated by the spirit of America, if after our best efforts for amendments, they could not be removed. I freely indulge those who may think this declaration too candid, in believing, that I hereby depart from the concealment belonging to the character of a statesman. Their censure would be more reasonable, were it not for an unquestionable fact, that the spirit of America depends upon a combination of circumstances, which no individual can control, and arises not from the prospect of advantages which may be gained by the arts of negotiation, but from deeper and more honest causes.

As with me the only question has ever been, between previous and subsequent amendments, so will I express my apprehensions, that the postponement of this convention, to so late a day, has extinguished the probability of the former without inevitable ruin to the union, and the union is the anchor of our political salvation; and I will assent to the lopping of this limb (meaning his arm) before I assent to the dissolution of the union. I shall not follow the hon. gentleman (Mr. Henry) in his enquiry."

* * * * * *

"In the whole of this business, I have acted in the strictest obedience to the dictates of my conscience, in discharging what I conceive to be my duty to my country. I refused my signature, and if the same reasons operated on my mind, I would still refuse; but as I think that those eight States which have adopted the constitution will not recede, I am a friend to the union."

[As the adoption by *eight States* was admitted by his Excellency to have determined him to cast his vote in favor of Ratification, it becomes important to know the *time when* that event occurred. The following table,* with that view, is inserted. It proves, without doubt, that the distinguished gentleman had but recently come to that resolution, and in this particular confirms the evidence contained in the text:

The Constitution was adopted on the 17th September, 1787, by the Convention appointed in pursuance of the resolution of the Congress of the Confederation, of the 21st February, 1787, and was ratified by the Conventions of the several States, as follows, viz:

By Convention	of	Delaware,	on the	7th December, 1787.
"	"	Pennsylvania,	"	12th December, 1787.
"	"	New Jersey	"	18th December, 1787.
"	"	Georgia,	"	2d January, 1788.

* From "The Constitution of the United States of America, with an Alphabetical Analysis," &c. By W. Hickey.

By Convention of		Connecticut,	on the	9th January,	1788.
"	"	Massachusetts,	"	6th February,	1788.
"	"	Maryland,	"	28th April,	1788.
"	"	South Carolina,	"	23d May,	1788.
"	"	New Hampshire,	"	21st June,	1788.
"	"	Virginia,	"	26th June,	1788.
"	"	New York,	"	26th July,	1788.
"	"	North Carolina,	"	21st November,	1789.
"	"	Rhode Island,	"	29th May,	1790.]

Extract from MR. HENRY'S *Speech in reply to* GOVERNOR RANDOLPH, (*Elliot's Debates*, vol. iii. pp. 124–126.)

"Now, Sir, I say, let us consider, whether the picture given of American affairs ought to drive us from those beloved maxims.

The honorable gentleman, (Governor RANDOLPH) has said, that it is too late in the day for us to reject this new plan. That system which was once execrated by the honorable member, must now be adopted, let its defects be ever so glaring. That honorable member will not accuse me of want of candor, when I cast in my mind what he has given the public,* and compare it to what has happened since. It seems to me very strange and unaccountable, that that which was the object of his execration, should now receive his encomiums. Something extraordinary must have operated so great a change in his opinion. *It is too late in the day!* Gentlemen must excuse me, if they should declare again and again, that it was too late and I should think differently. I never can believe, Sir, that it is too late to save all that is precious. If it be proper, and independently of every external consideration, wisely constructed, let us receive it: but Sir, shall its adoption by eight States induce us to receive it, if it be replete with the

* Alluding to his Excellency's letter on that subject to the Speaker of the House of Delegates.

most dangerous defects? They urge that subsequent amendments are safer than previous amendments, and that they will answer the same ends. At present we have our liberties and privileges in our own hands. Let us not relinquish them. Let us not adopt this system till we see them secure. There is some small possibility, that should we follow the conduct of Massachusetts, amendments might be obtained. There is a small possibility of amending any government; but, Sir, shall we abandon our most inestimable rights, and rest their security on a mere possibility? The gentleman fears the loss of the union. If eight States have ratified it unamended; and we should rashly imitate their precipitate example, do we not thereby disunite from several other States? Shall those who have risked their lives for the sake of union, be at once thrown out of it? If it be amended, every State will accede to it; but by an imprudent adoption in its defective and dangerous state, a schism must inevitably be the consequence: I can never, therefore, consent to hazard our most unalienable rights on an absolute uncertainty. You are told there is no peace, although you fondly flatter yourselves that all is peace—no peace—a general cry and alarm in the country—commerce, riches, and wealth, vanished—citizens going to seek comforts in other parts of the world—laws insulted—many instances of tyrannical legislation. These things, sir, are new to me. He has made the discovery—as to the administration of justice, I believe that failures in commerce, &c., cannot be attributed to it. My age enables me to recollect its progress under the old government. I can justify it by saying, that it continues in the same manner in this State, as it did under the former government. As to other parts of the continent, I refer that to other gentlemen. As to the ability of those who administer it, I believe they would not suffer by a comparison with those who administered it under the royal authority. Where is the cause of complaint if the wealthy go away? Is this, added to the other circumstances, of such enormity, and does it bring such danger over this Commonwealth as to warrant so important and so awful a change, in so precipitate a manner? As to insults offered to the laws, I know of none. In this respect, I believe this Commonwealth would not suffer by a comparison with the former government. The laws are as well executed, and as patiently acquiesced in, as they were under the royal administration. Compare the situation of the country—compare that of our citizens to what they were then, and decide whether persons and property are not as safe and as secure as they were at that time. Is there a man in this Commonwealth whose person can be insulted with impunity? Cannot redress be had here for personal insults or injuries, as well as in any part of the world—as well as in those countries where aristocrats and monarchs triumph and reign? Is not the protection of property in full operation here? The contrary cannot with truth be charged on this Commonwealth. Those severe charges which are exhibited against it, appear to me totally groundless. On a fair investigation, we shall be found to be surrounded by no real dangers. We have the animating fortitude and persevering alacrity of republican men to carry us through misfortunes and calamities. It is the fortune of a republic to be able to withstand the stormy ocean of human vicissitudes. I know of no danger awaiting us. Public and private security are to be found here in the highest degree. Sir, it is the fortune of a free people not to be intimidated by imaginary dangers. Fear is the passion of slaves. Our political and natural hemisphere are now equally tranquil. Let us recollect the awful magnitude of the subject of our deliberation. Let us consider the latent consequences of an erroneous decision—and let not our minds be led away by unfair misrepresentations and uncandid suggestions. There have been many instances of uncommon lenity and temperance used in the exercise of power in this Commonwealth. I could call your recollection to many that happened during the war and since—but every gentleman here must be apprised of them."

Extract from GOV. RANDOLPH'S *Rejoinder*, (*Elliott's Debates*, vol. iii. pp. 157–8.)

"Having consumed heretofore so much of your time, I did not intend to trouble you again so soon. But I now call on this committee, by way of right, to permit me to answer some severe charges against the friends of the new constitution. It is a right I am entitled to, and shall have. I have spoken twice in this committee. I have shown the principles which actuated the General Convention, and attempted to prove, that after the ratification of the proposed system by so many States, the preservation of the union depended on its adoption by us. I find myself attacked, in the most illiberal manner, by the honorable gentleman, (Mr. Henry.) I disdain his aspersions, and his insinuations. His asperity is warranted by no principle of parliamentary decency, nor compatible with the least shadow of friendship; and if our friendship must full—*let it fall, like Lucifer, never to rise to again!* Let him remember that it is not to answer him, but to satisfy this respectable audience, that I now get up. He has accused me of inconsistency in this very respectable assembly. Sir, if I do not stand on the bottom of integrity and pure love for Virginia, as much as those who can be most clamorous, I wish to resign my existence. Consistency consists in actions, and not in empty, specious words. Ever since the first entrance into that federal business, I have been invariably governed by an invincible attachment to the happiness of the people of America. Federal measures had been before that time repudiated. The augmentation of congressional powers was dreaded. The imbecility of the Confederation was proved and acknowledged. When I had the honor of being deputed to the Federal Convention to revise the existing system, I was impressed with the necessity of a more energetic government, and thoroughly persuaded that the salvation of the people of America depended on an intimate and firm union.

The honorable gentleman there can say, that, when I went thither, no man was a stronger friend to such an union than myself. I informed you why I refused to sign.

"I understand not him who wishes to give a full scope to licentiousness and dissipation, who would advise me to reject the proposed plan, and plunge us into anarchy.

[Here his Excellency Governor Randolph read the conclusion of his public letter, (wherein he says, that notwithstanding his objections to the constitution, he would adopt it rather than lose the Union,) and proceeded to prove the consistency of his present opinion with his former conduct, when Mr. Henry arose, and declared that he had no personal intention of offending any one—that he did his duty—but that he did not mean to wound the feelings of any gentleman—that he was sorry, if he offended the honorable gentleman without intending it—and that every gentleman had a right to maintain his opinion. His Excellency then said, that he was relieved by what the honorable gentleman said—that were it not for the concession of the gentleman, he would have made some men's hair stand on end by the disclosures of certain facts. Mr. Henry then requested, that if he had any thing to say against him to disclose it. His Excellency then continued—That, as there were some gentlemen there who might not be satisfied by the recantation of the honorable gentleman without being informed, he should give them some information on the subject. That his ambition had ever been to promote the union—that he was no more attached to it now than he always had been—and that he could, in some degree, prove it by the paper which he held in his hand, which was his public letter. He then read a considerable part of his letter, wherein he expressed his friendship to the union. He then informed the committee, that on the day of election of delegates to the convention for the county of Henrico, it being incumbent upon him to give his opinion, he told the respectable freeholders of that county his sentiments: that he wished not to become a member of that convention—that he had not attempted to create a belief that he would vote against the constitution—that he did really unfold to them his actual opinion, which was perfectly reconcileable with the suffrage he was going to give in favor of the constitution. He then read part of a letter which he had written to his constituents on the subject, which was expressive of sentiments amicable to an union with the other States. He then threw down the letter on the clerk's table, and declared that it might lie there for the *inspection of the curious and malicious!*]

"He then proceeded thus—I am asked, why I have thought proper to patronize this government? Not because I am one of those *illumined*, but because the felicity of my country requires it. The highest honors have no allurements to charm me. If he be as little attached to public places as I am, he must be free from ambition. It is true that I am now in an elevated situation; but I consider it as a far less happy or eligible situation than that of an inconsiderable land-holder. Give me peace—I ask no more. I ask no honor or gratification. Give me public peace, and I will carve the rest for myself. The happiness of my country is my first wish. I think it necessary for that happiness, that this constitution be now adopted; for, in spite of the representation of the honorable gentleman, I see a storm growling over Virginia. No man has more respect for Virginia, or a greater affection for her citizens, than I have; but I cannot flatter you with a kinder or more agreeable representation, while we are surrounded by so many dangers, and when there is so much rancor in the hearts of your citizens."

www.ingramcontent.com/pod-product-compliance
Lightning Source LLC
LaVergne TN
LVHW010243110826
845151LV00004B/1378
9781425525088